The NEW REAL BOOK

VOLUME 3

Publisher and Editor - Chuck Sher
(The World's Greatest!) Musical Editors - Sky Evergreen (formerly Bob Bauer) and Larry Dunlap
Music Copying - Mansfield Music Graphics and Ann Krinitsky, Berkeley, CA
Cover Design - Blackburn Design, Petaluma, CA
Cover Art - Computerized rendition of a raku pottery art piece, "Mu", by Kathryn McCleery.
Special thanks to Sandy Feldstein and all the staff at Warner Bros. Publications in Miami for their invaluable assistance.
As always, a heartfelt thanks to Sueann Sher for everything under the sun.

ISBN 1-883217-03-2

JAZZ CLASSICS

The Blue Note Era

JOE HENDERSON .... Inner Urge
Mamacita
Isotope
Short Story
Step Lightly
Punjab

HORACE SILVER .... Opus De Funk
Metamorphosis
Pyramid
Lonely Woman

FREDDIE HUBBARD .... Arietas
Blue Spirits
D Minor Mint
Super Blue

LEE MORGAN .... Ceora
The Double Up

HERBIE HANCOCK .... Dolphin Dance
Maiden Voyage
One Finger Snap

WAYNE SHORTER .... Black Nile
Toy Tune
El Gaucho

ART BLAKEY .... Backstage Sally
Bu's Delight
Look At The Birdie
That Old Feeling

JACKIE McLEAN .... Ballad For Doll
Appointment In Ghana
Kahill The Prophet
Cool Green

BOBBY HUTCHERSON ..... Herzog
Cirrus

GRANT GREEN .... Jean De Fleur

Swing Era

DUKE ELLINGTON .... Caravan
In A Sentimental Mood
Prelude To A Kiss
In A Mellow Tone
Daydream
Just Squeeze Me
Warm Valley
I Got It Bad
Solitude

GLENN MILLER .... Moonlight Serenade

FATS WALLER .... Jitterbug Waltz

BENNY GOODMAN .... Lullaby in Rhythm
Stompin' At The Savoy

More Jazz

JOHN COLTRANE .... Grand Central
Body And Soul
Autumn Serenade

BILL EVANS .... Since We Met
3/4 Skidoo
Emily
Spring Is Here

MILES DAVIS .... So Near, So Far
When Lights Are Low

CLIFFORD BROWN .... Tiny Capers

CHARLIE PARKER .... Wee (Allen's Alley)

STANLEY TURRENTINE .....Sugar

CHOICE STANDARDS

Almost Like Being In Love
And It All Goes Round And Round
Autumn Serenade
Blue Moon
Caravan
Close Your Eyes
Day Dream
Don't Be That Way
Don't Blame Me
Emily
Everything I Have Is Yours
For All We Know
Gentle Rain
A Ghost Of A Chance
I Fall In Love Too Easily
I Got It Bad
I Hear A Rhapsody
I'm Getting Sentimental Over You
I'm Through With Love
If You Could See Me Now
In A Mellow Tone
In A Sentimental Mood
Invitation
Just Friends
Just You, Just Me
Just Squeeze Me
The Lamp Is Low
Laura
Moon And Sand
Moonglow
Moonlight Serenade
On Green Dolphin Street
Over The Rainbow
Prelude To A Kiss
Ruby
The Second Time Around
Serenata
The Shadow Of Your Smile
Solitude
Spring Is Here
Stairway To The Stars
Star Eyes
Stars Fell On Alabama
Stompin' At The Savoy
Street Of Dreams
Sweet Lorraine
Taking A Chance On Love
That Old Feeling
There's A Lull In My Life
This Is New
What Are You Doing The Rest Of Your Life?
When I Look In Your Eyes
Where Are You?
You Must Believe In Spring
You Stepped Out Of A Dream
You've Changed

MOTOWN AND POP CLASSICS

STEVIE WONDER . . . . I Can't Help It
Part Time Lover
Bird Of Beauty
Another Star
That Girl
Smile Please
Creepin'
Too High

MARVIN GAYE . . . . Ain't That Peculiar
What's Going On?
I Heard It ThroughThe Grapevine
How Sweet It Is

SMOKEY ROBINSON . . . . Ooh Baby Baby
The Tracks Of My Tears

EDDIE FLOYD . . . . Knock On Wood

THE TEMPTATIONS . . . . My Girl
Get Ready
I'm Losing You

MARTHA & THE VANDELLAS . . Dancing In The Street
Heat Wave
Nowhere To Run

ANITA BAKER . . . . Sweet Love

AL GREEN . . . . Let's Stay Together

JOE COCKER . . . . You Are So Beautiful

VANESSA WILLIAMS . . . . Dreamin'

PATTI AUSTIN . . . . Baby Come To Me

ARETHA FRANKLIN . . . . Respect

THE FOUR TOPS . . . . Reach Out, I'll Be There

SAM AND DAVE . . . . Hold On, I'm Coming

TINA TURNER . . . . What's Love Got To Do With It

CONTEMPORARY JAZZ

CHICK COREA . . . . Bud Powell
Chick's Tune
Litha
Ritual

HERBIE HANCOCK . . . . Speak Like A Child
Actual Proof
Butterfly
Never Said (Chan's Song)

KENNY KIRKLAND . . . . Midnight Silence
Steepian Faith

TOM HARRELL . . . . It Always Is
Sail Away

NGUYEN LE . . . . Question Mark (?)
Isoar

MARIA SCHNEIDER . . . . Gush
Last Season

OTHELLO MOLINEUX . . . . Monk On The Run
No Way Out

KENNY BARRON . . . . I Wanted To Say

FRANK GAMBALE . . . . New Boots

SCOTT HENDERSON . . . . Sub Aqua

AYDIN ESEN . . . . Love's Haunts

JERRY BERGONZI . . . . Red's Blues

JULIAN JOSEPH . . . . Brothers of the Bottom Row

PEGGY STERN . . . . The Aerie

LARRY CARLTON . . . . Last Nite

ANDY LAVERNE . . . . In Love With Night

BRANFORD MARSALIS . . . . . Dienda

JUDE SWIFT . . . . Fall With Me

DONALD BROWN . . . . Daddy's Girl, Cynthia

MARC COPLAND . . . . Darius Dance

MULGREW MILLER . . . . From Day To Day

TRILOK GURTU . . . . Ballad For Two Musicians

BOB BERG . . . . American Gothic
Promise

YELLOWJACKETS . . . . Revelation
Freedomland
Man Facing North

EDDIE GOMEZ . . . . Next Future
Love Letter

EDDIE DANIELS . . . . Divertamento
Aja's Theme

ALAN BROADBENT . . . . Another Time
Don't Ask Why

RICHIE BEIRACH . . . . Riddles
Pendulum

PAUL McCANDLESS . . . . Rainland
Can't Stop The Wind

PHIL WOODS . . . . Real Life

BOB MINTZER . . . . Relentless

GARY BURTON . . . . Chairs And Children

JACO PASTORIUS . . . . (Used To Be A) Cha-Cha

WARREN BERNHARDT . . . . . Tuzz's Shadow

BOBBY WATSON . . . . In Case You Missed It

FRANCK AMSALLEM . . . . Out A Day

DAVID LIEBMAN . . . . Off Flow

DON GROLNICK . . . . One Bird, One Stone

PHIL MARKOWITZ . . . . Circular Motion

LYLE MAYS . . . . Hard Eights

JOHN ABERCROMBIE . . . . John's Waltz

ROBERT HURST . . . . Walk Of The Negress

JESSICA WILLIAMS . . . . Blue Tuesday

JOEY CALDERAZZO . . . . Dexter

BRANDON FIELDS . . . . B Sting

ALAN HOLDSWORTH . . . . . . Tokyo Dreams

ALPHABETICAL INDEX

TUNE	As Played &/or Written By:	Page
ACTUAL PROOF	Herbie Hancock	1
THE AERIE	Peggy Stern & Lee Konitz	2
AIN'T THAT PECULIAR	Marvin Gaye	4
AJA'S THEME	Eddie Daniels	6
ALMOST LIKE BEING IN LOVE		7
AMERICAN GOTHIC	Bob Berg	8
AND IT ALL GOES ROUND	Jaye P. Morgan	10
ANOTHER STAR	Stevie Wonder	12
ANOTHER TIME	Alan Broadbent	15
APPOINTMENT IN GHANA	Jackie McLean	16
ARIETAS	Freddie Hubbard	19
AUTUMN SERENADE	John Coltrane & Johnny Hartman	22
B-STING	Brandon Fields & Billy Childs	24
BABY COME TO ME	Patti Austin	26
BACKSTAGE SALLY	Art Blakey	28
A BALLAD FOR DOLL	Jackie McLean	31
BALLAD FOR TWO MUSICIANS	Trilok Gurtu & Joe Zawinul	32
BIRD OF BEAUTY	Stevie Wonder	34
BLACK NILE	Wayne Shorter	37
BLUE MOON		38
BLUE SPIRITS	Freddie Hubbard	40
BLUE TUESDAY	Jessica Williams	45
BODYAND SOUL	John Coltrane	46
BROTHERS OF THE BOTTOM ROW	Julian Joseph	48
BU'S DELIGHT	Art Blakey	50
BUD POWELL	Chick Corea	54
BUTTERFLY	Herbie Hancock	56
CAN'T STOP THE WIND	Paul McCandless	58
CARAVAN	Duke Ellington	62
CEORA	Lee Morgan	65
CHAIRS AND CHILDREN	Gary Burton	66
CHICK'S TUNE	Chick Corea	68
CIRCULAR MOTION	Phil Markowitz	70
CIRRUS	Bobby Hutcherson	72
CLOSE YOUR EYES		76
COOL GREEN	Jackie McLean	77
CREEPIN'	Stevie Wonder	78
D MINOR MINT	Freddie Hubbard	81
DADDY'S GIRL, CYNTHIA	Donald Brown	82
DANCING IN THE STREET	Martha & The Vandellas	84
DARIUS DANCE	Marc Copland	86
DAY DREAM	Duke Ellington	88
DEXTER	Joey Calderazzo	89
DIENDA	Branford Marsalis	91
DIVERTAMENTO	Eddie Danials	92
DOLPHIN DANCE	Herbie Hancock	95
DON'T ASK WHY	Alan Broadbent	96
DON'T BE THAT WAY		97
DON'T BLAME ME		98
THE DOUBLE UP	Lee Morgan	99
DREAMIN'	Vanessa Williams	100
EL GAUCHO	Wayne Shorter	103

TUNE	As Played &/or Written By:	Page
EMILY	Bill Evans	104
EVERYTHING I HAVE IS YOURS		105
FALL WITH ME	Jude Swift	106
FOR ALL WE KNOW		108
FREEDOMLAND	Yellowjackets	109
FROM DAY TO DAY	Mulgrew Miller	110
THE GENTLE RAIN	Luis Bonfa	113
GET READY	The Temptations	114
A GHOST OF A CHANCE		117
GRAND CENTRAL	John Coltrane	118
GUSH	Maria Schneider	120
HARD EIGHTS	Lyle Mays	122
HEAT WAVE	Martha & The Vandellas	124
HERZOG	Bobby Hutcherson	126
HOLD ON, I'M COMING	Sam & Dave	129
HOW SWEET IT IS	Marvin Gaye	130
I CAN'T HELP IT	Stevie Wonder	132
I FALL IN LOVE TOO EASILY		133
I GOT IT BAD		134
I HEAR A RHAPSODY		137
I HEARD IT THROUGH THE GRAPEVINE	Marvin Gaye	138
I WANTED TO SAY	Kenny Barron	140
I'M GETTING SENTIMENTAL OVER YOU		141
I'M LOSING YOU	The Temptations	142
I'M THROUGH WITH LOVE		144
IF YOU COULD SEE ME NOW	Bill Evans	146
IN A MELLOW TONE		149
IN A SENTIMENTAL MOOD	Duke Ellington	150
IN CASE YOU MISSED IT	BobbyWatson	152
IN LOVE WITH NIGHT	Andy LaVerne	154
INNER URGE	Joe Henderson	155
INVITATION		156
ISOAR	Nguyen Le	158
ISOTOPE	Joe Henderson	161
IT ALWAYS IS	Tom Harrell	162
JEAN DE FLEUR	Grant Green	166
THE JITTERBUG WALTZ	Fats Waller	168
JOHN'S WALTZ	John Abercrombie	169
JUST FRIENDS		170
JUST SQUEEZE ME	Duke Ellington	171
JUST YOU, JUST ME		173
KAHLIL THE PROPHET	Jackie McLean	174
KNOCK ON WOOD	Eddie Floyd	176
THE LAMP IS LOW		179
LAST NITE	Larry Carlton	180
LAST SEASON	Maria Schneider	182
LAURA		185
LET'S STAY TOGETHER	Al Green	186
LITHA	Chick Corea	188
LONELY WOMAN	Horace Silver	191
LOOK AT THE BIRDIE	Art Blakey	192
LOVE LETTER	Eddie Gomez	195
LOVE'S HAUNTS	Aydin Esen	196
LULLABY IN RHYTHM	Benny Goodman	199

TUNE	As Played &/or Written By:	Page
MAIDEN VOYAGE	Herbie Hancock	200
MAMACITA	Joe Henderson	201
MAN FACING NORTH	Yellowjackets	204
METAMORPHOSIS	Horace Silver	206
MIDNIGHT SILENCE	Kenny Kirkland	210
MONK ON THE RUN	Othello Molineaux	212
MOON AND SAND		214
MOONGLOW		216
MOONLIGHT SERENADE		217
MY GIRL	The Temptations	218
NEVER SAID (Chan's Song)	Herbie Hancock & Diane Reeves	220
NEW BOOTS	Frank Gambale	223
NEXT FUTURE	Eddie Gomez	224
NO WAY OUT	Othello Molineaux	226
NOWHERE TO RUN	Martha & The Vandellas	228
OFF FLOW	Dave Liebman	230
ON GREEN DOLPHIN STREET		232
ONE BIRD, ONE STONE	Don Grolnick	234
ONE FINGER SNAP	Herbie Hancock	239
OOO BABY BABY	Smokey Robinson	240
OPUS DE FUNK	Horace Silver	242
OUT A DAY	Franck Amsallem	244
OVER THE RAINBOW		246
PART-TIME LOVER	Stevie Wonder	248
PENDULUM	Richie Beirach	250
PRELUDE TO A KISS	Duke Ellington	251
PROMISE	Bob Berg	252
PUNJAB	Joe Henderson	254
PYRAMID	Horace Silver	256
QUESTION MARK	Nguyen Le	259
RAINLAND	Paul McCandless	260
REACH OUT, I'LL BE THERE	The Four Tops	266
REAL LIFE	Phil Woods	268
RED'S BLUES	Jerry Bergonzi	271
RELENTLESS	Bob Mintzer	272
RESPECT	Aretha Franklin	274
REVELATION	Yellowjackets	276
RIDDLES	Richie Beirach	278
RITUAL	Chick Corea	280
RUBY		282
SAIL AWAY	Tom Harrell	284
THE SECOND TIME AROUND		287
SERENATA		288
THE SHADOW OF YOUR SMILE		291
SHORT STORY	Kenny Dorham	292
SINCE WE MET	Bill Evans	294
SMILE PLEASE	Stevie Wonder	297
SO NEAR, SO FAR	Miles Davis	298
SOLITUDE		301
SPEAK LIKE A CHILD	Herbie Hancock	302
SPRING IS HERE	Bill Evans	304
STAIRWAY TO THE STARS		305
STAR EYES		306
STARS FELL ON ALABAMA		309
STEEPIAN FAITH	Kenny Kirkland	310

TUNE	As Played &/or Written By:	Page
STEP LIGHTLY	Joe Henderson	313
STOMPIN' AT THE SAVOY		314
STREET OF DREAMS		315
SUB AQUA	Scott Henderson & Tribal Tech	316
SUGAR	Stanley Turrentine	319
SUPER BLUE	Freddie Hubbard	320
SWEET LORRAINE		322
SWEET LOVE	Anita Baker	324
TAKING A CHANCE ON LOVE		326
THAT GIRL	Stevie Wonder	328
THAT OLD FEELING (Standard version)		331
THAT OLD FEELING	Art Blakey	332
THERE'S A LULL IN MY LIFE		334
34 SKIDOO	Bill Evans	336
THIS IS NEW		337
TINY CAPERS	Clifford Brown	338
TOKYO DREAM	Alan Holdsworth	340
TOO HIGH	Stevie Wonder	342
TOY TUNE	Wayne Shorter	345
THE TRACKS OF MY TEARS	Smokey Robinson	346
TUZZ'S SHADOW	Warren Bernhardt	348
(USED TO BE A) CHA-CHA	Jaco Pastorius	350
WALK OF THE NEGRESS	Bob Hurst	353
WARM VALLEY	Duke Ellington	354
WEE	Charlie Parker	355
WHAT ARE YOU DOING THE REST OF YOUR LIFE		356
WHAT'S GOING ON?	Marvin Gaye	358
WHAT'S LOVE GOT TO DO WITH IT	Tina Turner	360
WHEN I LOOK IN YOUR EYES		362
WHEN LIGHTS ARE LOW	Miles Davis	364
WHERE ARE YOU?		366
YOU ARE SO BEAUTIFUL	Billy Preston	367
YOU MUST BELIEVE IN SPRING	Bill Evans	368
YOU STEPPED OUT OF A DREAM		370
YOU'VE CHANGED		371

APPENDIX - SOURCES 372

GENERAL RULES FOR USING THIS BOOK

FORM

1. Key signatures will be found at the top of page one, and at the top of page three for tunes longer than two pages. Any change of key will be noted not only where it occurs but also at the start of the next line. The key signature holds even if there is a change of clef, and is not restated. A change of key to C Major will appear as a clef followed by the naturals needed to cancel the previous key signature.
2. The Coda sign is to be taken only when ending the tune unless otherwise stated. Some tunes have dual Codas (𝄌1 and 𝄌2) to make it possible to fit a complex tune on two pages.
3. All repeats are observed during a 'D.C. al Coda' or 'D.S. al Coda' except in the following cases:
   a) when a Coda sign appears in a repeated section; the Coda is taken before repeating (unless marked 'on repeat').
   b) when an instruction to the contrary appears (e.g. 'D.S. al 2nd ending al Coda').
4. A Coda sign just within repeats is taken before repeating. A Coda sign just outside of repeats is taken after repeating.
5. When no solo form is specified, the whole tune is used for solos (except any Coda).
6. Till Cue On Cue signifies dual endings for a section that repeats indefinitely. The 'till cue' ending is played until cue, at which point the 'on cue' ending is played instead.
7. A section marked '4x's' is played four times (repeated three times).
8. A section marked 'ENDING' is played to end a tune; it directly follows the last bar of the head.

CHORDS

9. Chords fall on the beat over which they are placed.
10. Chords carry over to the next bar when no other chords or rests appear.
11. Chords in parentheses are optional except in the following cases:
    a) turn arounds
    b) chords continued from the line before
    c) verbal comment explaining thier use (for solos, for bass but not piano, only at certain times, etc.)
12. Optional chords in parentheses last as long as the chord they are written over or until the closing parenthesis is encountered, whichever is longer.
13. Written-out piano or guitar voicings are meant to be played as written. Chord symbols appearing with such voicings often will not describe the complete voicing; they are meant to aid sight reading and are often used for solos.
14. Multiple voices playing different rhythms are separated by having their stems lie in opposite directions whenever possible.

TERMS

15. An 'altered ' dominant chord is one in which neither the fifth nor the ninth appears unaltered. Thus it contains b5 &/or #5, and b9 &/or #9.
16. 'Freely' signifies the absense of a steady tempo.
17. During a 'break......♩' piano, bass and drums all observe the same rests. The last beat played is notated as ♪ or x to the left of the word 'break'.
18. A 'sample bass line', 'sample solo', or 'sample fill' is a transcribed line given as a point of reference.

TRANSPOSITIONS

19. Bass lines are always written to be read by a bass player, i.e. one octave higher than they sound.
20. Tenor sax and guitar lines are often written an octave higher than they sound and flute lines an octave lower to put them in a more readable range. There will be a verbal note to this effect in every case.
21. All horn and harmony parts are written in concert key (not transposed).

ABBREVIATIONS

15ma .... two octaves higher
15ma b. .... two octaves lower
8va .... one octave higher
8va b. .... one octave lower
accel. .... accelerando
alt .... altered
bari .... baritone saxophone
bkgr. .... background
bs. .... bass
cresc. .... crescendo
decres. .... decrescendo
dr. .... drums
elec. bs. ..... electric bass
elec. pn. ..... electric piano
fl. .... flute
gliss. .... glissando
gtr. .... guitar
indef .... indefinite (till cue)
L.H. .... piano left hand
Med. .... Medium
N.C. .... No Chord
Orig. .... Original
perc. .... percussion
pn. .... piano
rall. .... rallentando
R.H. .... piano right hand
rit. .... ritardando
sop. .... soprano saxophone
stac. .... staccato
susp. .... suspended
synth. .... synthesizer
ten. .... tenor saxophone
trb. .... trombone
trbs. .... trombones
trp. .... trumpet
trps. .... trumpets
unis. .... unison
V.S. .... Volti Subito (quick page turn)
w/ .... with
x .... time
x's .... times

ORNAMENTS AND SYMBOLS

Slide into the note from a short distance below

Slide into the note from a greater distance below

Fall away from the note a short distance

Fall away from the note a greater distance

Top note of a complete voicing

A rapid variation of pitch upward, much like a trill

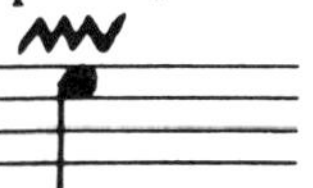

Mordent

A muted or optional pitch

Note with indeterminate pitch

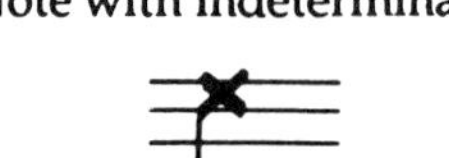

Rhythm played by drums or percussion

CHORD SYMBOLS

The chord symbols used in this book follow (with some exceptions) the system outlined in "Standard Chord Symbol Notation" by Carl Brandt and Clinton Roemer. It is hoped you will find them clear, complete and unambiguous.

Below are two groups of chord spellings:

1) The full range of chords normally encountered, given with a C root, and

2) Some more unusual chords, all of which appear in tunes in this book. (Note: some groups of notes below could be given different names, depending on context. See previous page for a definition of 'altered' chords).

PREFACE TO THE Bb AND Eb VERSIONS

Here are a few points that we hope will clear up any possible confusion in using the transposed versions:

1. All pitches and chord names in the Bb and Eb versions are transposed to be read by Bb or Eb horn players respectively (even if guitar, piano or other instruments that read in a different key are indicated.) Instrumental markings (e.g., ten., trp., gtr., pn.) indicate only the instrumentation on the particular recording of the tune that was used to derive the chart.

2. All melodies and horn parts in the concert version have been included in the Bb and Eb versions. Bass parts, most keyboard parts and some intros, endings and piano/guitar voicings have been omitted if they were likely to be of little interest to horn players. The number of bars and the form is unchanged from the concert version.

3. In the Bb version, pitches have generally been transposed up a major second from the concert version, although sometimes up a major ninth to make it easier for both tenor and trumpet to read. Since we cannot know whether a given line will be played on trumpet, tenor, clarinet or soprano, such octave indications as 'ten. 8va b.' and 'loco' do not necessarily apply to the notes on the page; rather, they apply to the original pitches in the concert version. Use your own best sense in choosing the appropriate octave for your instrument.

In the Eb version, pitches have been transposed to place the melody in the middle range of alto and baritone saxophones.

ENJOY!

Actual Proof

Herbie Hancock

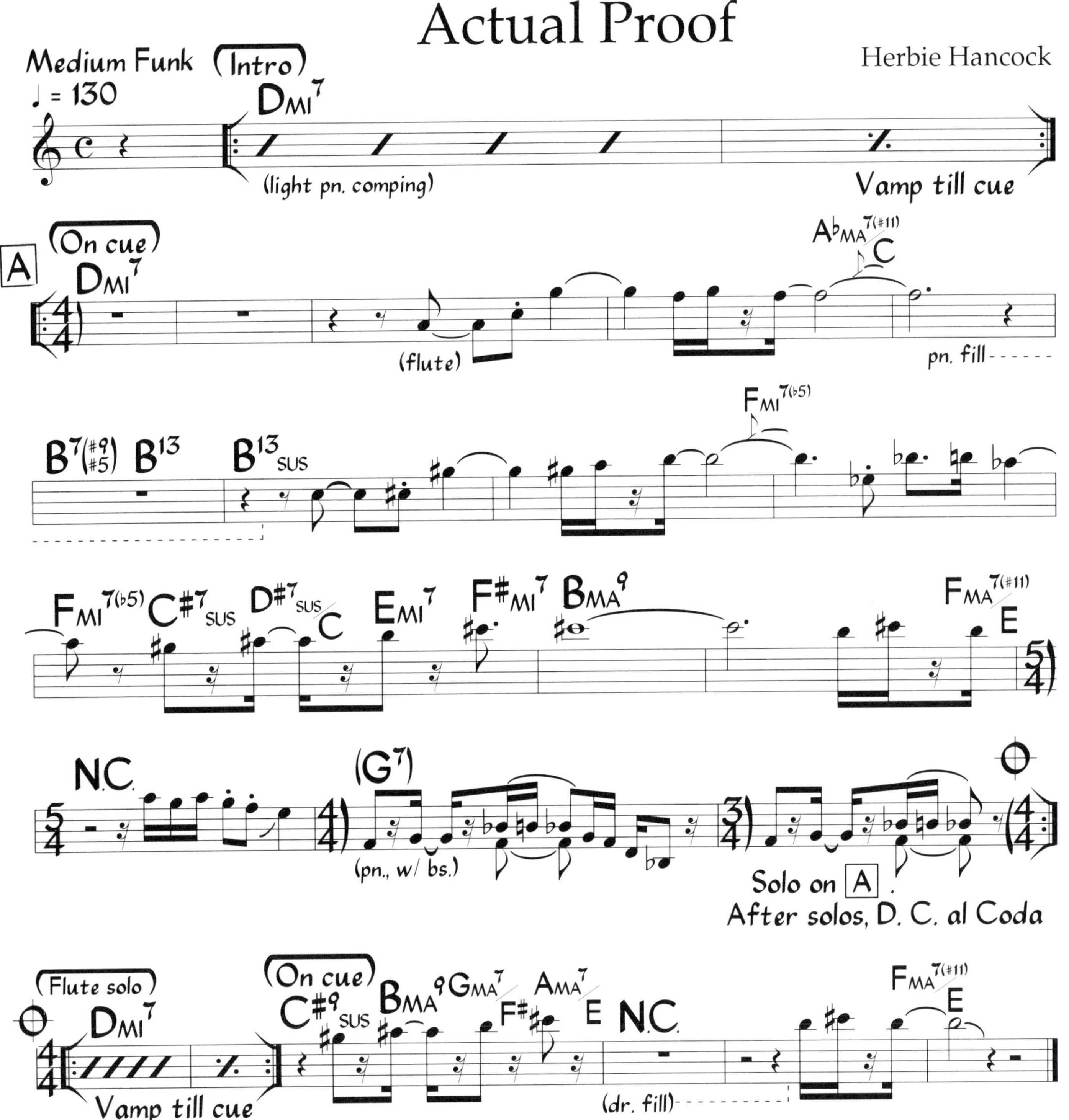

First two bars of A may be repeated.
Head is played twice before solos.

The Aerie

Peggy Stern

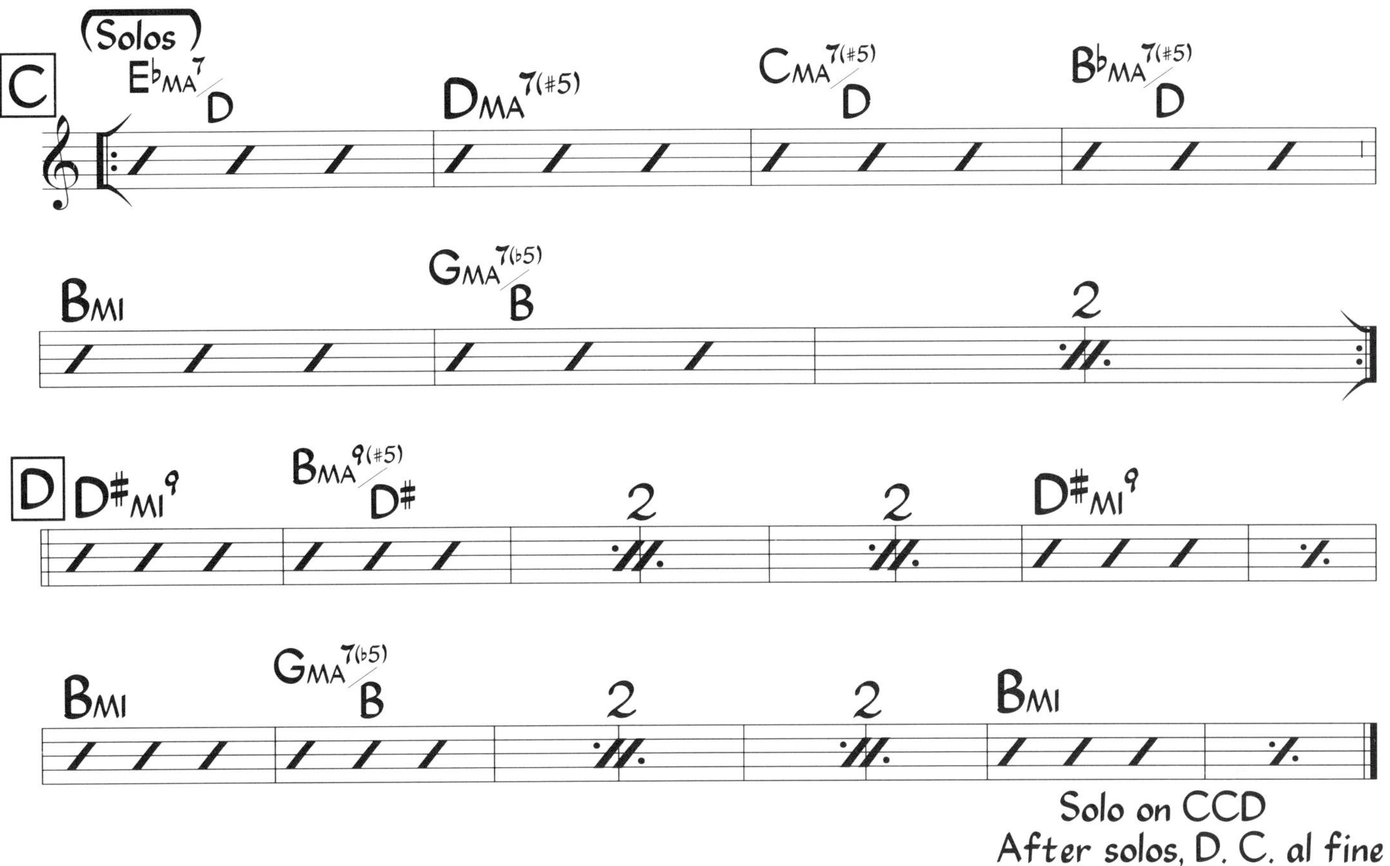

Head is played twice before solos, once after solos.

Ain't That Peculiar

Eddie Holland & Norman Whitfield
(As sung by Marvin Gaye)

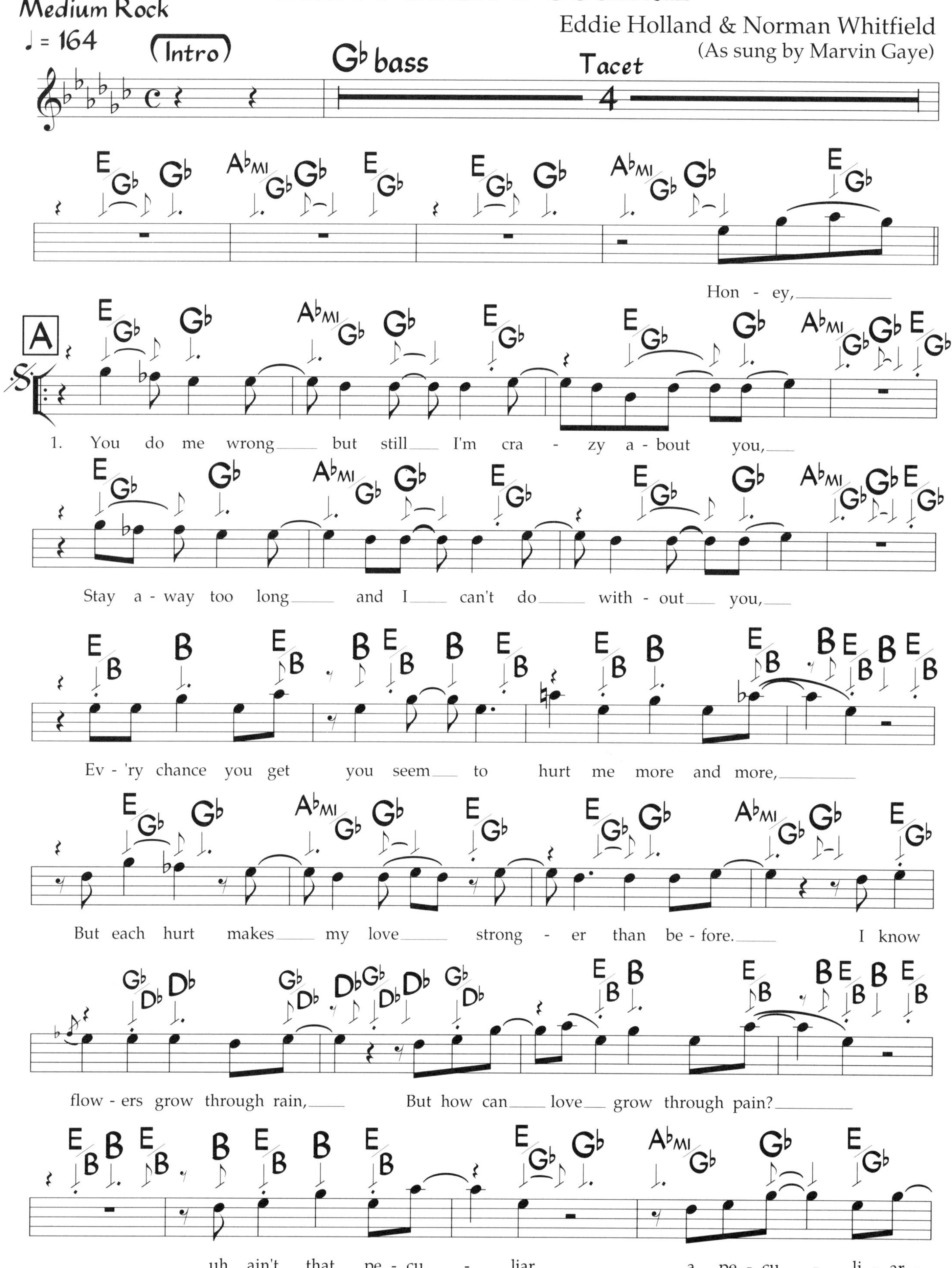

Second verse:
You tell me lies, that should be obvious to me,
But I'm so much in love, baby, till I don't want to see
That things you do and say are designed to make me blue,
It's a doggone shame my love for you makes all your lies seem true.
If the truth makes love last longer,
why do lies make my love stronger?
Uh—Ain't that peculiar…

Third verse:
I've cried so much, just like a child that's lost a toy,
Maybe, baby, you think these tears I cry are tears of joy,
A child can cry so much until you do everything they say,
But unlike a child my tears don't help me to get my way.
I know love can last through years,
but how can love last through tears?
Uh—Ain't that peculiar…

Aja's Theme

Torrie Zito
(As played by Eddie Daniels)

Solos and out head are in time.
For solos, each bar may be two bars of swing.
Melody is freely interpreted.

Almost Like Being in Love

Lyric: Alan Jay Lerner
Music: Frederick Lowe

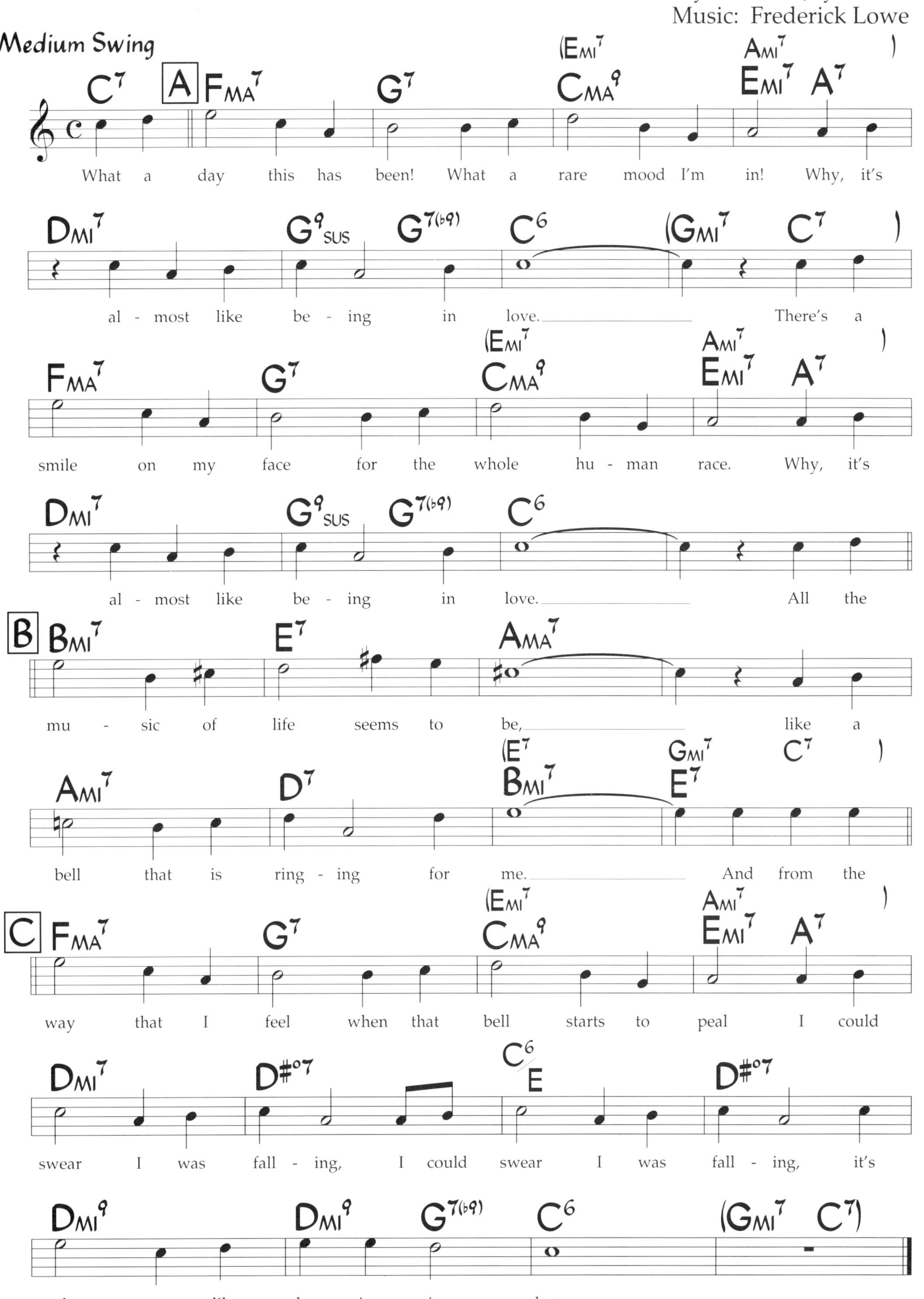

American Gothic
Bob Berg
Med. Funk (Intro)
♩ = 126
Esus(add 9)
Tacet
8
cym. fills
(pn.)
A
E(omit 3)
(E6/9)
D6/9
E(omit 3)
Bbass
B/C
C#MI11
Abass
Bbass
Cbass
C/D
(ten. w/ pn.)
B
G(omit 3)
F(omit 3)
(FMA9)
G(omit 3)
Dbass
D/Eb
EMI11
F(omit 3)
G(omit 3)
Eb(omit 3)
F(omit 3)
C(omit 3)
D(omit 3)
F(omit 3)
G(omit 3)
(pn.)
C
C
D(add 9)
(add ten.)
C
D(add 9)
Ebass
E(add 9)
-omit on D.S.-
AMI
E/A
C#MI
G#SUS
G#/C#
G#MI(add 9)/B
G(add 9)/B
(ten. only on melody)
BMA7
G(add 9)/B
CMI9
GMI9
BMI
F#MI7
EbMA7(#11)
(Tenor Solo, Half-Time Feel)
D
D/G
EMI7
EbMA9
F6/9
G(add 9 omit 3)
(omit letter D on D.S.)
(ten.)
(Orig. Feel)
E
Gbass
Gbbass
Fbass
EMI7
Ebbass
Dbass
Dbbass
C13(#11)

Tenor plays 8va (sounds as written)

(And) It All Goes 'Round and 'Round

Bernard Ighner
(As sung by Jaye P. Morgan)

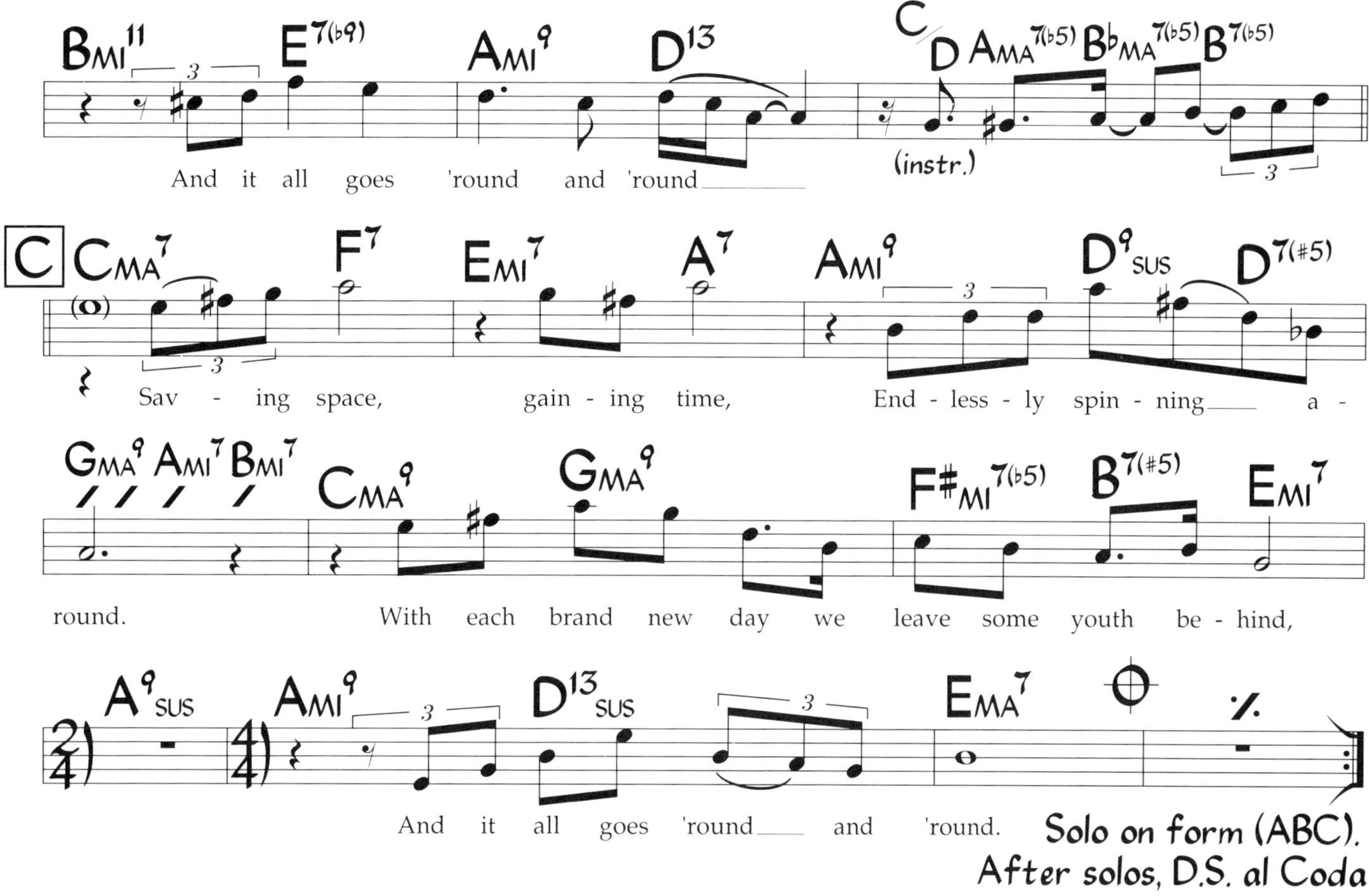

Lyric at letters B and C, last time:

Life is like a school,
And some folk never learn the rules.
But here we are,
Much wiser now than we were then,
And it all goes 'round and 'round.

No way to turn back the time,
Endlessly spinning around.
With each brand new day
We leave some youth behind
And it all goes 'round and 'round.

Melody is freely interpreted.
On recording, letter C and the Coda are 1/2 step higher the last time.
On recording, solo is letter A only, vocal in at letter B.

Another Star

Stevie Wonder

Horns and background vocals at letter B are like letter A each time (horns on bars 9-16 only).

Second and Third verses:

2. For you, love might be a toast of wine,
But with each sparkle know the best for you
I pray.
For you, love might be for you to find,
But I will celebrate our love of yesterday.

3. For you, there might be another star,
But through my eyes the light of love is all
I see.
For you, there might be another song,
But in my heart your melody will stay with me.

Photo by Tom Copi

MILES DAVIS

Another Time

Alan Broadbent

Solos in 4. Chords in parentheses are used for solos.

Appointment in Ghana
Jackie McLean
Slow, even 1/8's
♩ = 71
Intro
(trp.)
Fast Swing
♩ = 234
N.C.
A
E bass
B
C
D
Solos
E
F
Solo on DEF.
After solos, D.S. al Coda
alto fills

Appointment in Ghana (Harmony)

Tenor and alto sound one octave lower than written. (In correct range if played by tenor.)

Photo by Paul Hoeffler, Toronto

ERIC DOLPHY

Arietas

Freddie Hubbard

Chords in parentheses are used for solos.
Break is not used for solos.

Arietas (Harmony)

Medium-Fast Swing
♩ = 228

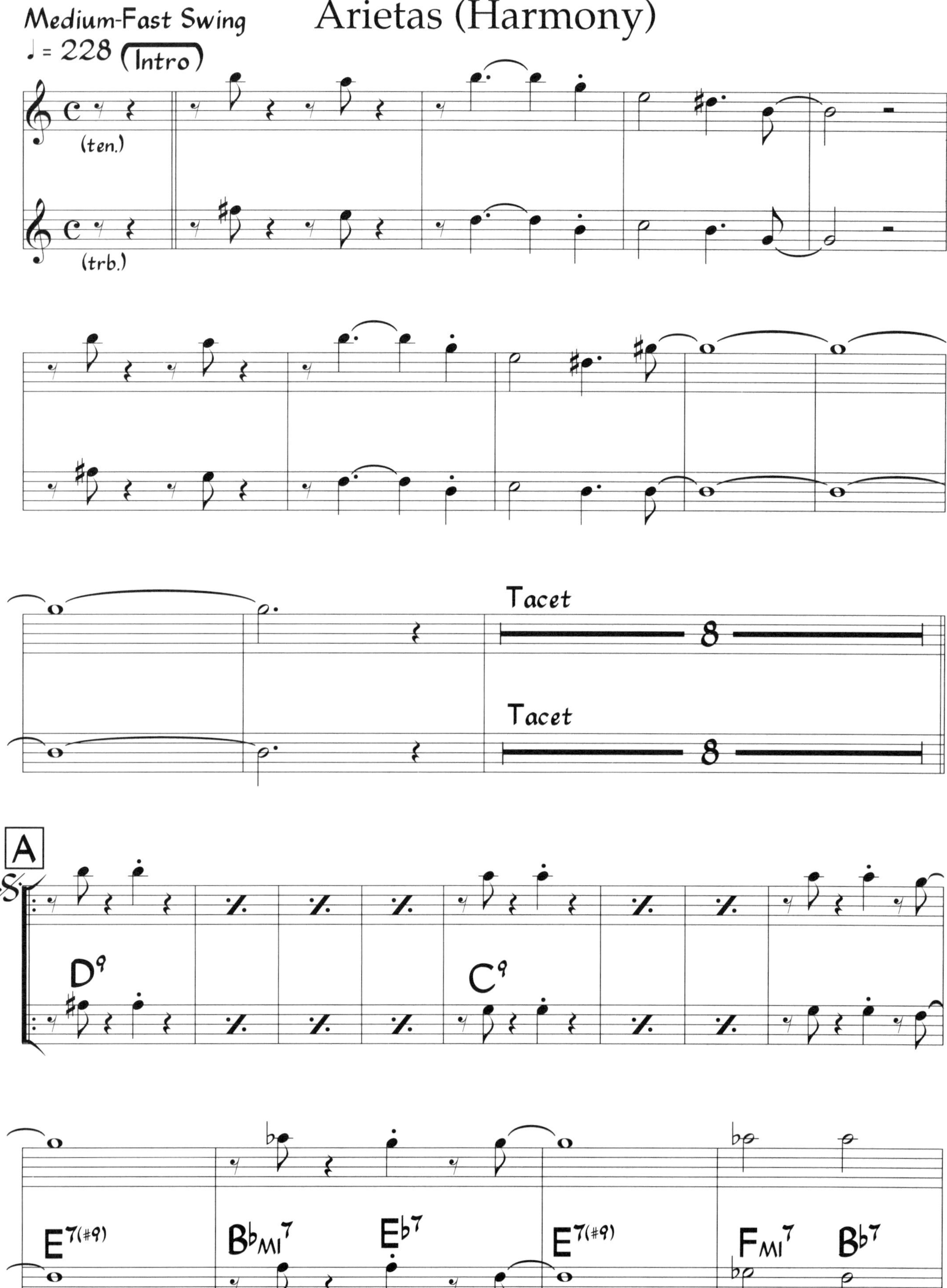

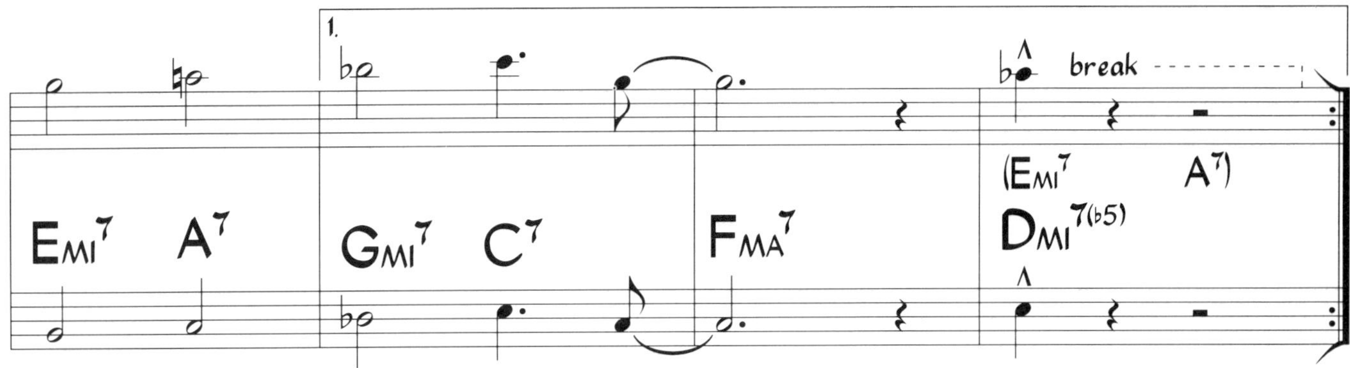

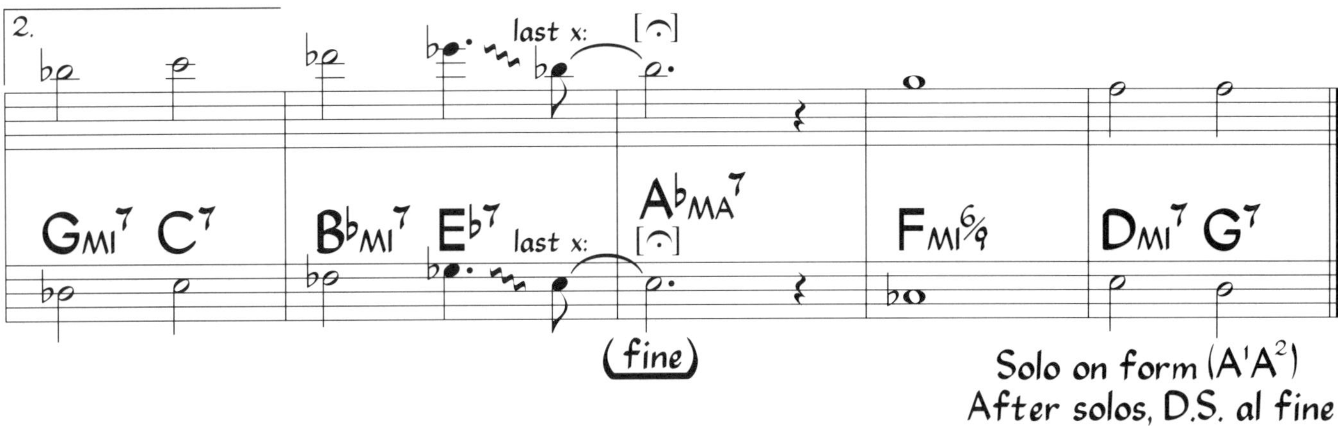

Tenor and trombone lines sound one octave lower than written.
Chords in parenthesis are used for solos.
Break is not used for solos.

Autumn Serenade

Lyric: Sammy Galop
Music: Peter De Rose
(As played by John Coltrane & Johnny Hartman)

Medium Latin
♩ = 112 N.C. (Intro)

FMI6/9 | Gb13 | FMI6/9

Gb7(#11 #9) | FMI6/9 | Gb13

Through the

A

FMI(MA7) | C7(#9 #5)

trees___ comes au - tumn with her ser - e - nade,___ Mel - o -

FMI(MA7) | Bb13(#11)

dies,___ the sweet - est mu - sic ev - er played,___ Au - tumn

GMI7 | C7(b9) | FMA7 | DMI7/A

kiss - es we knew are beau - ti - ful sou - ve - nirs,___ As I

AMI7(b5) | D7(alt.) | GMI7 | C13(b9)

pause to re - call the leaves seem to fall like tears. Sil - ver

B

FMI(MA7) | C7(#9 #5)

stars___ were cling - ing to an au - tumn sky,___ Love was

FMI(MA7) | Bb13

ours___ un - til Oc - to - ber wan - dered by,___ Let the

Break at bar 16 of letter A is not played for solos.

B-Sting

Brandon Fields
Billy Childs

Horns play letter A in unison 1st time only.
Second time and on D.S. play harmonies. (Trumpet/Alto/Tenor)

Baby, Come To Me

Rod Temperton
(As sung by Patti Austin
& James Ingram)

Second verse lyric:

Spendin' every dime to keep you talkin' on the line, that's how it was,
And all those walks together, out in any kind of weather, just because.
There's a brand new way of looking at your life
When you know that love is standing by your side.

Backstage Sally

Wayne Shorter
(As played by Art Blakey)

Head is played twice before and after solos.

Backstage Sally (Harmony)

Head is played twice before and after solos.

Tenor plays lines as written (sounding an octave lower).

Photo by Francis Wolff, courtesy of Mosaic Images

JACKIE McLEAN

A Ballad for Doll

Jackie McLean

Chords in parentheses are used for head only.
Tenor and alto sound one octave lower than written.

Ballad for Two Musicians
Joe Zawinul
(as played by Trilok Gurtu)
Ballad
♩ = 63
Tacet
("sax")
("sax")
A
B
(ad lib.)
C
(omit 1st x)
(Ad lib. on D.S.)
D
(Ad lib.)
(8va on D.S.)
(as is)

Note: Melody is very freely interpreted, particularly on D.S.

("Sax" is a synth. sound)

Bird of Beauty

Stevie Wonder

Second verse:

Simon says that your mind is requesting a furlough,
Let it find the answers to things that you've
always wanted to know.
There's a fair of many places that you've
always wanted to go, yeah,
And to me that sure sounds best,
'cause it means happiness for you.

Third verse:

Tudo bem, você deve descançar a sua mente.
Não faz mal, o que vai acontecer
daqui pra frente,
Vai cantar, alegria que chegou
tão de repente
Você coracão assim,
tão feliz já vai cantar, Carnaval.

Photo © W. Patrick Hinely

WAYNE SHORTER

Black Nile

Wayne Shorter

Blue Moon

Lyric: Lorenz Hart
Music: Richard Rodgers

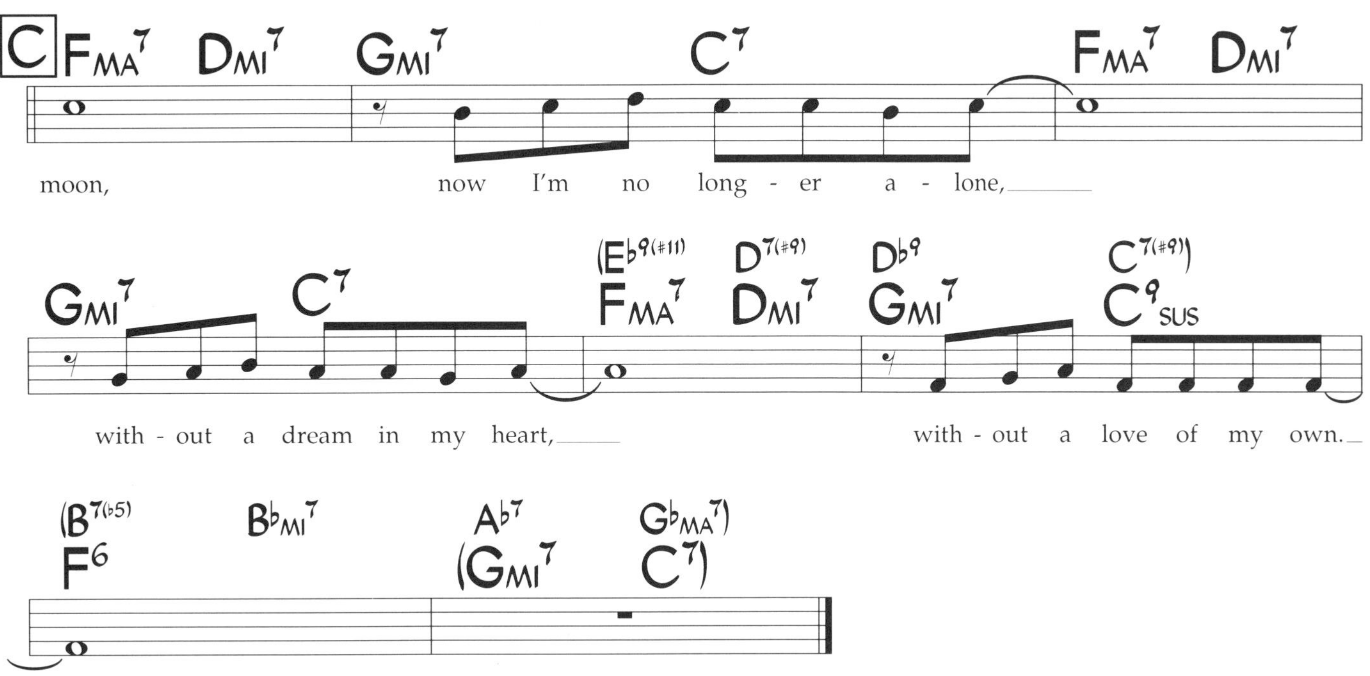

Alternate chords are as played by Art Blakey.

Blue Spirits

Freddie Hubbard

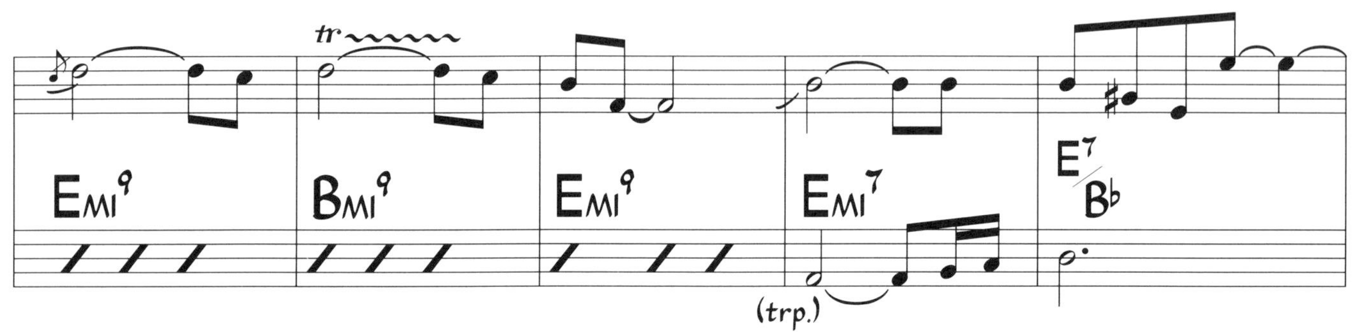

D.S. al 3rd ending al fine.
Solo on form (AABA).
After solos, D.S.S. al Coda
(play entire head
before taking Coda).

BMI9 EMI9

(trp.- play 4x's, then solo)

(Vamp, solo & fade)

Chords in parentheses are used for solos.

Blue Spirits (Harmony)

Chords in parentheses are used for solos.
Tenor and trombone are in correct range if played by tenor.
On recording, trombone parts are played by euphonium.

Photo by Carole Reiff

CHET BAKER

Blue Tuesday

Jessica Williams

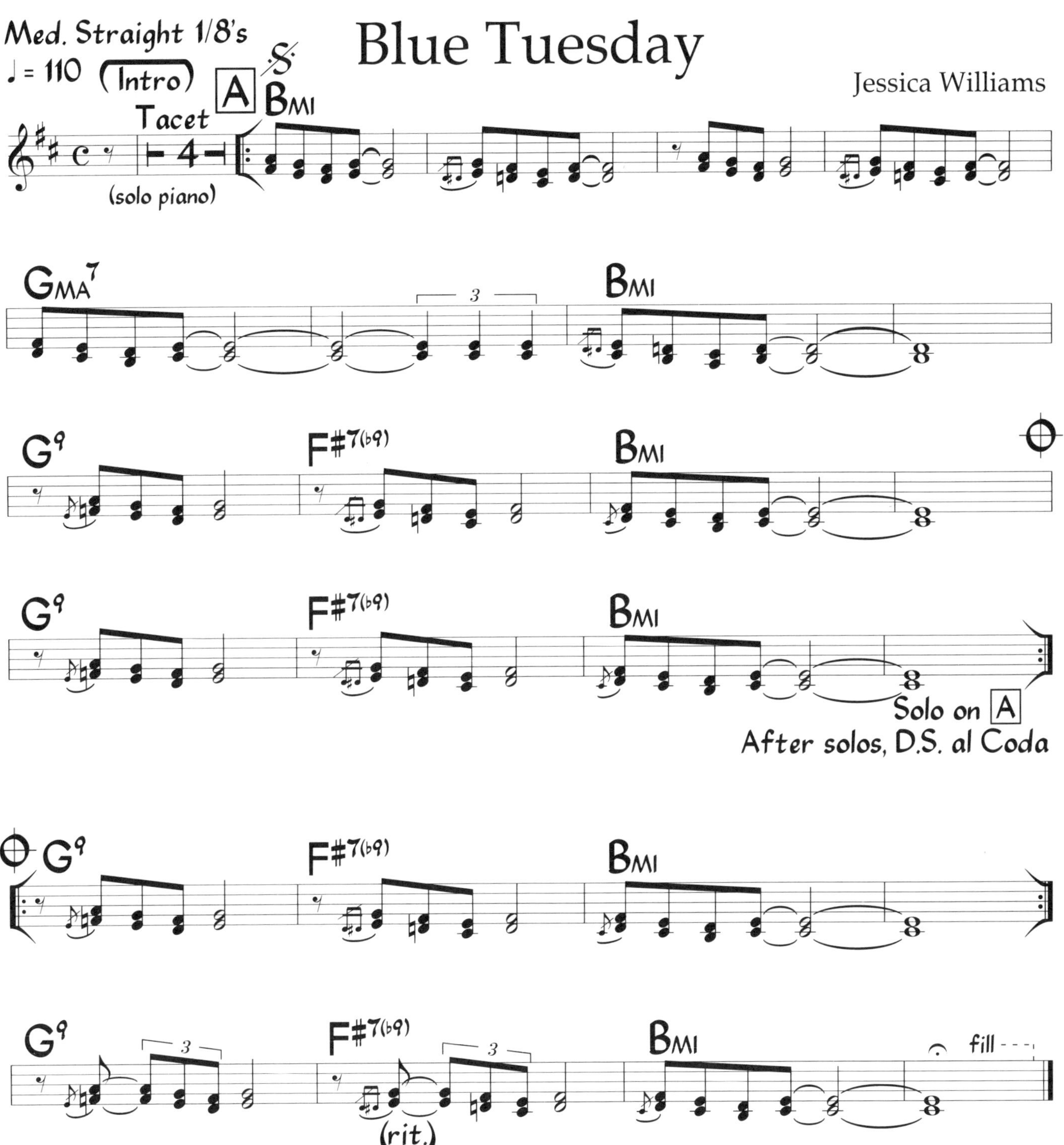

Head is played twice before solos, once after, with variation.

Body and Soul
Music by Johnny Green
(As played by John Coltrane)
Medium Swing (in 2)
♩ = 144
Intro
(ten.)
A
(ten.)
(tenor fill)
B
(tenor fill)
(tenor fill)
C

Chords in parentheses are not used for solos. Ab pedal is used for solos. Kicks are not played for solos.
Piano rhythm is played with variation. Melody is transcribed directly from the first chorus.

Brothers of the Bottom Row

Julian Joseph

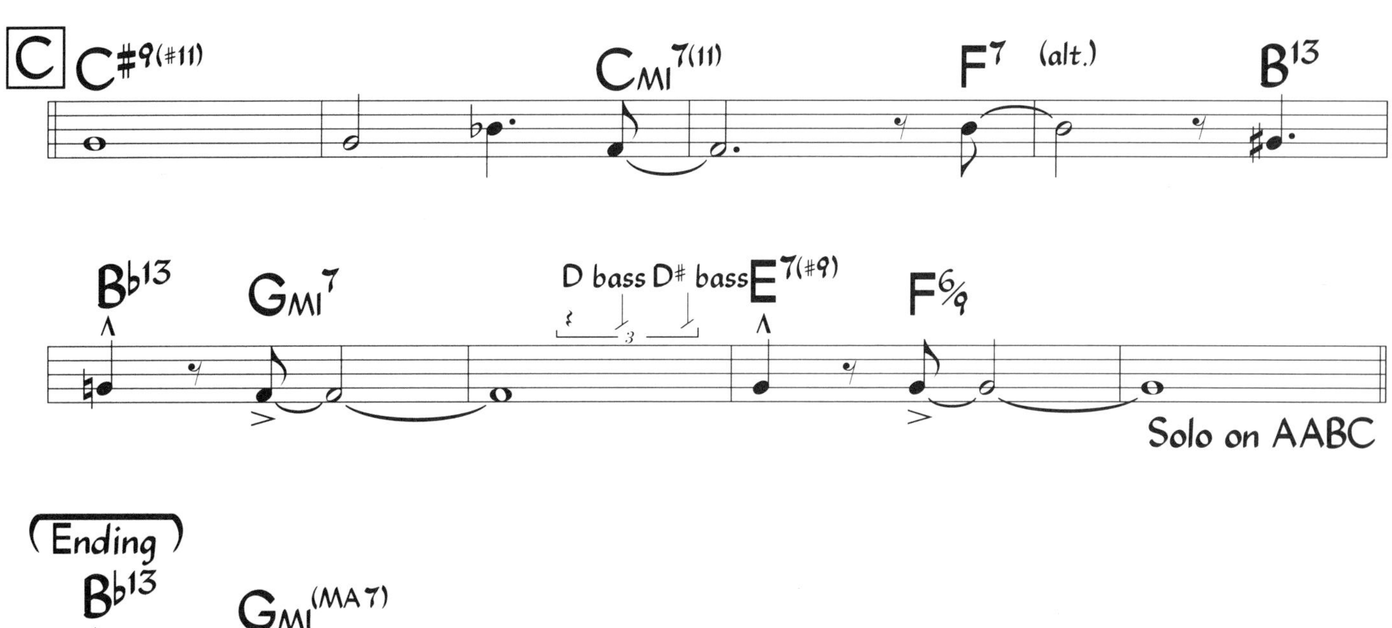

Ending

Bb13 GMI(MA7)

Melody at A is freely interpreted
(bottom staff is a sample interpretation).

Bu's Delight

Curtis Fuller
(As played by Art Blakey)

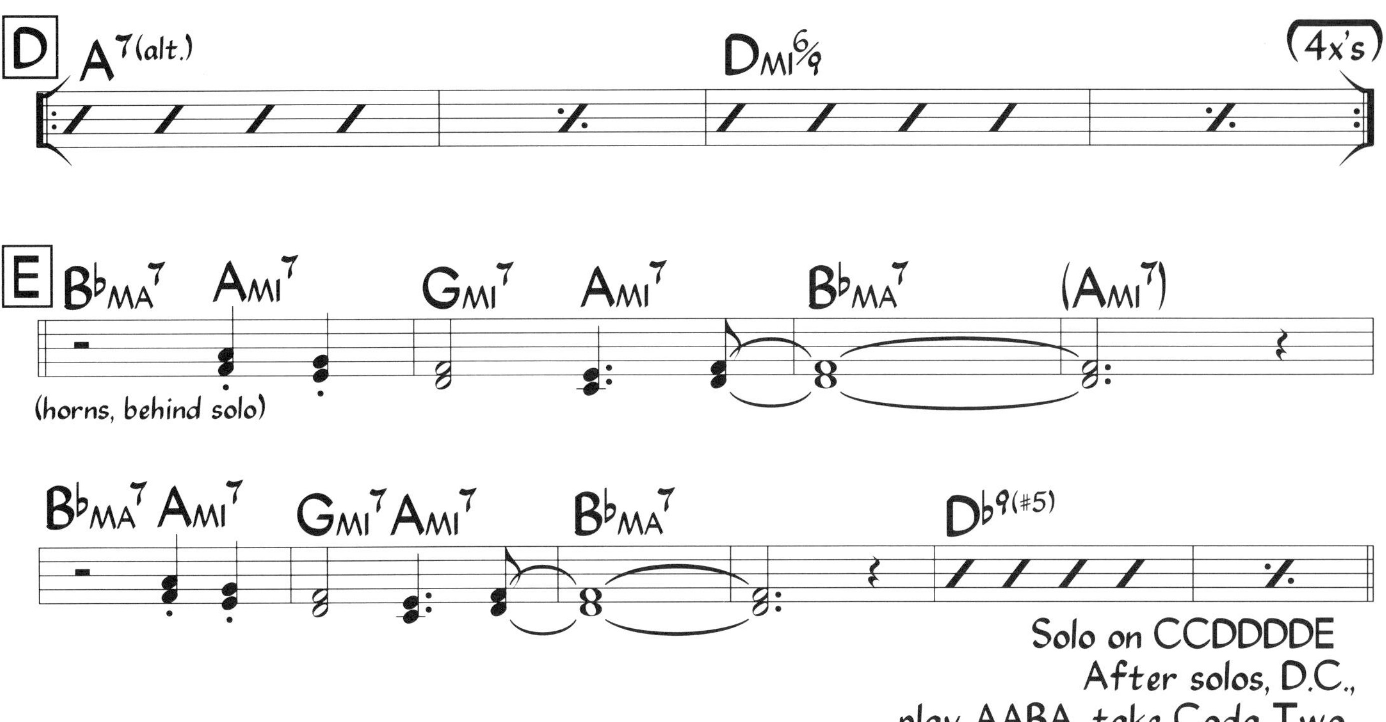
D
A7(alt.)
Dmi6/9
(4x's)
E
B♭ma7
Ami7
Gmi7
Ami7
B♭ma7
(Ami7)
(horns, behind solo)
B♭ma7
Ami7
Gmi7
Ami7
B♭ma7
D♭9(#5)
Solo on CCDDDDE
After solos, D.C.,
play AABA, take Coda Two

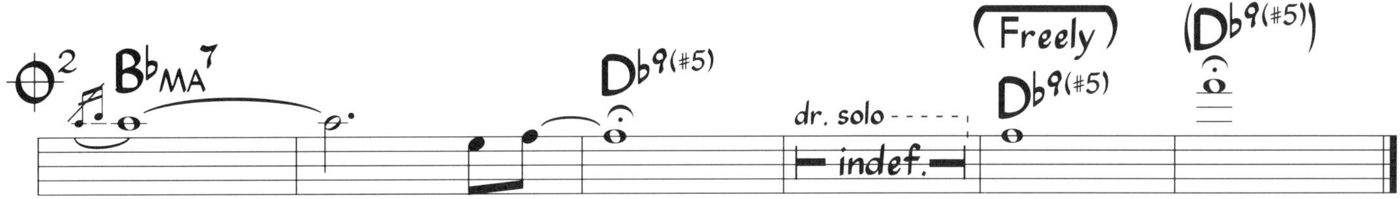
2
B♭ma7
D♭9(#5)
dr. solo
indef.
(Freely)
D♭9(#5)
(D♭9(#5))

Bu's Delight (Harmony)

Trombone and tenor lines are in correct range if played by tenor sax.
Horns at letter E rotate, depending on soloist.

Bud Powell

Chick Corea

Kicks and breaks are not played for solos (except the last 2 bars of letters A & C).

Butterfly
Herbie Hancock
(As played by Norman Connors)
(Arr. by Jacques Burvick)
Medium Latin/Funk
♩ = 124
break
(pn.)
1. Pre - cious
A
day wings,
lights your rain - bow
(horns)
way, waves,
Rest your Touch my
wings. mind.
(fine) (perc. break)
Stay a - while. Be so fine.
You're the sun in my sky, But - ter - fly.
When you're gone peo - ple cry, But - ter - fly.
D bass
(horns)
break
You don't know the peace you bring. You show me the se - crets and the ways to
love ev - 'ry mo - ment of the day, and flow - ers you kiss all come to life. 2. Soar - ing

2.
N.C.
(horns)
B
(Voice solo)
GMI9
B7(#9 #5)
Bb13 SUS
CMI9
CMA9
AbMA7/C
EbMA9(#11)
EMI9
FMA9(#11) GbMA9(#11) FMA9(#11) DbMA9(#11) EMI11
A7(alt.)
(horns)
C
(Piano solo)
DMI9
G7
GMI9
C13
FMI7(11)
Bb13
FMI7(11)
Bb13
GbMA7
D
(Trumpet solo)
GMI9
(GMI9 D7(#9 #5))
(Vamp till cue)
(On cue)
GMI9
(GMI9)
(horns)
D.S. al Coda
(GbMA7)
GMI7
BMI7 GMI7
BMI7 GMI7
To give all the love we knew, to see all the light that we can see, and
GMI7
BMI7 GMI7
BMI7 N.C.
teach all our chil - dren not to lie, and may - be one day we'll learn to fly. 2. Soar - ing
D.S.S. al fine
(2nd verse)
Alternate solo section
(replaces letters B, C & D):
GMI7
4
(Vamp till cue)
(On cue)
C13
3
Till cue
On cue
BMA9(#11)

Can't Stop the Wind

Paul McCandless

Bars with two chords in them are divided 3 beats per chord.

Can't Stop the Wind (Background Part)

On the recording, parts at letter A are somewhat different each time.

Caravan

Duke Ellington
Irving Mills & Juan Tizol

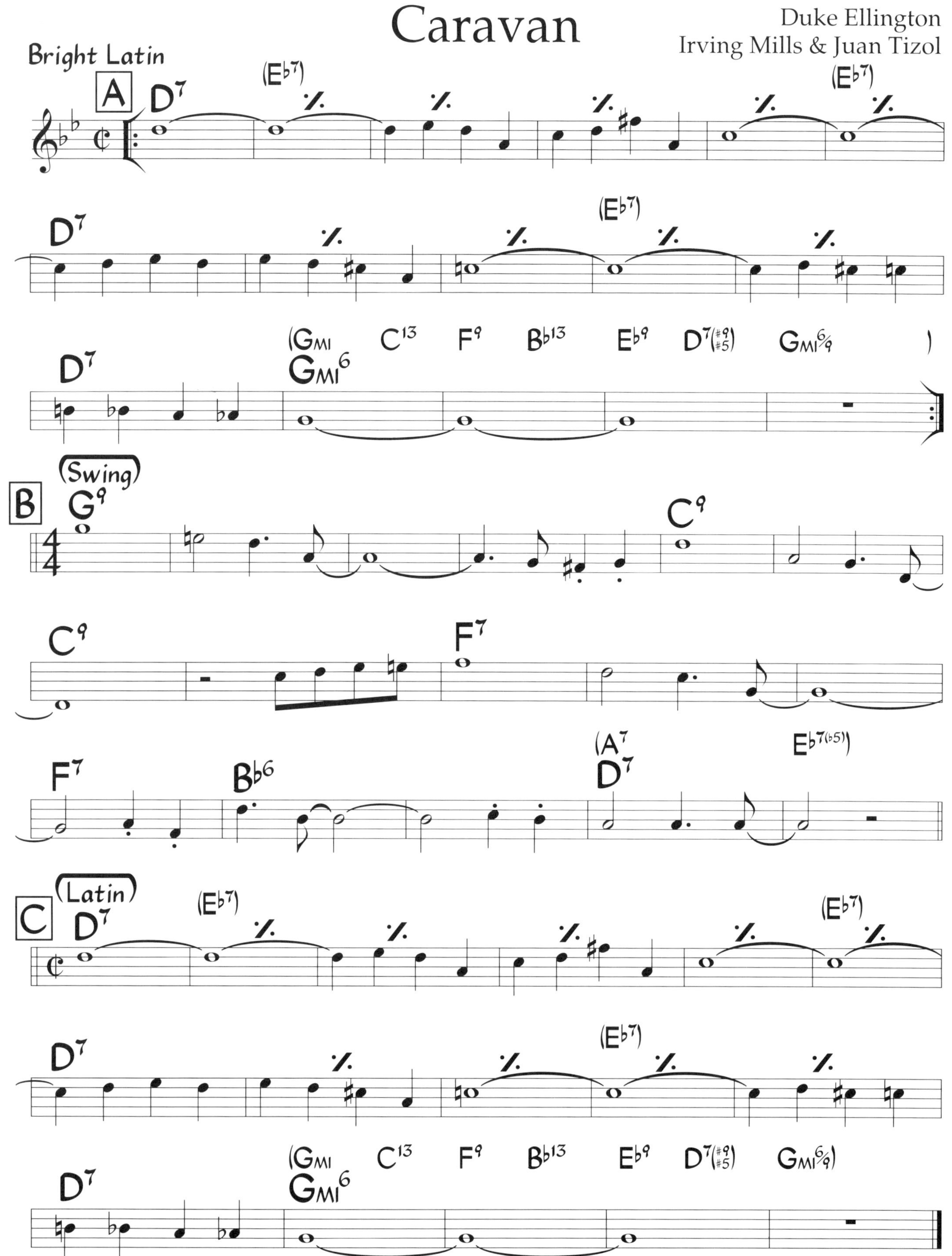

Solos may swing throughout.

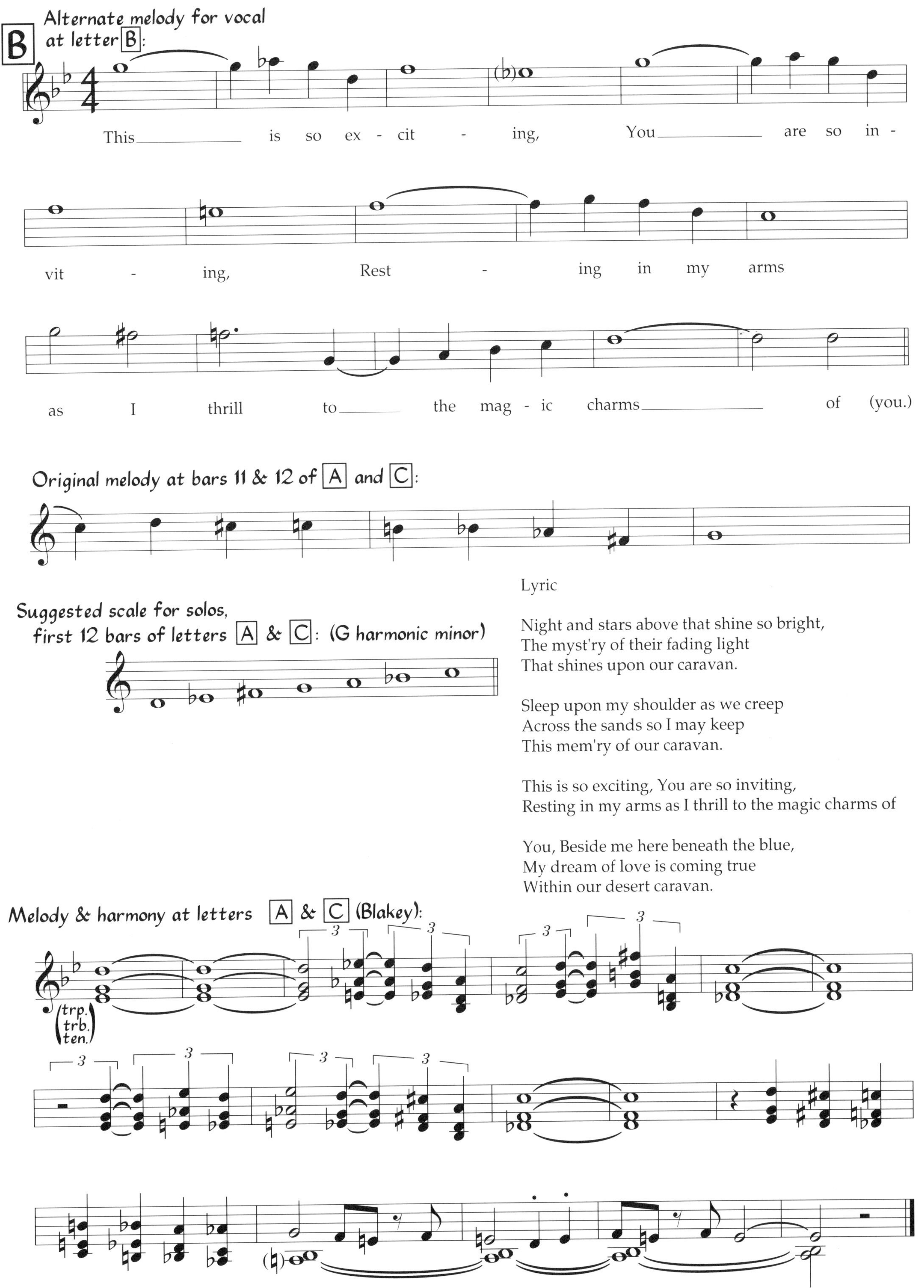
B
Alternate melody for vocal at letter B:
This is so ex - cit - ing, You are so in - vit - ing, Rest - ing in my arms as I thrill to the mag - ic charms of (you.)
Original melody at bars 11 & 12 of A and C:
Suggested scale for solos, first 12 bars of letters A & C: (G harmonic minor)
Lyric
Night and stars above that shine so bright,
The myst'ry of their fading light
That shines upon our caravan.
Sleep upon my shoulder as we creep
Across the sands so I may keep
This mem'ry of our caravan.
This is so exciting, You are so inviting,
Resting in my arms as I thrill to the magic charms of
You, Beside me here beneath the blue,
My dream of love is coming true
Within our desert caravan.
Melody & harmony at letters A & C (Blakey):
(trp. trb. ten.)

Photo by Paul Hoeffler, Toronto

LEE MORGAN

Ceora

Lee Morgan

Tenor plays as written, except 8va for bars 5-8 of letters A & B (and the first beat of bar 9).
Breaks are not used for solos. Chords in parentheses are used for solos.
On recording, piano solos over a complete chorus before the head.

Chairs and Children

Vince Mendoza
(As played by Gary Burton)

Head is played twice before solos.
Note: C#sus/E# may be substituted for C#(add9)/E# throughout.

Chick's Tune

Chick Corea
(As played by Blue Mitchell)

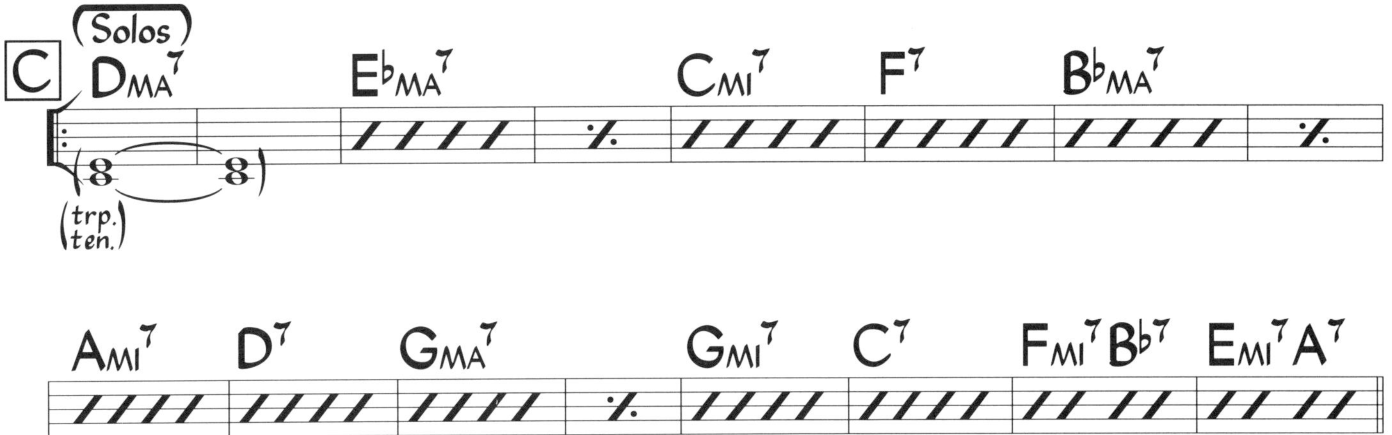

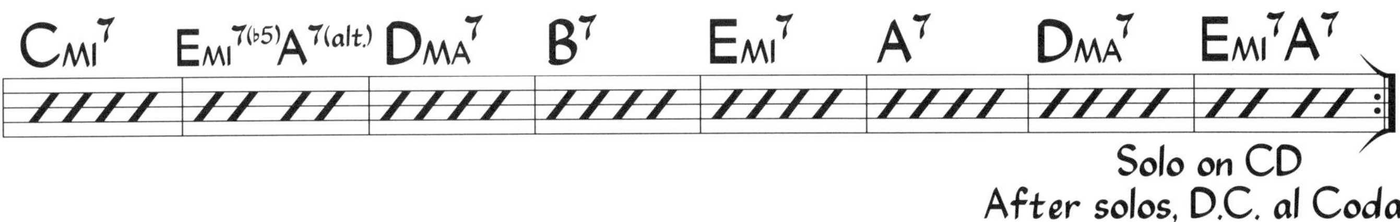

Tenor plays an octave higher on unison and harmony parts only, except at Coda.

Based on the changes to "You Stepped Out of a Dream".

Circular Motion

Phil Markowitz

Head is played twice before and after solos.

MARIA SCHNEIDER

Cirrus

Bobby Hutcherson

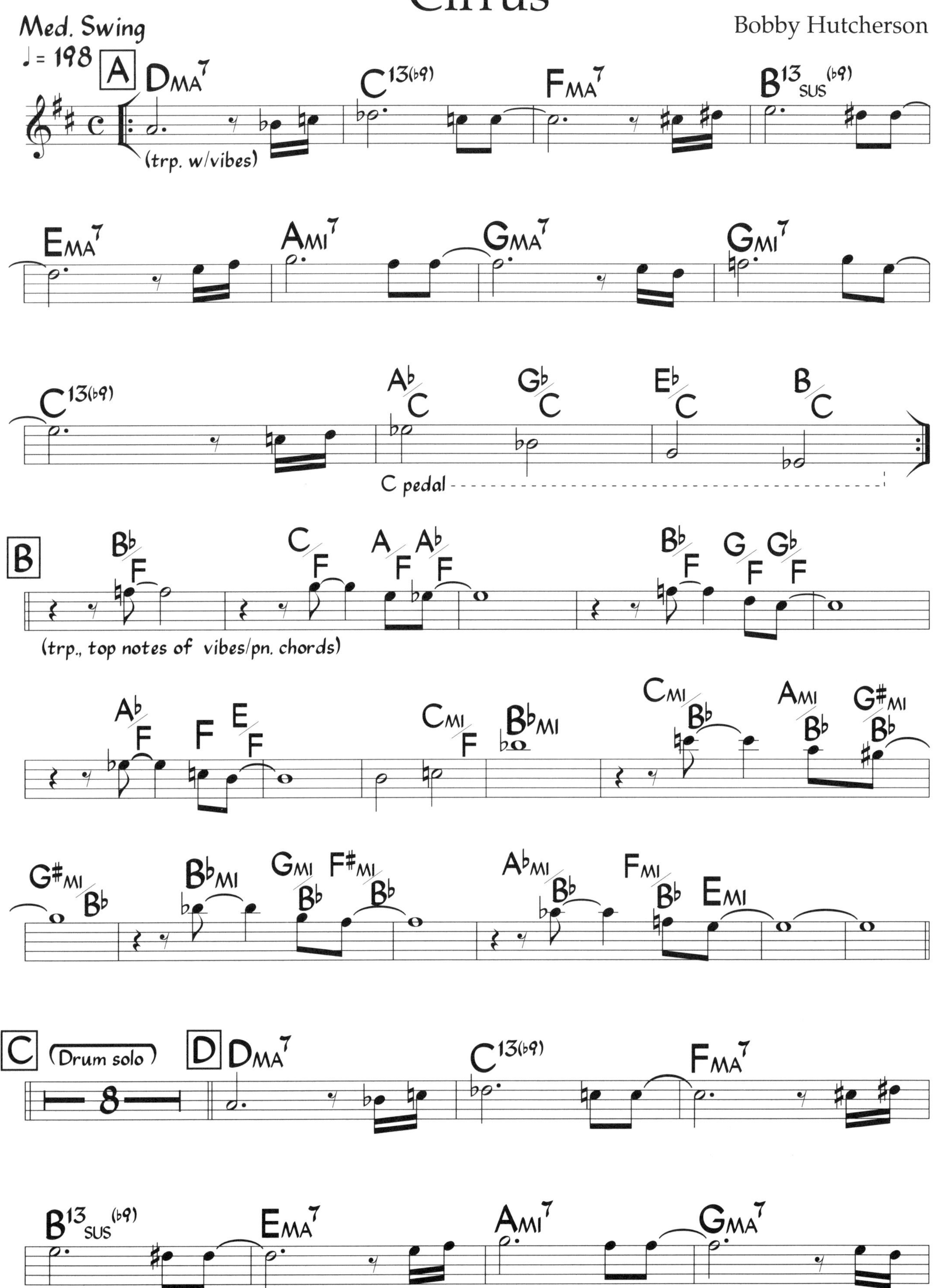

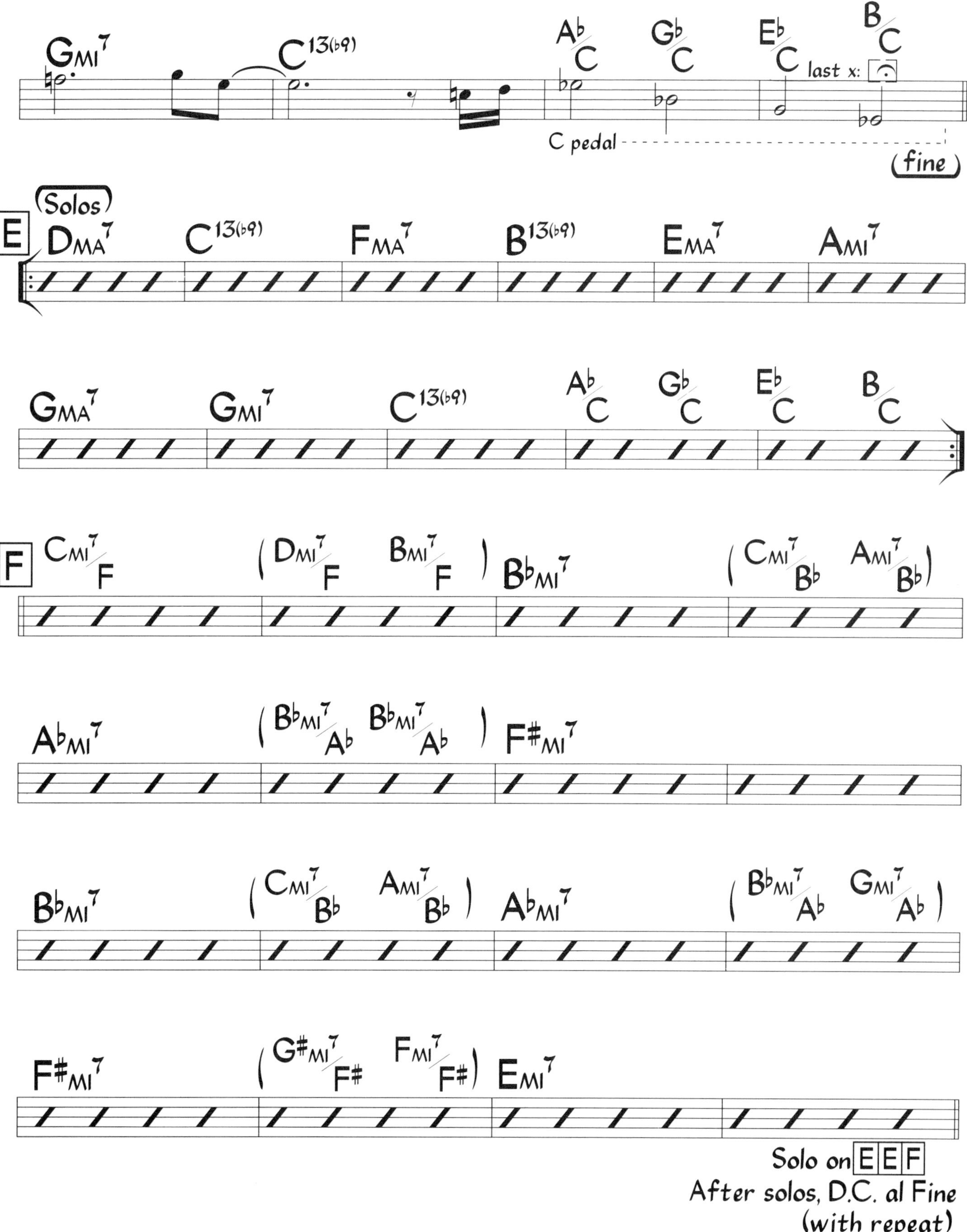

Soloist may ignore chords in parentheses at letter F.

Cirrus (Harmony)
Med. Swing
♩ = 198
A
ten. 1
ten. 2
DMA7
C13(b9)
FMA7
B13SUS(b9)
EMA7
AMI7
GMA7
GMI7
C13(b9)
Ab/C
F#/C
Eb/C
B/C
B
Bb/F
C/F
A/F
Ab/F
Bb/F
G/F
F#/F
(ten. 1 ten. 2) (F pedal for 8 bars)
F#/F
Ab/F
F
E/F
CMI/F
BbMI
CMI/Bb
AMI/Bb
G#MI/Bb
BbMI
GMI/Bb
F#MI/Bb
(Bb pedal for 6 bars)
F#MI/Bb
AbMI/Bb
FMI/Bb
EMI
C
Tacet
8
(dr. solo)
D
DMA7
C13(b9)
FMA7
B13SUS(b9)

Soloist may ignore chords in parentheses at letter F.
Tenor sounds one octave lower than written.

Close Your Eyes

Bernice Petkere

Cool Green

Kenny Drew
(As played by Jackie McLean)

Head is played twice before and after solos.
Tenor plays an octave higher except 2 bars in Intro. as indicated.

Creepin'

Stevie Wonder

CMA7
DMI7 EMI7 FMA7
FMI6
C/E
When you sleep at night, ba - by, I won - der do I creep in - to your dreams, or
GMI7(11)
CMI7
Gb/C
could it be I sleep a - lone in my fan - ta - sy? Oh,
C
FMI7
DbMA7
love is so a - maz - ing, Guess you will be stay - in'
Ab/Eb
F7/A
BbMI
EMA7
EbMI7
so let it be that you al - ways creep in - to my dreams.
In my dreams.
Dbsus/Ab
Csus/Ab
(synth.)
Dbsus/Ab
Csus/Ab
Ab(add 9)/C
D.S. al 2nd ending al Coda
(harmonica solo at letter [A]).
Dbsus/Ab
Csus/Ab
Dbsus/Ab
Csus/Ab
(dreams.) In my dreams, In my
(synth. like Intro)
(Vamp & fade)

Photo by Val Wilmer

BOBBY HUTCHERSON

D Minor Mint

Freddie Hubbard

Daddy's Girl Cynthia

Donald Brown

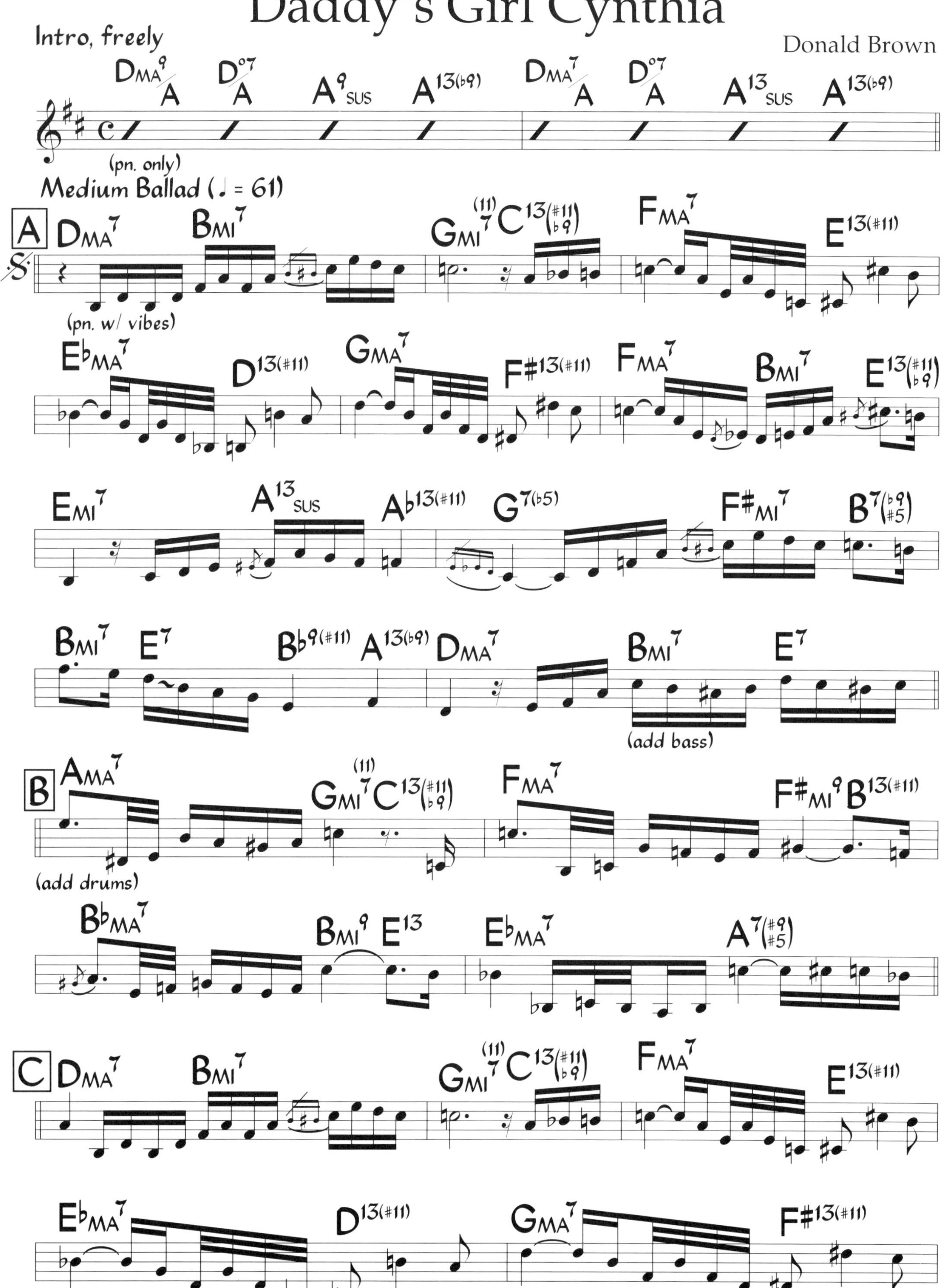

FMA7
BMI7
E13(#11 b9)
EMI7
A13sus
Ab13(#11)
G7(b5)
F#MI7
B7(b9 #5)
BMI7 E7
Bb9(#11) A13(b9)
DMA7 F°7 EMI7 A7
Solo on form (ABC).
After solos, D.S. al Coda
DMA7 G13 F#MI7 B7
E9(#11) E9
Bb9(#11) A13(b9)
D/A E/A F/A F#/A G/A G#/A
DMA9

Dancing in the Street

William Stevenson
Marvin Gaye, Ivy Hunter
(As sung by Martha Reeves
and the Vandellas)

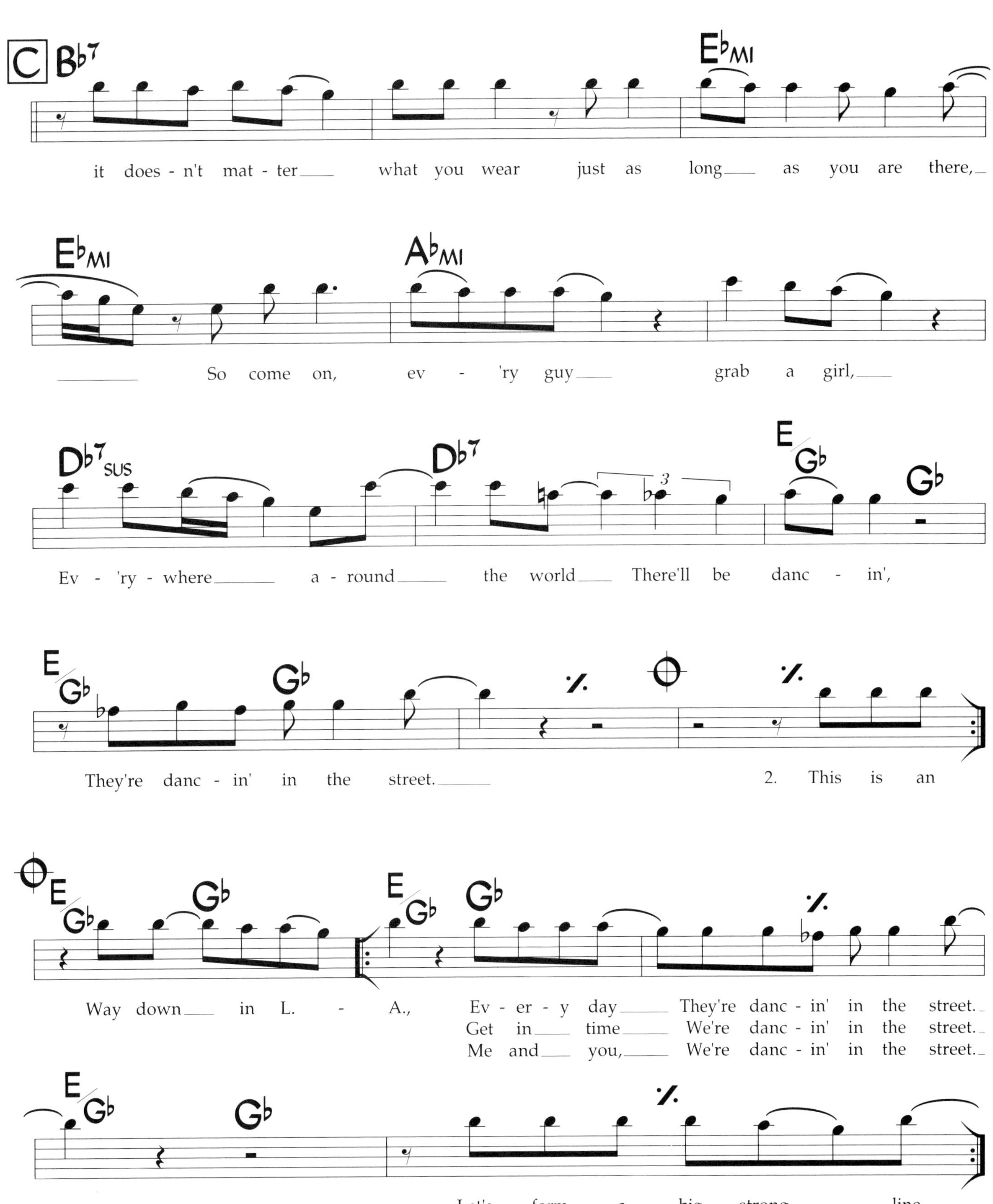

Second verse lyric:

This is an invitation across the nation, a chance for folks to meet,
There'll be laughin', singin', music swingin', dancin' in the street,
Philadelphia, P.A., Baltimore and D.C., now,
Can't forget the motor city,
All we need is music… (etc.)

Darius Dance

Marc Copland

FMI9
FMI11(MA7 b5)
D7(#11 #9)
GMI11
BbMI11
DbMA7/Eb
FMI9
FMI11(MA7 b5)
D7(#11 #9)
GMI11
BbMI11
C
Piano solo
EMI6
F#MI7(b5)
B7(alt.)
4
2
2
(bass walks in 2)
EMI6
F#MI7(b5)
B7(alt.)
4
2
2
(Repeat back to letter B)
D
Solos
FMI6
GMI7(b5)
C7(alt.)
4
2
2
E
EMI6
F#MI7(b5)
B7(alt.)
4
2
2
Solos start at letter C, then repeat DDEE, DDEE, etc.
Play letter A between solos. After last solo, D.C., play ABC,
vamp & fade on letter A (drum solos).

Day Dream
Duke Ellington
& Billy Strayhorn
Medium Ballad
A
Day Dream, Why do you haunt me so? Deep in a ros - y
glow, the face of my love you show.
Day Dream, I walk a - long on air, Build - ing a cas - tle
there for me and my love to share.
B
Don't know the time, Lord - y, I'm in a daze.
Sun in the sky, while I moan a - round feel - ing haz - y.
C
Day Dream, Don't break my rev - er - ie, un - til I find that
she is day - dream - ing just like me.

Dexter

Medium Jazz Ballad

Jerry Bergonzi
(As played by Joey Calderazzo)

Melody is freely interpreted.
Melody includes embellishments from the recording.

Photo by Jerry Stoll

DEXTER GORDON

Dienda

Kenny Kirkland
(As played by Branford Marsalis)

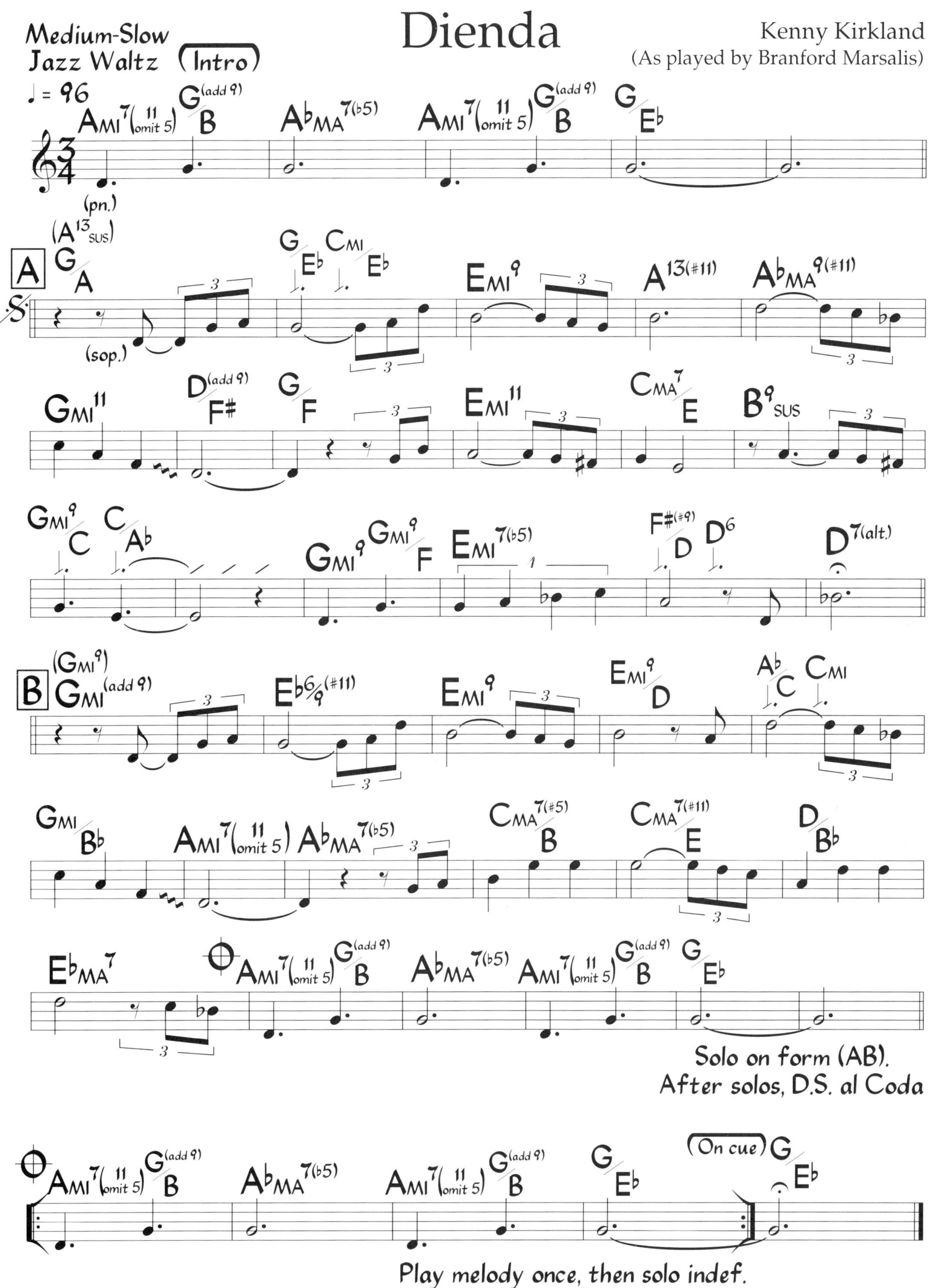

Melodic rhythm is freely interpreted. Fermata is ignored for solos.
On recording, piano plays the head once ad lib. before the Intro.
Chords in parenthesis are used for solos.

Divertimento

Torrie Zito
(As played by Eddie Daniels)

D♭MA7(♭5)
G13(♭9)
CMA7(♭5)
BMA7(♭5)
B♭MA7(♭5)
B♭13(♭5)
DMA7/A
8va
F/A
A13(♭9)
Solo on form (ABC).
Last solo ends at letter B, play B, C, Ending
Ending
(D)
(rit.)
D

Photo by Tom Copi

TONY WILLIAMS, JACO PASTORIUS & HERBIE HANCOCK

Dolphin Dance

Herbie Hancock

After first solo, each solo (and the out head) begins at B2.

Don't Ask Why (for Irene Kral)

Alan Broadbent

Don't Be That Way

Music: Benny Goodman
& Edgar Sampson
Lyric: Mitchell Parish

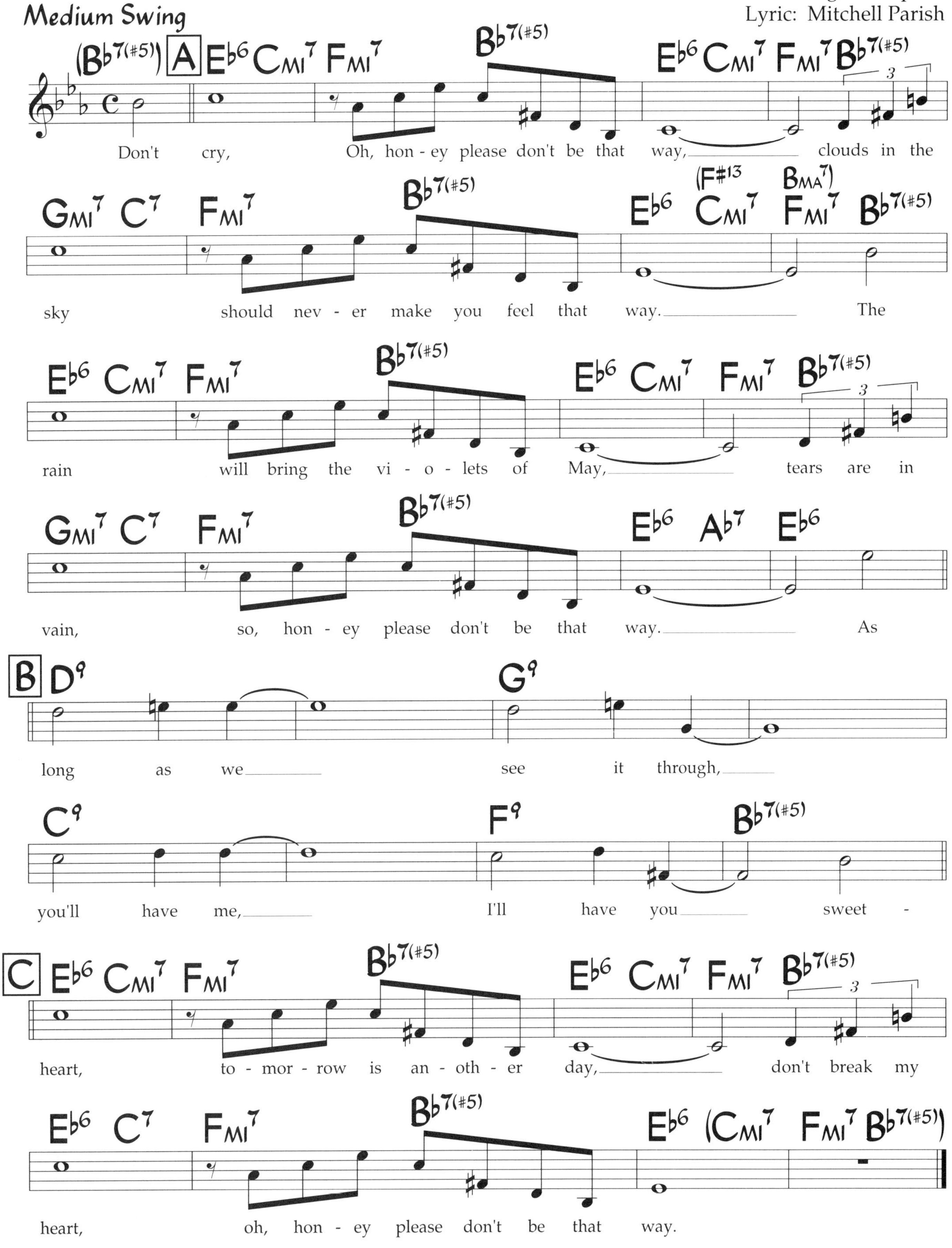
Medium Swing
(Bb7(#5)) A Eb6 Cmi7 Fmi7 Bb7(#5) Eb6 Cmi7 Fmi7 Bb7(#5)
Don't cry, Oh, hon - ey please don't be that way, clouds in the
Gmi7 C7 Fmi7 Bb7(#5) Eb6 (F#13) Cmi7 (BMA7) Fmi7 Bb7(#5)
sky should nev - er make you feel that way. The
Eb6 Cmi7 Fmi7 Bb7(#5) Eb6 Cmi7 Fmi7 Bb7(#5)
rain will bring the vi - o - lets of May, tears are in
Gmi7 C7 Fmi7 Bb7(#5) Eb6 Ab7 Eb6
vain, so, hon - ey please don't be that way. As
B D9 G9
long as we see it through,
C9 F9 Bb7(#5)
you'll have me, I'll have you sweet -
C Eb6 Cmi7 Fmi7 Bb7(#5) Eb6 Cmi7 Fmi7 Bb7(#5)
heart, to - mor - row is an - oth - er day, don't break my
Eb6 C7 Fmi7 Bb7(#5) Eb6 (Cmi7 Fmi7 Bb7(#5))
heart, oh, hon - ey please don't be that way.

Alternate changes at letter B: ‖ Ami7 | D7 | G#mi7(b5) | C#7(b5) | Gmi7 | C7 | F#mi7(b5) B7(#9 #5) | Bb7(#5) ‖

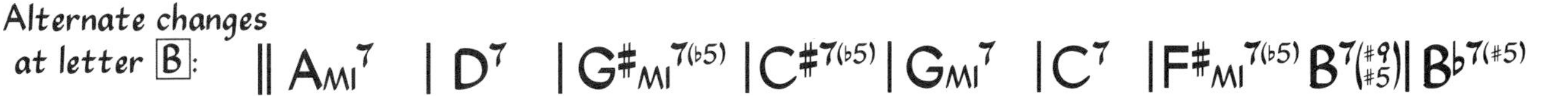

Don't Blame Me

Lyric: Dorothy Fields
Music: Jimmy McHugh

The Double Up

Lee Morgan

Recording has one chorus in front (piano solo).
Head is played twice before and after solos.
Tenor play as written except harmony notes at letter B and Coda, which should be played an octave higher.

Dreamin'
Lisa Montgomery
Geneva Paschal
(As sung by Vanessa Williams)
Med. Funk (Intro)
♩ = 84
N.C.
(voices only)
Now I'm liv - ing in the mid - dle of a dream, a dream with a lit - tle bit of fan - ta - sy.
N.C.
B♭MI9 A♭SUS B♭ G♭MA7 G♭(add 9 omit 3)
1.,2.
3.
1st x: synth.
2nd x: voice
(3rd x: tenor sax)
(add bass & drums)
A
A♭/B♭ B♭MI7 A♭/B♭ B♭MI7 A♭ G♭MA9
1. For the life of me, I nev - er thought that it could be the way it stands right now,
(3rd x: tenor solo for 8 bars)
A♭/B♭ B♭MI7 A♭/B♭ B♭MI7 A♭ G♭MA9
e - mo - tions run - ning high, ev - 'ry night I wish that I could tell you how I
G♭MA9 FMI7 G♭MA9 A♭MI7
(end solo)
feel. Those words are here in my heart, oh, but there
A♭MI7 B♭7 B♭7(♯5) B♭7 E♭MI9 break FMI7 G♭MA7
is just one miss - ing part: How to put it to - geth - er,
break G♭MA7 CMI7(11 omit 5) F7(♯9 ♯5)
how to say it right, and let you know that ev - 'ry night I'll be

2nd verse:

2. Let me take time out to try and find out if this could be real.
'Cause reality scares me, I've been living a fantasy, how should I feel?

SAM JONES, JOE ZAWINUL, NAT & CANNONBALL ADDERLEY, CHARLES LLOYD

Photo © Lee Tanner

El Gaucho

Wayne Shorter

No kicks or bass licks during solos.
Head is played twice before and after solos.

Emily

Music: Johnny Mandel
Lyric: Johnny Mercer
(As played by Bill Evans)

Lyric:

Emily, Emily, Emily has the murmuring sound of May,
All silver bells, coral shells, carousels,
And the laughter of the children at play, say

Emily, Emily, Emily, and we fade to a marvelous view,
Two lovers alone and out of sight, seeing images in the firelight,
As my eyes visualize a family, they see dreamily, Emily, too.

Everything I Have Is Yours

Fall With Me

Music: Jude Swift
Lyric: Jude Swift & Lorraine Feather

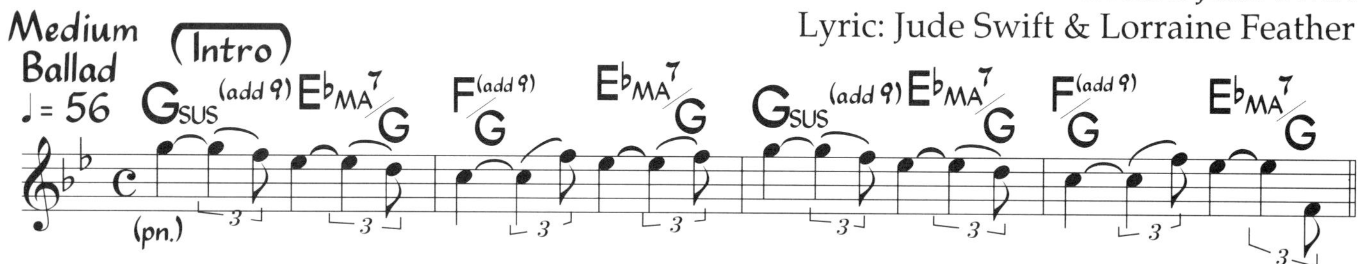

D
DMI9 CMI9 Bb13SUS AbMA7(#11)
AbMA7(#11) A13SUS A13 D6/9
time I hold you through the night, I can't fight the truth.
DMI9 GMI9 CMI9 Bb13SUS Ab/Bb A/B Bb/C C/D
If this grows sweet-er, strong-er and deep-er, I think we're wise to try and risk it
G13SUS G7SUS(b9) Eb6/9 AMI7(11 omit 5) DMI7(11 omit 5)
all, Would you like to fall, fall with
GSUS(add 9) EbMA7/G F(add 9)/G EbMA7/G GSUS(add 9) EbMA7/G F(add 9)/G EbMA7/G
(pn.)
me?
D.S. al Ending (pn. solo at A & B, vocal returns at C)
(Ending)
GSUS(add 9) EbMA7/G F(add 9)/G EbMA7/G
(pn. & ten. fill)
(Vamp, fill & fade)

For All We Know

Music: J. Fred Coots
Lyric: Sam M. Lewis

Freedomland
Russ Ferrante
(As played by the Yellowjackets)
Med. Funk/Latin
♩ = 122
(synth.)
1st x: tenor doubles synth. melody
2nd x: tenor solos
(tenor)
(synth.)
drums & perc. fill
D.C., play AABB (tenor solos over synth. melody at A). Then continue to letter C.
(4x's)
(Synth. solo)
(bass)
Vamp & solo till cue. On cue, D.C. al Coda.
1st x: tenor plays melody
2nd x on: tenor solos
(synth.)
(tenor fill)
(Vamp, solo & fade)
Tenor should play an octave higher than written.

Medium Jazz Waltz
♩ = 178
From Day to Day
Mulgrew Miller
Intro
(pn.)

Chords in parentheses optional for head and solos.
Note: This chart is based primarily on the composer's score.

Photo by Paul Hoeffler, Toronto

MULGREW MILLER

The Gentle Rain
Med. Ballad (or Slow Bossa)
Lyric: Matt Dubey
Music: Luiz Bonfá
We both are lost and a - lone in the world, walk with
me in the gen - tle rain.
Don't be a - fraid, I've a hand for your hand, and I
will be your love for a while.
B
I feel your tears as they fall on my cheek, they are
warm like the gen - tle rain.
Come, lit - tle one, you have me in the world, And our
love will be sweet, will be sad, like the gen - tle rain,
like the gen - tle rain, like the gen - tle rain.

Medium Motown Rock
♩ = 132
Get Ready
William "Smokey" Robinson
Intro
N.C.
(drs. tacet)
(bs./pn./low horns)
(dr. fill)
(strings)
(bs./low horns)
A
I nev - er met a girl who makes me feel the way that you do. (You're all right.) When - ev - er I'm asked who makes my dreams real, I say that you do. (You're out - ta sight.) So
B
fee fi fo fum. Look out, ba - by, 'cause here I come.
C
And I'm bring - in' you a love that's true so get read - y, so get read - y.
(bkgr. vocals) Ah get read - y, get read - y.
E A G C Ami7 D7

Second verse:
If you wanna play hide and seek with love let me remind you. (It's all right.)
The lovin' you're gonna miss and the time it takes to find you. (It's outta sight.)
So fiddleleedee, fiddleleedum. Look out, baby, 'cause here I come. etc.

Third verse:
All my friends shouldn't want you, too, I understand it. (It's all right.)
I hope I get to you before they do, the way I planned it. (It's outta sight.)
So tweedleleedee, tweedleleedum. Look out, baby, 'cause here I come. etc.

Photo by Paul Hoeffler, Toronto

AL COHN

A Ghost of a Chance

Music: Victor Young
Lyric: Bing Crosby & Ned Washington

Grand Central

John Coltrane

Note: On piano solo omit figures except last x of letter F.
Tenor should play an octave higher than written.

Gush

Maria Schneider

This chart has been simplified from the composer's score.

Hard Eights

Lyle Mays

Melody at letters A & C may be played an octave higher.
Melody is freely interpreted.

Heat Wave

Eddie Holland
Lamont Dozier
Brian Holland

(As sung by Martha Reeves and the Vandellas)

Horn line at 2nd ending of letter A is played at every "break".

Second and third verses

2. Whenever he calls my name, soft, low, sweet and plain,
I feel, yeah, yeah, I feel that burnin' flame.
Has high blood pressure got a hold on me
Or is this the way love's supposed to be?
It's like a heat wave…

3. Sometimes I stare in space, tears all over my face.
I can't explain it, don't understand it, I ain't never felt like this before.
Now that funny feelin' has me amazed,
I don't know what to do, my head's in a haze.
It's like a heat wave…

Herzog

Bobby Hutcherson

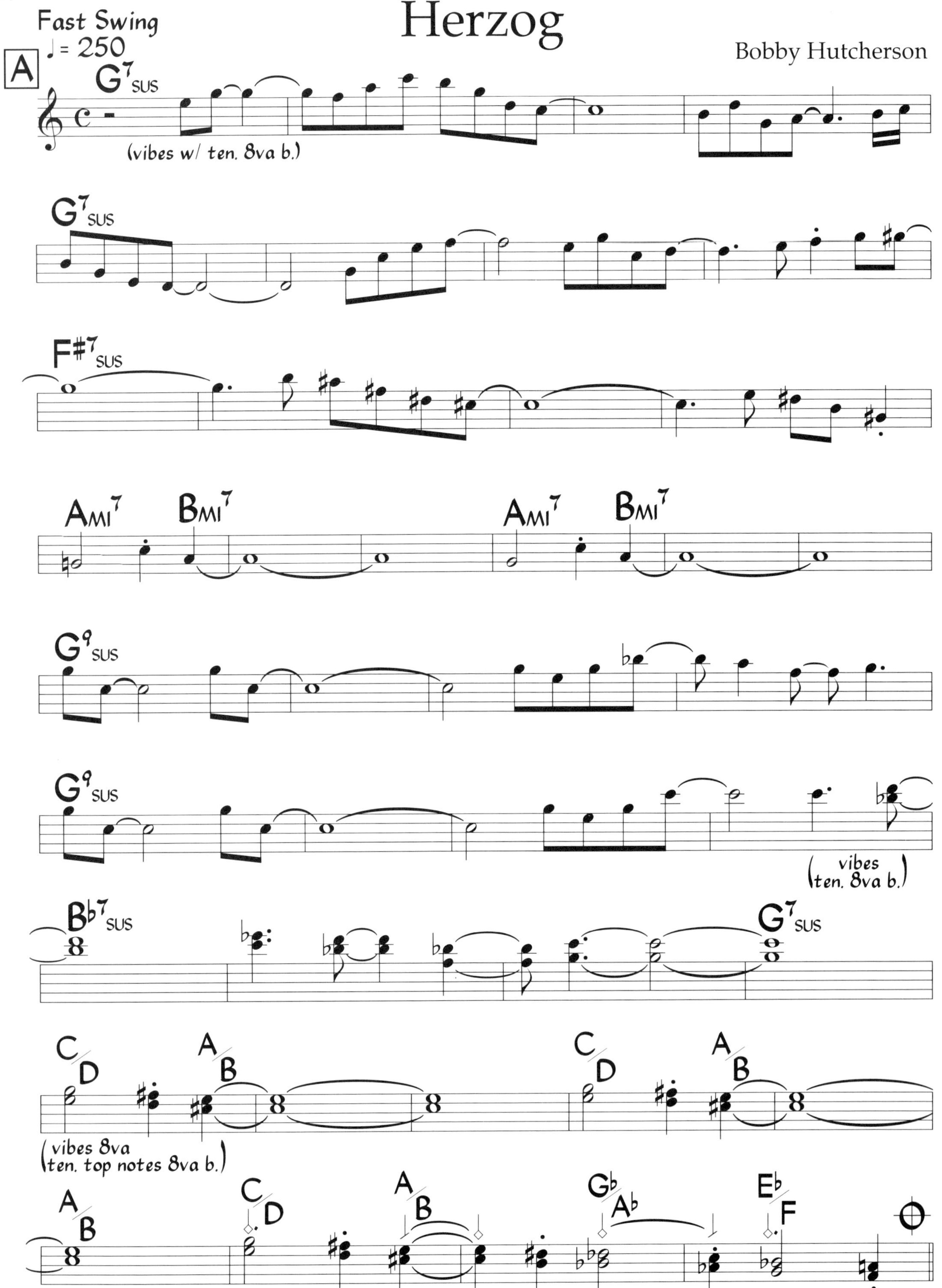

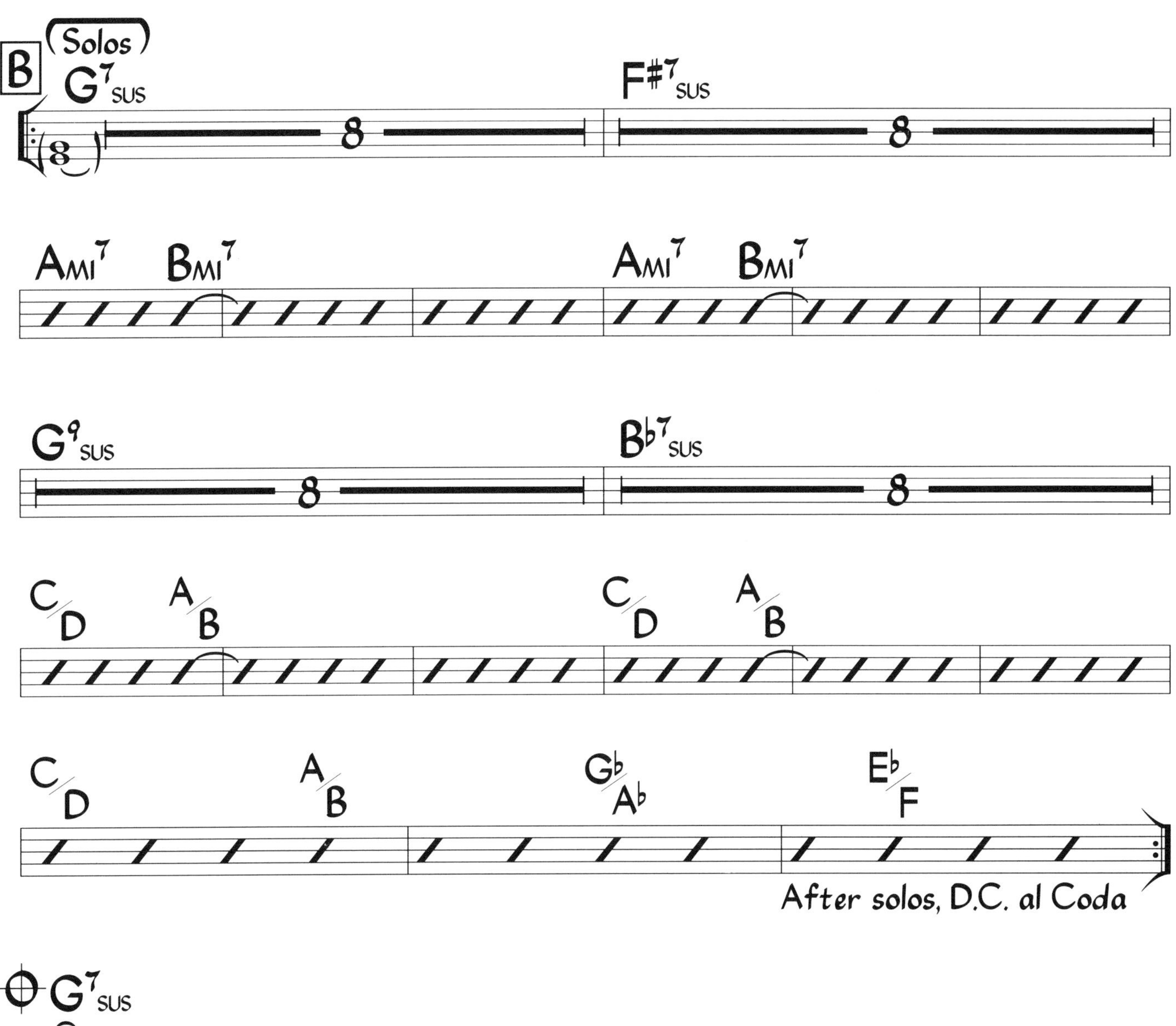
B
Solos
G7sus
F#7sus
Ami7
Bmi7
Ami7
Bmi7
G9sus
Bb7sus
C/D
A/B
C/D
A/B
C/D
A/B
Gb/Ab
Eb/F
After solos, D.C. al Coda
G7sus

Photo © Hyou Vielz

ALLAN HOLDSWORTH

Hold On I'm Coming

Isaac Hayes
& David Porter
(As sung by Sam & Dave)

2nd verse: I'm on my way, your lover,
If you get cold I'll be your cover
Don't have to worry, 'cause I'm here,
No need to suffer, 'cause I'm here.

How Sweet It Is (To Be Loved By You)

Eddie Holland, Lamont Dozier & Brian Holland
(As sung by Marvin Gaye)

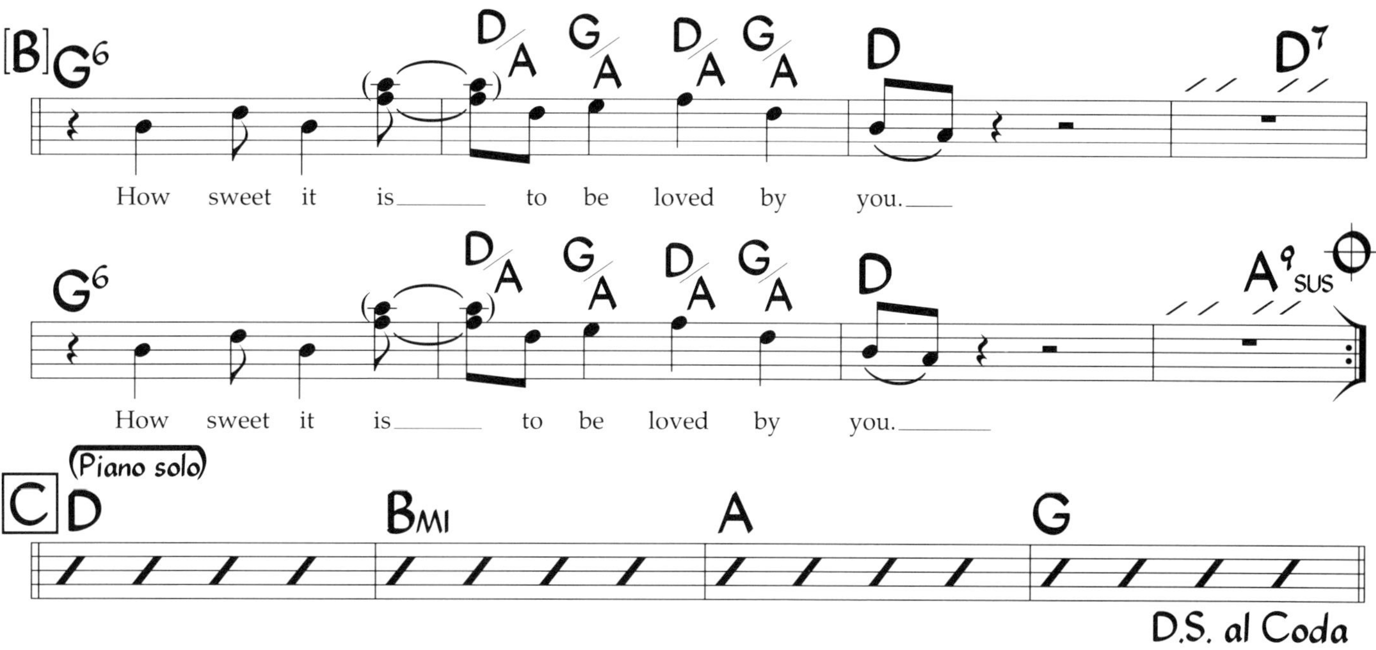

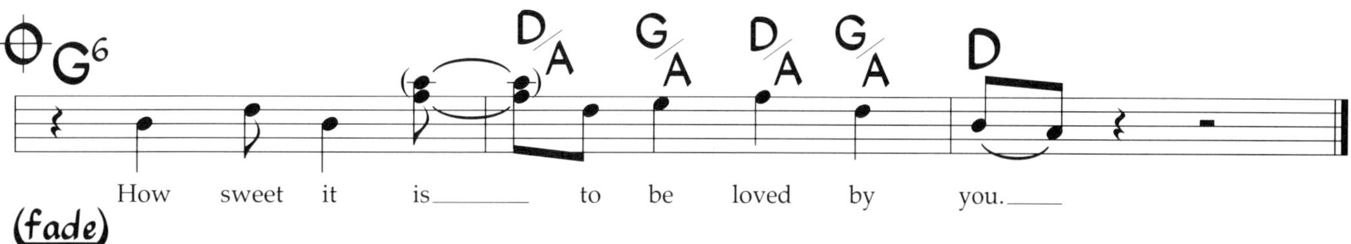

Second verse:

I close my eyes at night,
Wonderin' where would I be without you in my life.
Ev'rything I did was just a bore.
Ev'rywhere I went, seems I've been there before.
But you brighten up for me all of my days
With a love so sweet in so many ways
I want to stop (etc.)

Third verse: (begins at the sign, D.S.)

You were better to me than I was to myself.
For me there's you and there ain't nobody else.
I want to stop (etc.)

I Can't Help It

Susaye Green
Stevie Wonder
(As performed by Michael Jackson)

Second verse: Love to run my fingers softly while you sigh.
Love came and possessed you, bringing sparkles to your eyes.
Like a trip to heaven, heaven is the prize.
And I'm so glad I found you, yeah. You're an angel in disguise.
I can't help it. etc.

I Fall In Love Too Easily

Medium Ballad

Music: Jule Styne
Lyric: Sammy Cahn

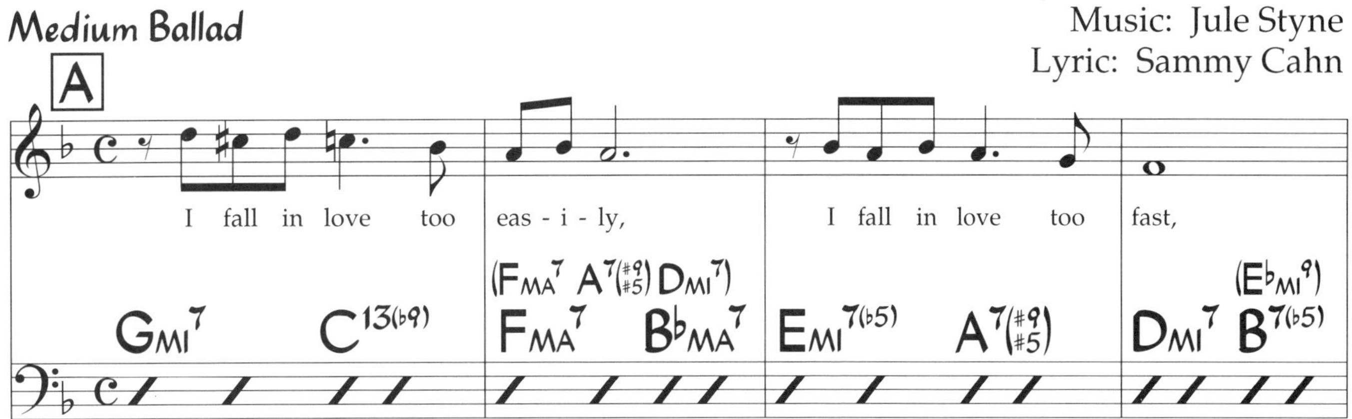

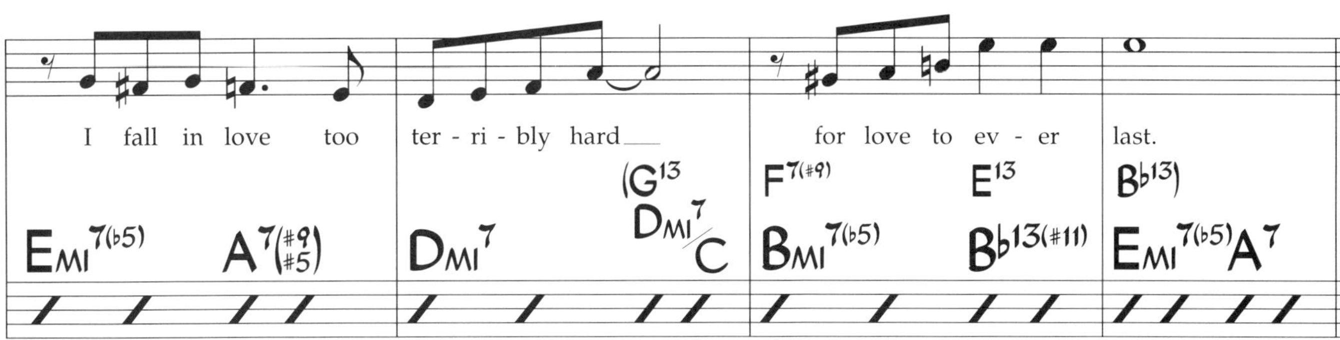

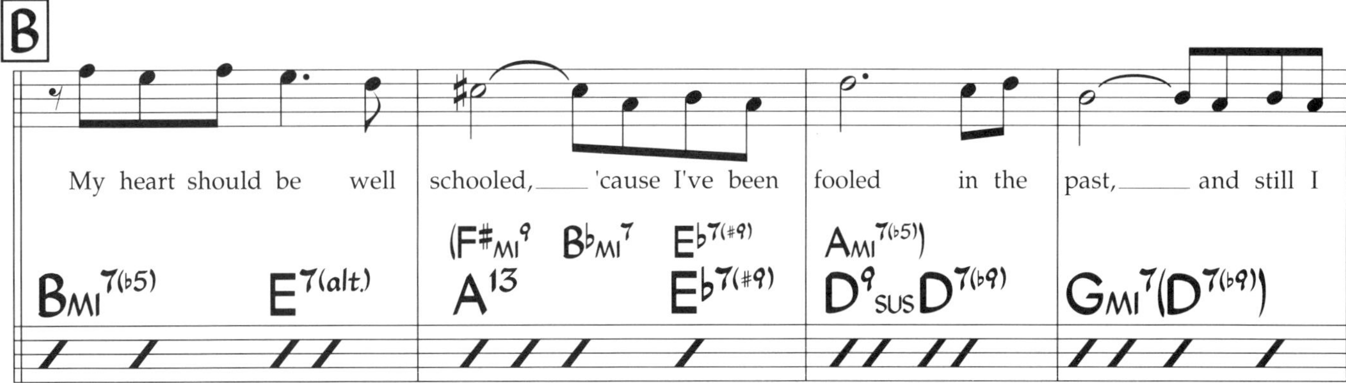

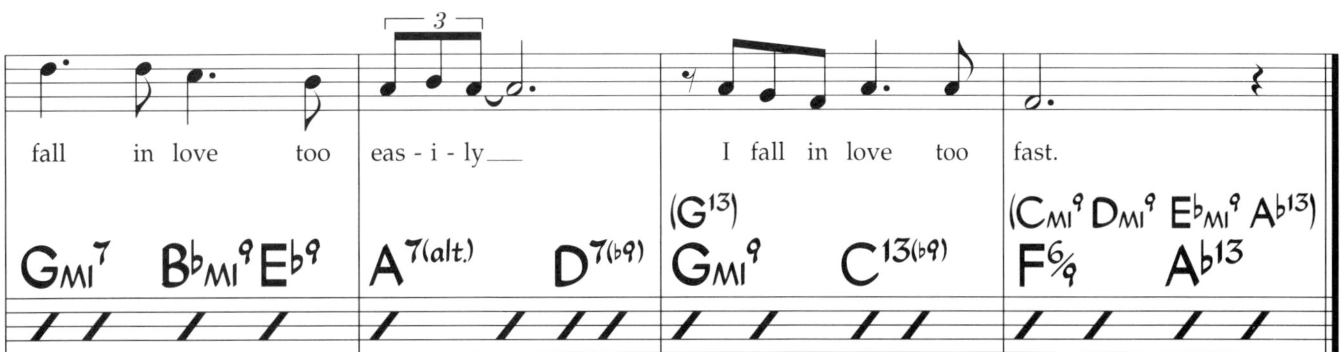

C sharp in bar 1 of A and F sharp in bar 5 may be played as naturals.

I Got It Bad
(And That Ain't Good)

Lyric: Paul Webster
Music: Duke Ellington

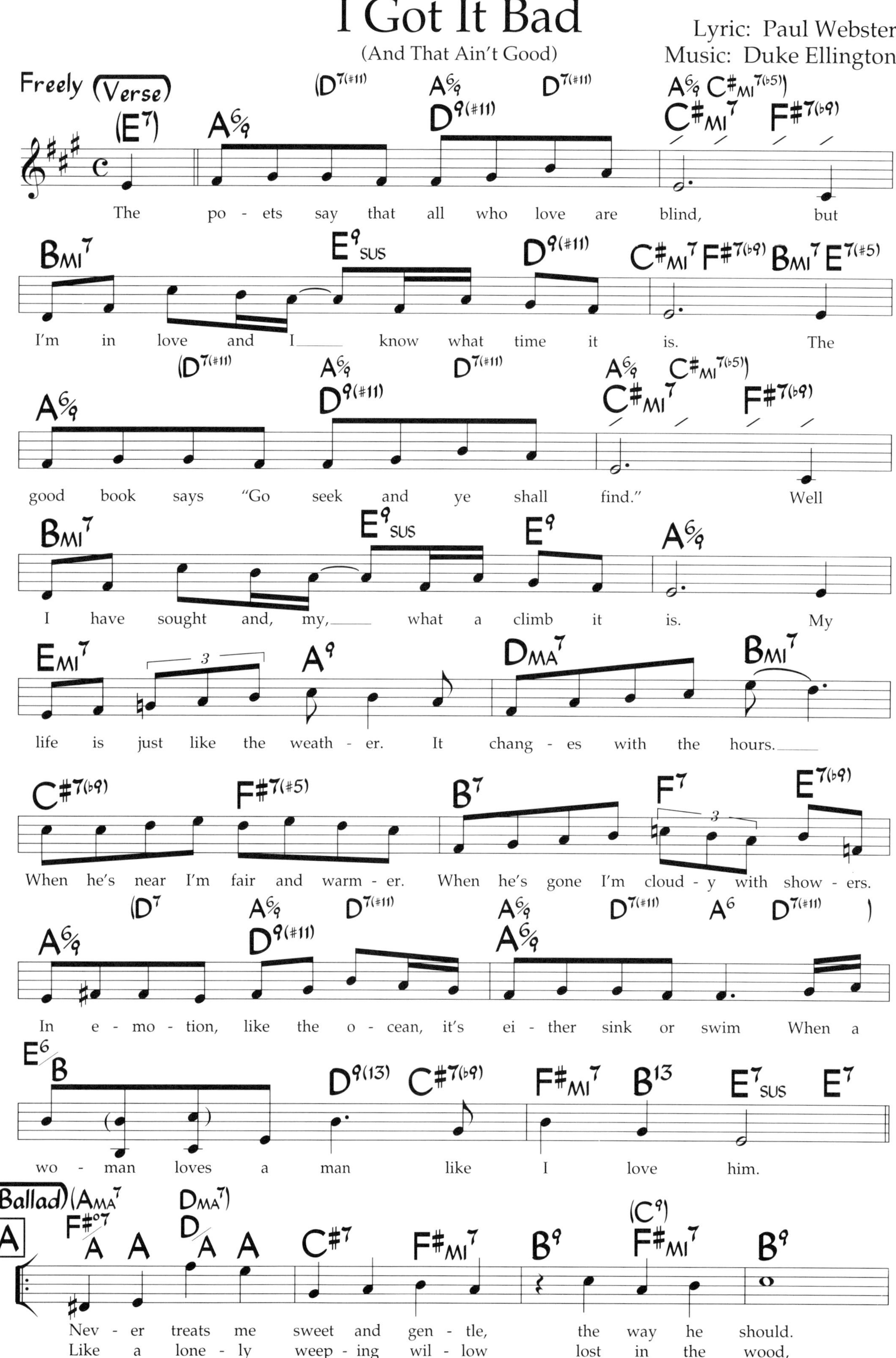

BMI7 C#7(#5) F#7 B7 E13 A6 F#MI7 BMI7 E7

I got it bad and that ain't good!

(AMA7 DMA7) F#°7/A A D/A A C#7 F#MI7 B9 (C9) F#MI7 B9

My poor heart is sen - ti - men - tal, not made of wood.
And the things I tell my pil - low no wom - an should.

BMI7 C#7(#5) F#7 B7 E13 A6 D#°7 EMI7 A7

I got it bad and that ain't good!___________ But
Tho'

B D6 G7

when the week - end's o - ver and Mon - day rolls a - round I
folks with good in - ten - tions tell me to save my tears, I'm

AMA7 (G#MI7 G7 F#MI7) C#MI7 F#7 BMI7 (F7(#5)) E9SUS E7(b9)

end up like I start out, just cry - in' my heart out.
glad I'm mad a - bout him. I can't live with - out him.

C (AMA7 DMA7) F#°7/A A D/A A C#7 F#MI7 B9 (C9) F#MI7 B9

He don't love me like I love him. No - bod - y could.
Lord a - bove me, make him love me the way he should.

BMI7 C#7(#5) F#7 B7 E13 A6 (F#MI7 BMI7 E7)

I got it bad and that ain't good.

Solo on form (ABC)

Alternate lyric at letter B:

But when the fish are jumpin'
And Friday rolls around,
My man and me, we gin some
And sin some and then some.

Alternate changes (Bill Evans) (Actually played in G)
Letters **A** & **C**:

G#/A A D#7(#9 #5) G#7(b9 #5) C#MI9 G9 F#MI11 C13(#11) B9(#11) BMI9 A9(#5)

G9(#11) F#7(#11 b9) F9 E7(#11 b9) 1. A6/C# F#7(b9 #5) B9 E7(b9 #5) 2. A6/9 C#7(#9 #5) F#13(b9) B7(#9) E13(#9) A9 Eb9 **B** (DMA7(add 6) (etc.)

Photo by Francis Wolff. Courtesy of Mosaic Images

JOHN COLTRANE

I Hear a Rhapsody

George Fragos, Jack Baker
& Dick Gasparre

Note: Bottom changes are Bill Evans'; more standard changes in parentheses.

I Heard It Through the Grapevine

Norman Whitfield
Barrett Strong
(As sung by Marvin Gaye)

Second and Third Verse lyrics:

2. I know a man ain't supposed to cry,
But these tears I can't hold inside.
Losin' you would end my life, you see,
'Cause you mean that much to me.
You could have told me yourself
That you loved someone else.
Instead, I heard it through the grapevine (etc.)

3. People say believe half of what you see,
Son, and none of what you hear,
But I can't help bein' confused.
If it's true please tell me, dear.
Do you plan to let me go
For the other guy you loved before?
Don't you know, I heard it through the grapevine (etc.)

I Wanted to Say
Medium Swing (in 2)
♩= 136
Victor Lewis
(As played by Kenny Barron)
A
(muted trp. w/ ten. 8va b.)
B
(trp. 8va b.)
C
Solo on form (ABC).
After solos, D.C. al Coda
(pn. fills)
(Vamp & fade)
Chords in parentheses are optional for solos.
On recording, solos are 2 choruses each, the first in 2 and the second in 4.

I'm Getting Sentimental Over You

Lyric: Ned Washington
Music: George Bassman

(I Know) I'm Losing You

Cornelius Grant
Norman Whitfield
Eddie Holland
(As sung by the Temptations)

Second verse:

When I look into your eyes,
A reflection of a face I see.
I'm hurt, down-hearted and worried, girl,
'Cause that face doesn't belong to me.

It's all over your face, Someone's taken my place,
Ooh, baby, I'm losing you.
You try hard to hide the emptiness inside,
Ooh, baby, I'm losing you.

Repeat of letter D:

Oh, my dear, what happened to the love we shared?
Ooh, baby, I'm losing you.
I know it's true, there's someone new,
Ooh, baby, I'm losing you.

I'm Through with Love

Lyric: Gus Kahn
Music: Matt Malneck
& Fud Livingston

AMI7
(E7(b9 #5))
AMI7
D7(b9)
deep e - mo - tion, de - vo - tion to you. Good -
C
GMA7
Bb°7
AMI7
D7
(DMI7)
GMA9
G7
bye to Spring, and all it meant to me, It can nev - er bring the
CMA7
F7
BMI7
E7(b9 #5)
AMI7
(E7(b9 #5))
thing that used to be, for I must have you or no - one,
(A7)
AMI7
D7(b9)
G6
(D7(b9))
and so I'm through with love.

If You Could See Me Now

Lyric: Carl Sigman
Music: Tadd Dameron

Note: These are Bill Evans' changes, transposed.

Photo by Paul Hoeffler, Toronto

DUKE ELLINGTON

In a Mellow Tone

Lyric: Milt Gabler
Music: Duke Ellington

In a Sentimental Mood

Duke Ellington, Irving Mills
& Manny Kurtz

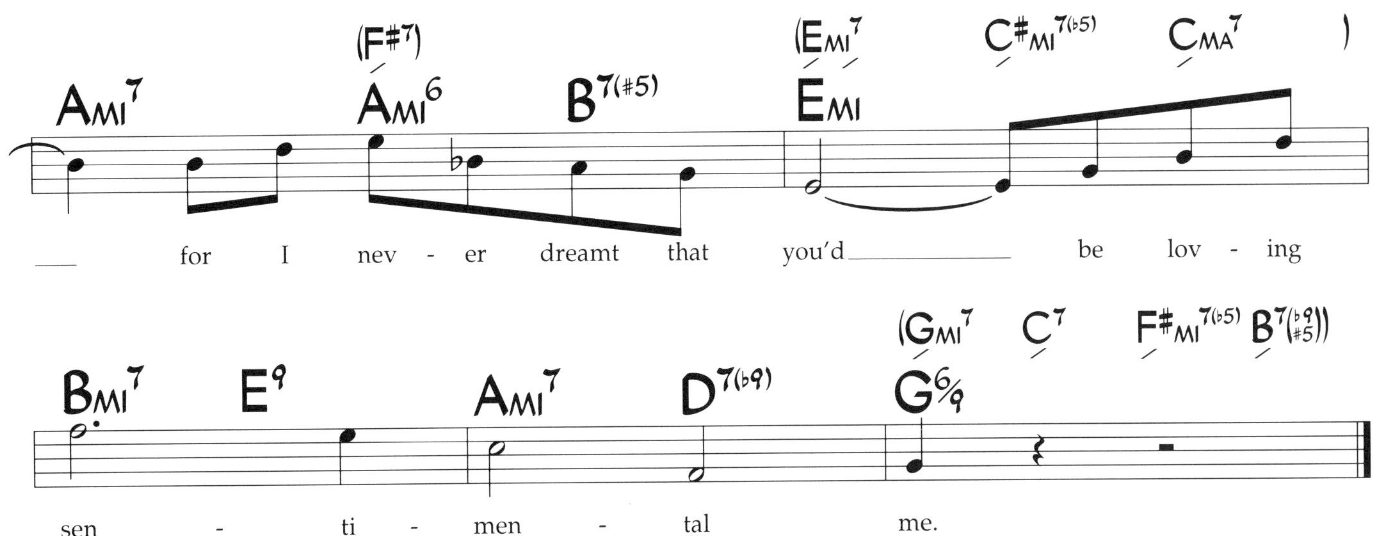

Chords in parentheses are Bill Evan's changes for head.

In Case You Missed It

Bobby Watson

Kicks are played for solos (first 16 bars of A may be played straight ahead after first chorus of each solo).

In Love With Night
Bright Jazz Waltz
♩ = 170
Andy LaVerne
(tenor)
(add pn., loco)
last x: rit.
(Fine)
Solo on form (A A B)
After solos, D.C. al Fine

Head is played twice before and after solos.

Invitation

Medium Swing or Ballad
(or 12/8 Latin)

Lyric: Paul Francis Webster
Music: Bronislau Kaper

D
DMI9
long must I stay in a world of il - lu - sion, be where you
DMI9
(G13(♭9/♭5))
G13
(C13(♭9/♭5))
C13
are, so near yet so far a - part,
E
FMI9
D♭9(#11)
Hop - ing you'll say, with a warm in - vi - ta - tion, "Where have you
G7(#9)
C7(#9)
FMI(MA7)
(E7 A7)
been? Dar - ling come in, come in - to my heart."

Isoar

Nguyên Lê

D
C#MI7
CMA7
G/B
C/Ab
B/D
(gtr.)
EMI7
C#MI9(b5)
F#7SUS
F#13(b9)
BMA9/D#
DMA7(#5)
AMA7/C#
D/G
(add sop.)
(gtr.)
(gtr.)
B9SUS
(sop.)
D9SUS
G#MI7
F#9SUS
F#9SUS
A/F
DMI13
Solo on A
Play BCC after each solo.
After last solo, play BCCD
to Coda.
DMI13
(Vamp, fill & fade)
Recording has an Intro not included on this chart.

Photo by Val Wilmer

JOE HENDERSON

Isotope

Joe Henderson

Head is played twice before and after solos.

It Always Is

Tom Harrell

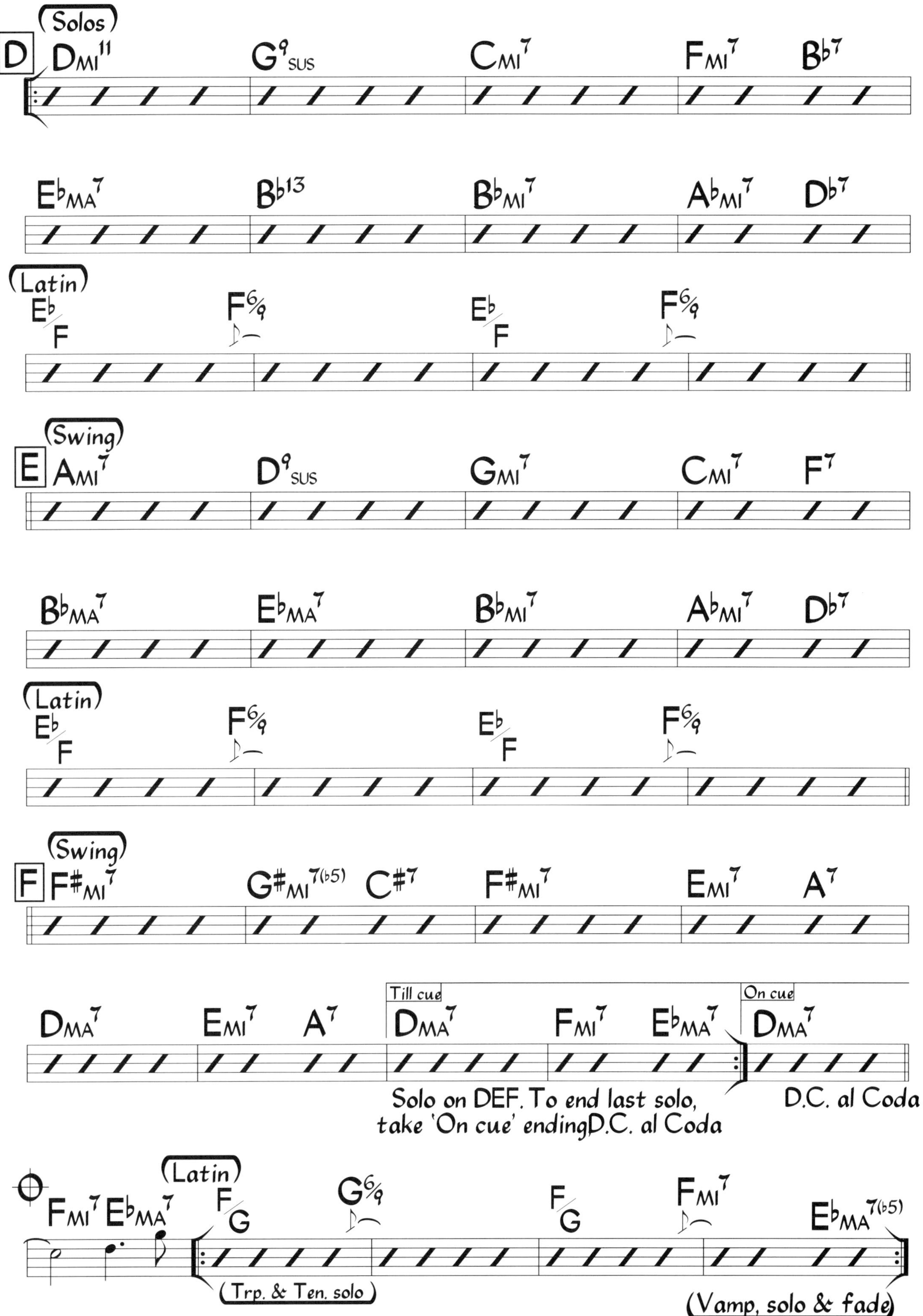

(Solos)
D
DMI11
G9SUS
CMI7
FMI7
B♭7
E♭MA7
B♭13
B♭MI7
A♭MI7
D♭7
(Latin)
E♭/F
F6/9
E♭/F
F6/9
(Swing)
E
AMI7
D9SUS
GMI7
CMI7
F7
B♭MA7
E♭MA7
B♭MI7
A♭MI7
D♭7
(Latin)
E♭/F
F6/9
E♭/F
F6/9
(Swing)
F
F♯MI7
G♯MI7(♭5)
C♯7
F♯MI7
EMI7
A7
DMA7
EMI7
A7
Till cue
DMA7
FMI7
E♭MA7
On cue
DMA7
Solo on DEF. To end last solo, take 'On cue' endingD.C. al Coda
D.C. al Coda
FMI7
E♭MA7
(Latin)
F/G
G6/9
F/G
FMI7
E♭MA7(♭5)
(Trp. & Ten. solo)
(Vamp, solo & fade)

It Always Is (Harmony)
Med.-Fast Swing
♩ = 230
A
(ten.)
(Latin)
B
(Swing)
dr. fill
dr. fill
dr. fill
(Latin)
C
(Swing)
D
(Solos)
DMI11
G9SUS
CMI7
FMI7
Bb7
EbMA7
Bb13
BbMI7
AbMI7
Db7
(Latin)
Eb/F
F6/9
Eb/F
F6/9

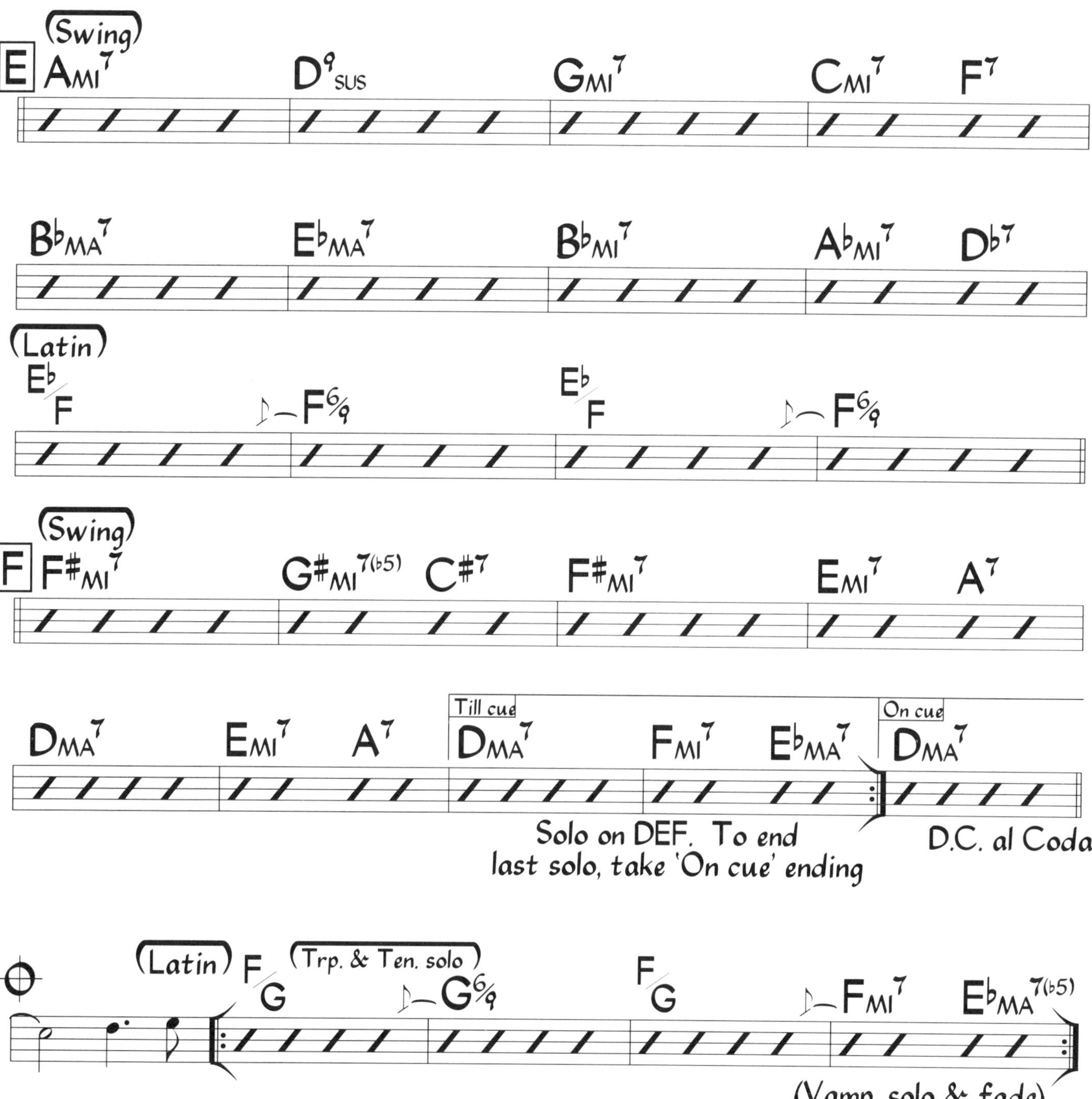

(Swing)
E
AMI7
D9SUS
GMI7
CMI7
F7
B♭MA7
E♭MA7
B♭MI7
A♭MI7
D♭7
(Latin)
E♭/F
F6/9
E♭/F
F6/9
(Swing)
F
F#MI7
G#MI7(♭5)
C#7
F#MI7
EMI7
A7
DMA7
EMI7
A7
Till cue
DMA7
FMI7
E♭MA7
On cue
DMA7
Solo on DEF. To end last solo, take 'On cue' ending
D.C. al Coda
(Latin)
F/G
(Trp. & Ten. solo)
G6/9
F/G
FMI7
E♭MA7(♭5)
(Vamp, solo & fade)

Jean de Fleur

Grant Green

Tenor plays an octave higher except at letter B.

The Jitterbug Waltz

Thomas "Fats" Waller

John's Waltz

John Abercrombie

Head is played once before and after solos.
Melody is freely interpreted.

On recording, head is played as an Intro:

20 bars rubato, guitar solos
10 bars in time, guitar plays melody. (Then play entire head in time.)

Just Friends

Music: John Klenner
Lyric: Sam M. Lewis

Just Squeeze Me

Photo by Francis Wolff, courtesy of Mosaic Images

BOBBY HUTCHERSON

Just You, Just Me

Lyric: Raymond Klages
Music: Jesse Greer

Kahlil the Prophet

Jackie McLean

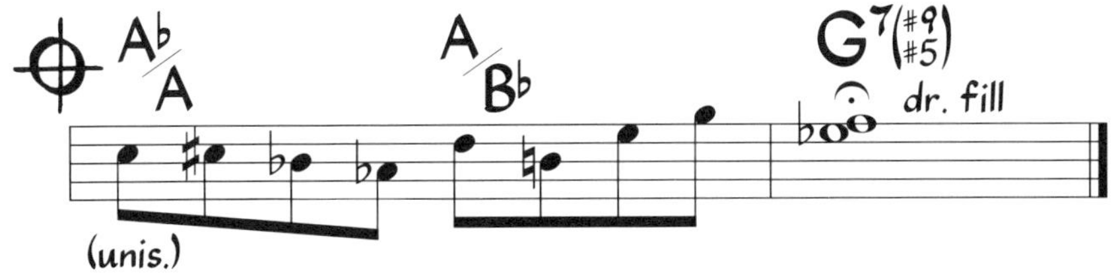

Letter A is repeated before and after solos. On the repeat of the out head, alto plays one octave higher, starting in bar 9 of letter A. All notes sound an octave lower than written.

Knock on Wood

Eddie Floyd
& Steve Cropper

Second verse:

I'm not superstitious about ya,
but I can't take no chance.
Got me spinnin', baby.
Baby, I'm in a trance.
'Cause your love is better
than any love I know.
It's like thunder… (like 1st verse)

Third verse:

No secret, that woman
fills my lovin' cup.
'Cause she sees to it
that I get enough.
Just one touch from her,
you know it means so much.
It's like thunder… (like 1st verse)

Photo by Jerry Stoll

LARRY DUNLAP & BOBBE NORRIS

The Lamp Is Low

Lyric: Mitchell Parish
Music: Peter De Rose
& Bert Shefter

This is based on Maurice Ravel's "Pavane for a Dead Princess."

Last Nite

Larry Carlton

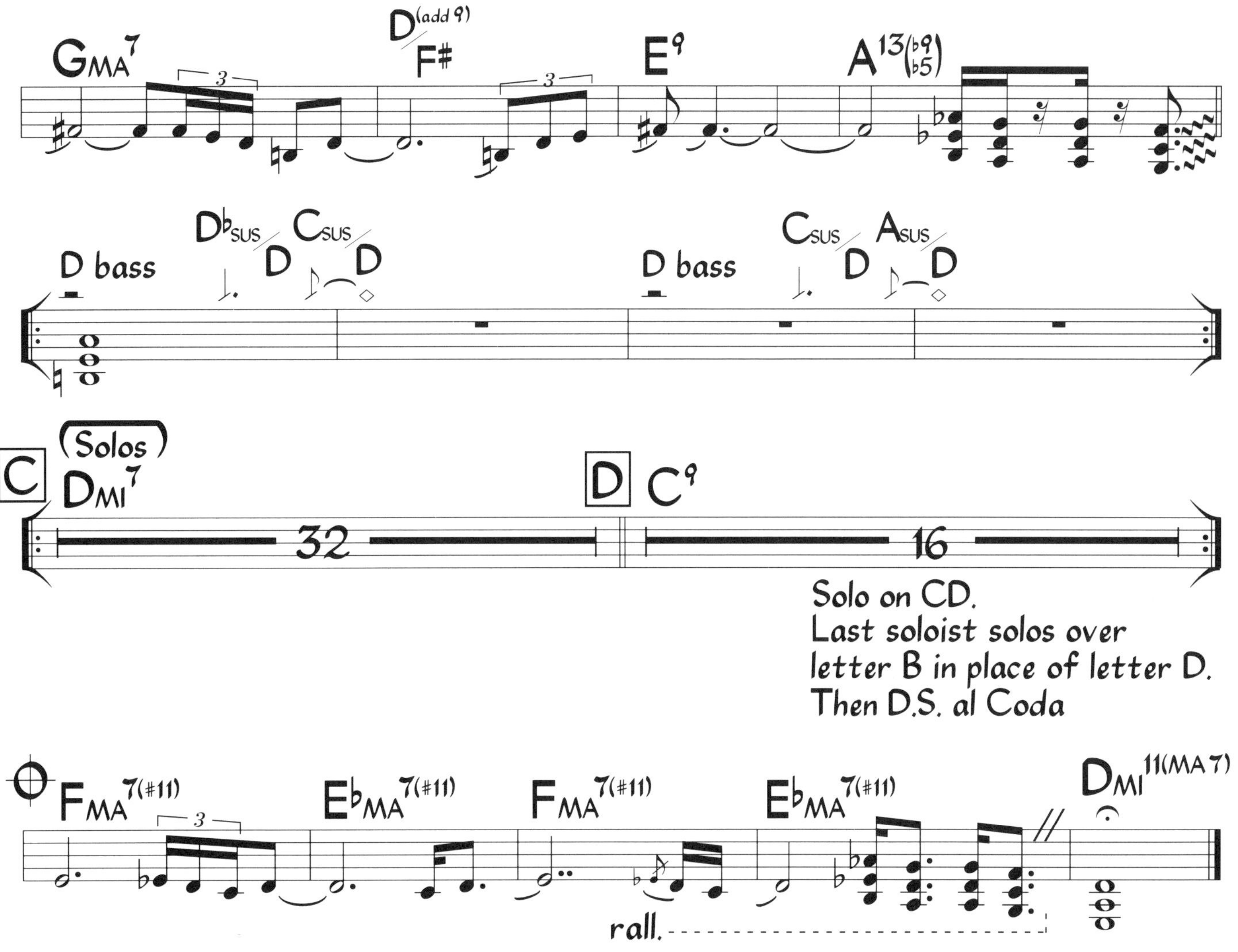

Melody is somewhat freely interpreted.

Last Season

Maria Schneider

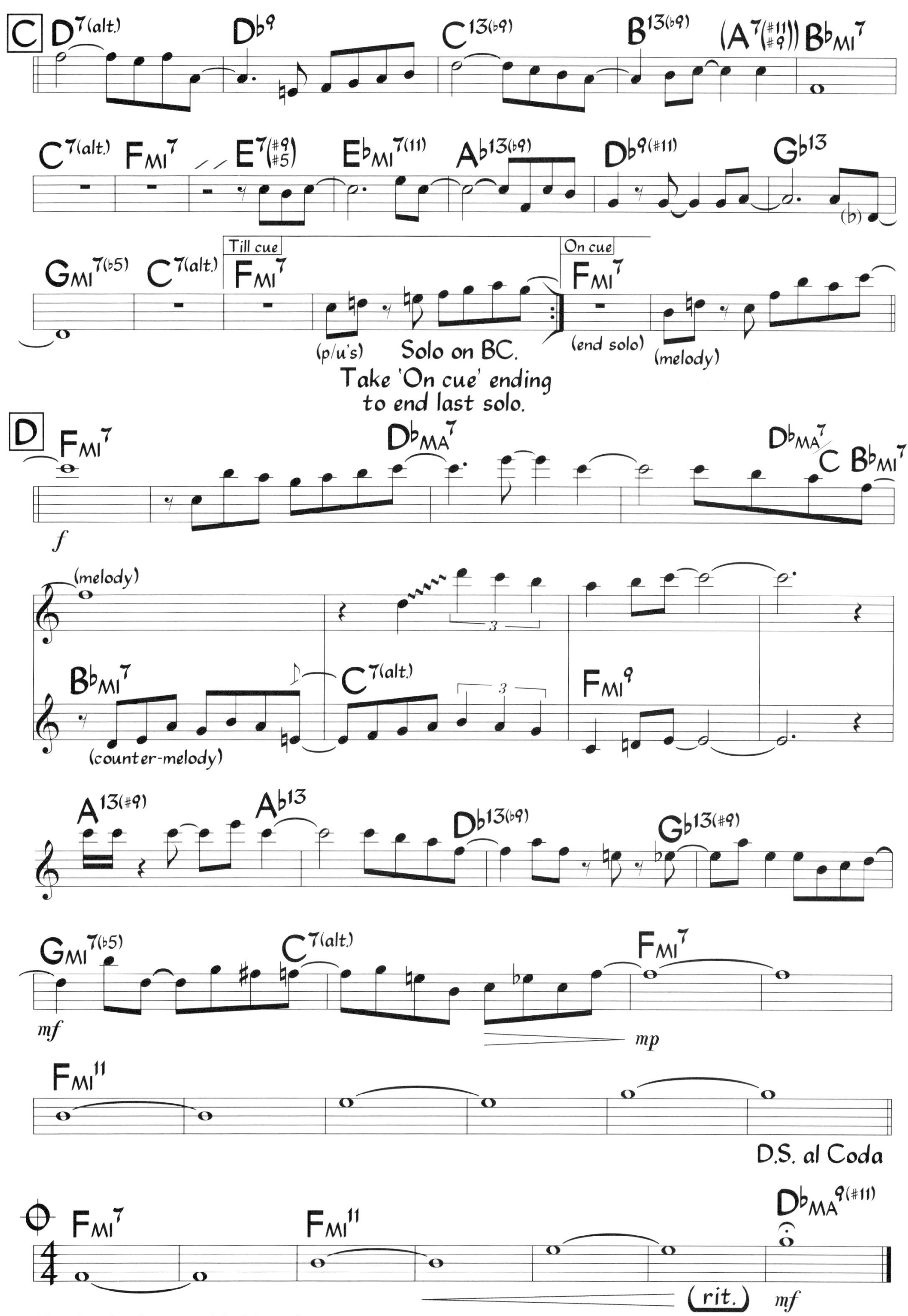

This chart has been simplified from the composer's score.

Photo by Francis Wolff. Courtesy of Mosaic Images

LEE MORGAN

Laura

Lyric: Johnny Mercer
Music: David Raksin

Let's Stay Together

Willie Mitchell
Al Green
Al Jackson
(As sung by Al Green)

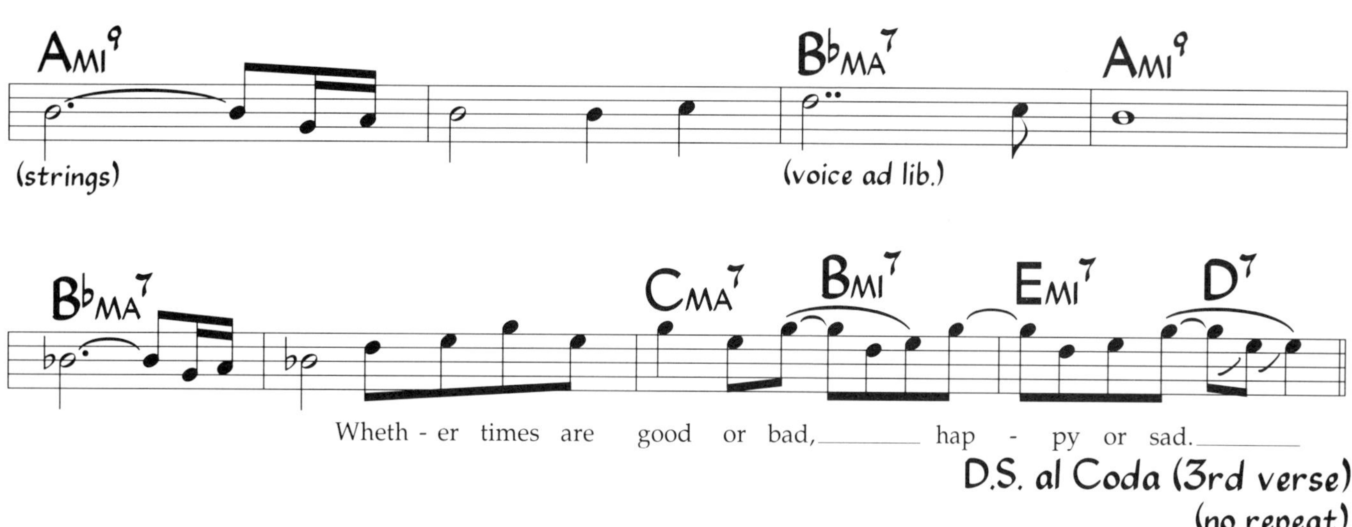

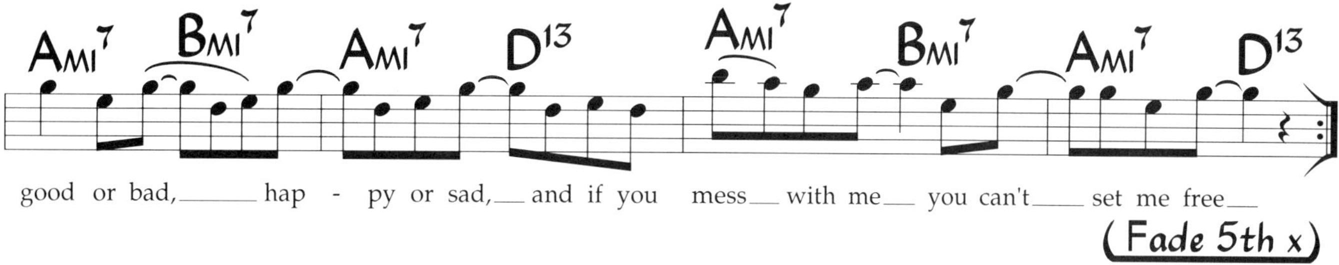

Second verse:

Let me say since, since we've been together,
Loving you forever is what I need.
Let me be the one you come running to,
And I'll never be untrue.

Third verse:

Why, somebody, why people break up,
Oh, and turn around and make up I just can't see.
You'd never do that to me, would you, baby?
Just being around you is all I see.

Letter B is played even faster than ♩. = 𝅗𝅥 ; (♩ = 138).

Head is played twice before solos.

Litha (Harmony)

Head is played twice before solos.

Photo by Tom Copi

EDDIE DANIELS

Lonely Woman

Horace Silver

Chords in parentheses are used for head only.

Look at the Birdie

Wayne Shorter
(As played by Art Blakey)

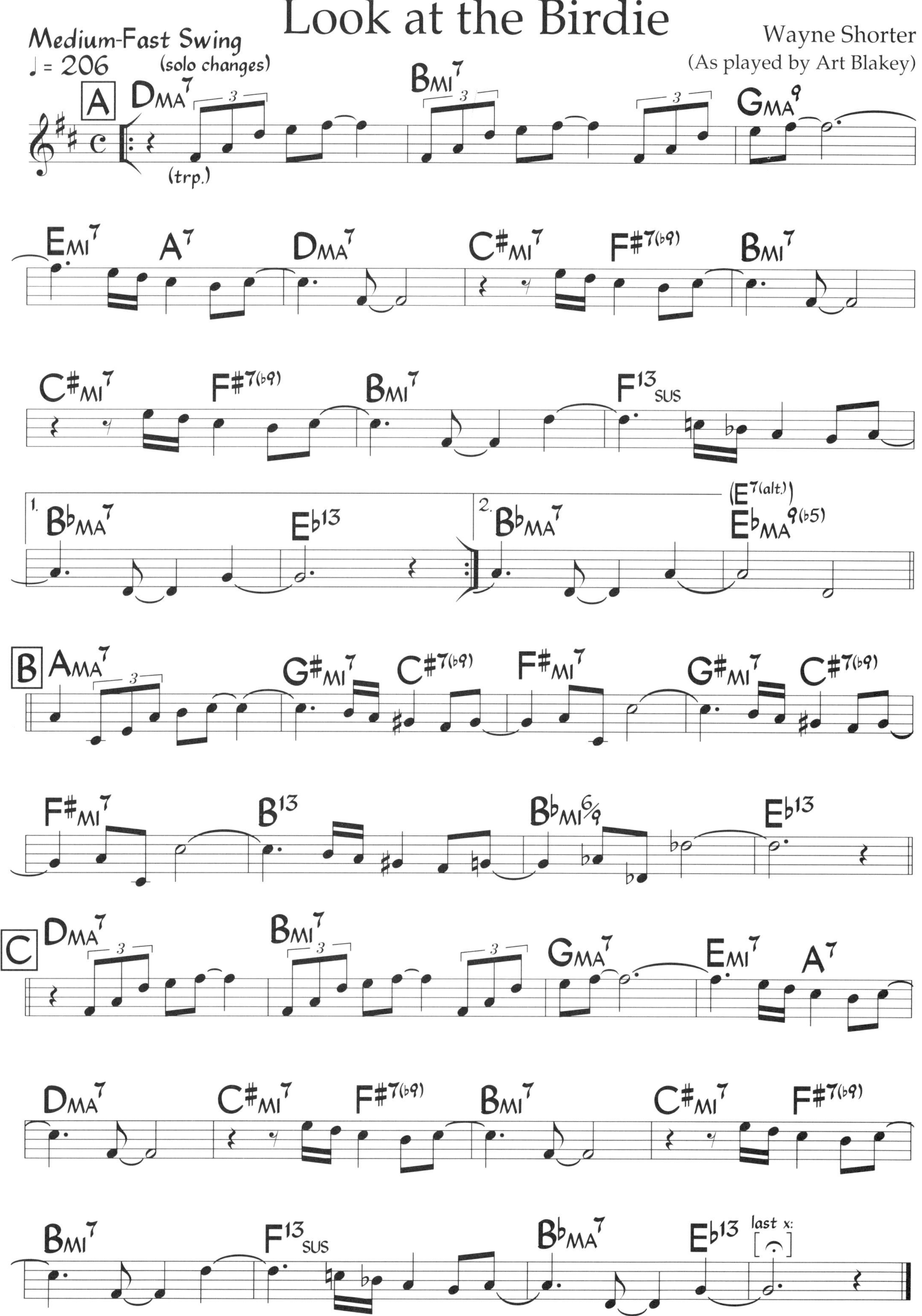

Chord in parentheses is used for solos.

Look at the Birdie (Harmony)

Chord in parentheses is used for solos.

Photo by Paul Hoeffler, Toronto

ABDULLAH IBRAHIM (Dollar Brand)

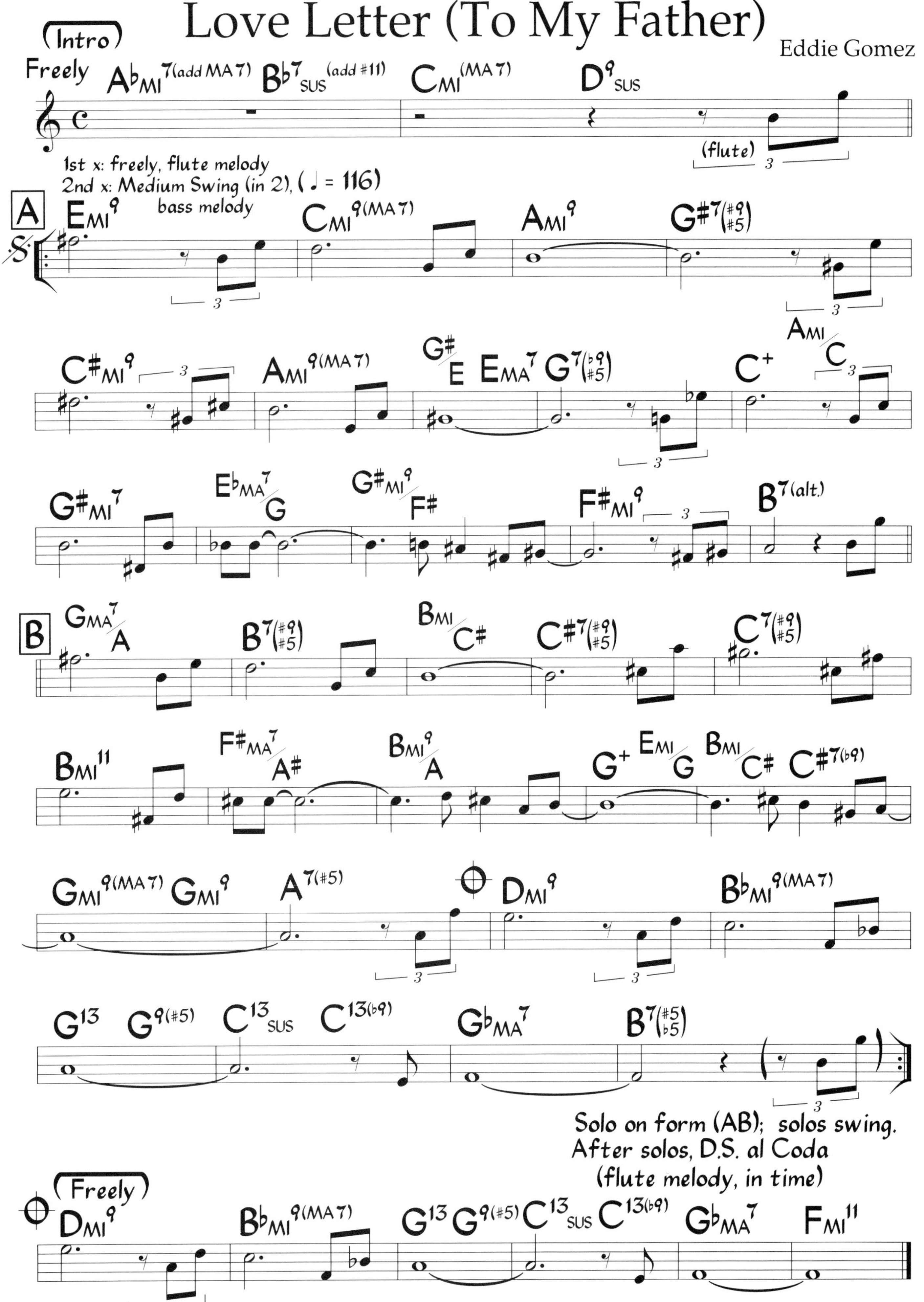
Love Letter (To My Father)
Eddie Gomez
Intro
Freely
(flute)
1st x: freely, flute melody
2nd x: Medium Swing (in 2), (♩ = 116)
bass melody
A
B
Solo on form (AB); solos swing.
After solos, D.S. al Coda
(flute melody, in time)
(Freely)

Love's Haunts

Aydin Esen

E
F
♩ = 𝅗𝅥 (Double-Time Swing, in 2)
(horns, behind solo)
(end solo)
𝅗𝅥 = ♩ (Original tempo)
G
(pn. w/ trp.)
(trp.)
(trp.)
N.C.
H
(freely)
Melody is freely interpreted.
Original melody at A & B
is mostly whole notes:
(etc.)

Photo by Tom Copi

RAHSAAN ROLAND KIRK

Lullaby in Rhythm

Benny Goodman,
Edgar Sampson,
Clarence Profit
& Walter Hirsch

Maiden Voyage

Herbie Hancock

Tenor play as written, except harmony 8va bars 17-24 of letter A.

Mamacita

Joe Henderson

Head is played twice before and after solos.

Mamacita (Harmony)

Head is played twice before and after solos.
Tenor and trombone sound one octave lower than written.

Man Facing North

Bob Mintzer, Will Kennedy,
Russ Ferrante, Jimmy Haslip
(As played by the Yellowjackets)

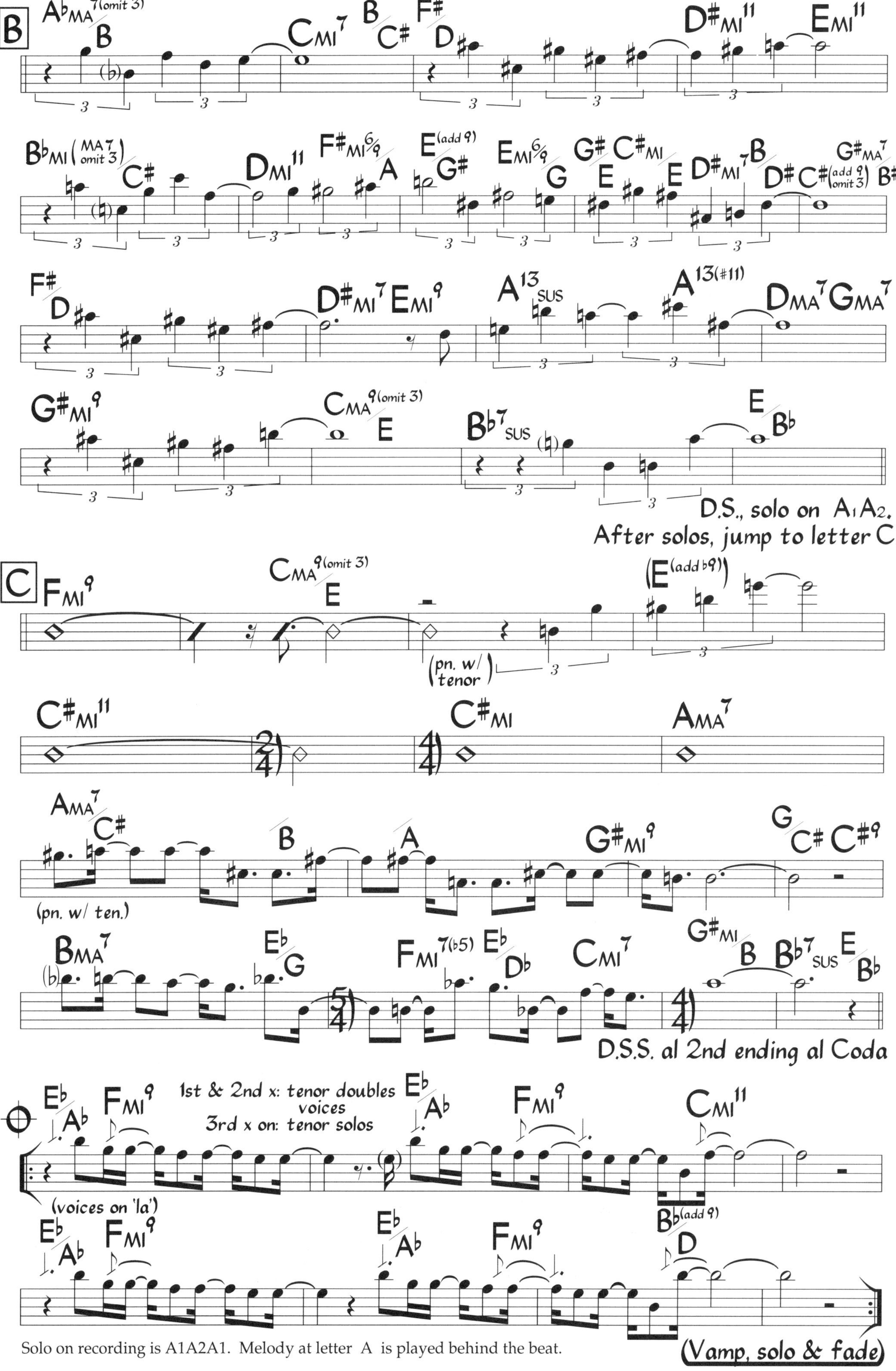
B
D.S., solo on A1A2.
After solos, jump to letter C.
C
(pn. w/ tenor)
(pn. w/ ten.)
D.S.S. al 2nd ending al Coda
1st & 2nd x: tenor doubles voices
3rd x on: tenor solos
(voices on 'la')
Solo on recording is A1A2A1. Melody at letter A is played behind the beat.
(Vamp, solo & fade)

Metamorphosis

Horace Silver

Med.-Fast Swing (Stop Time)
♩ = 200

A

Emi7 A7 | Dma7 D#°7 | Emi7 A7 | (Dma7)

(trp.)

Dmi7 G7 | Cma7 C#°7 | Dmi7 G7 | Fmi7 Bb7 Ebma7

Ebma7 | Ebmi7 Ab7 | Dbma7 | C#mi7 F#7 Bma7

Bma7 | 1., 3. Fmi7(11) Bb7 | Eb6/9 | 2. Fmi7(11) Bb7 | Eb6/9

B

(Beguine)

Gmi7 | C7(#5) | Ami7 | D7 | Gmi7

C9sus | 1. (Fma7) Ami7 | Ami7 D7(#9) break | 2. B13sus | (B13sus) F#mi9 Fmi9

D.C. al 3rd ending. Solo on form (AABBA).
After last solo, continue to letter **C**.

C

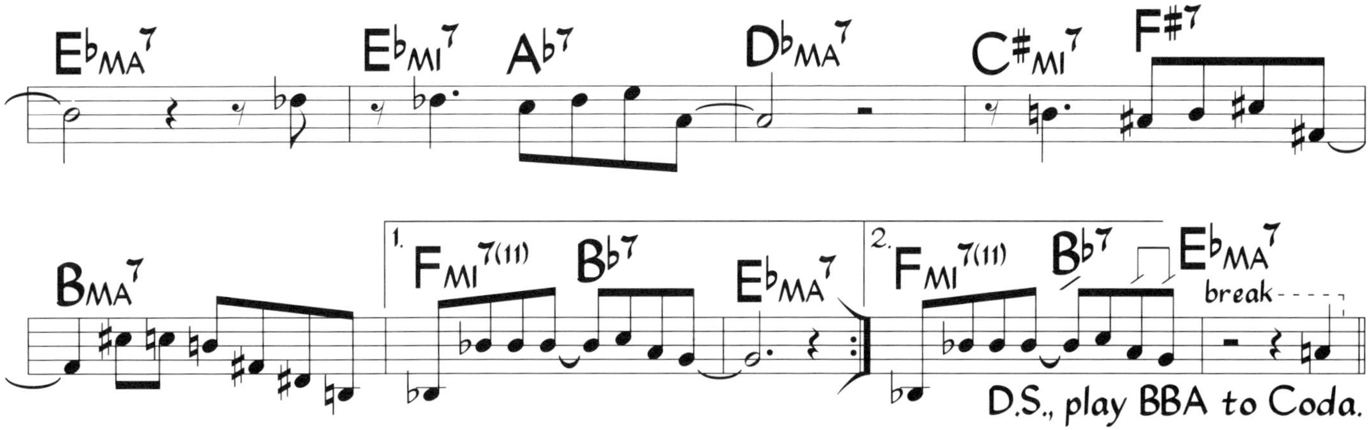

Chords in parentheses are used for solos. Solos swing throughout.

Metamorphosis (Harmony)

Chords in parentheses are used for solos. Solos swing throughout.

Midnight Silence

Kenny Kirkland

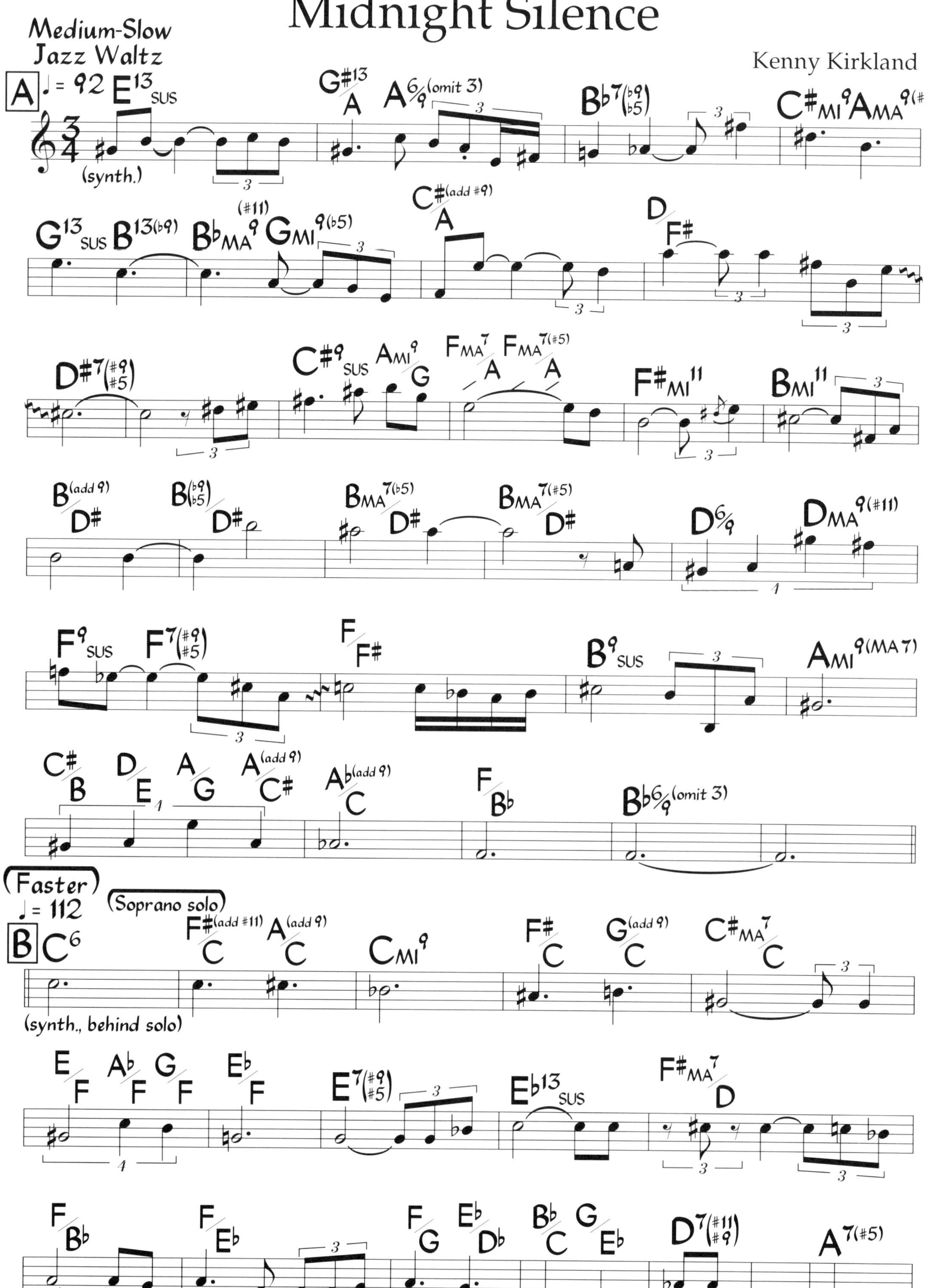

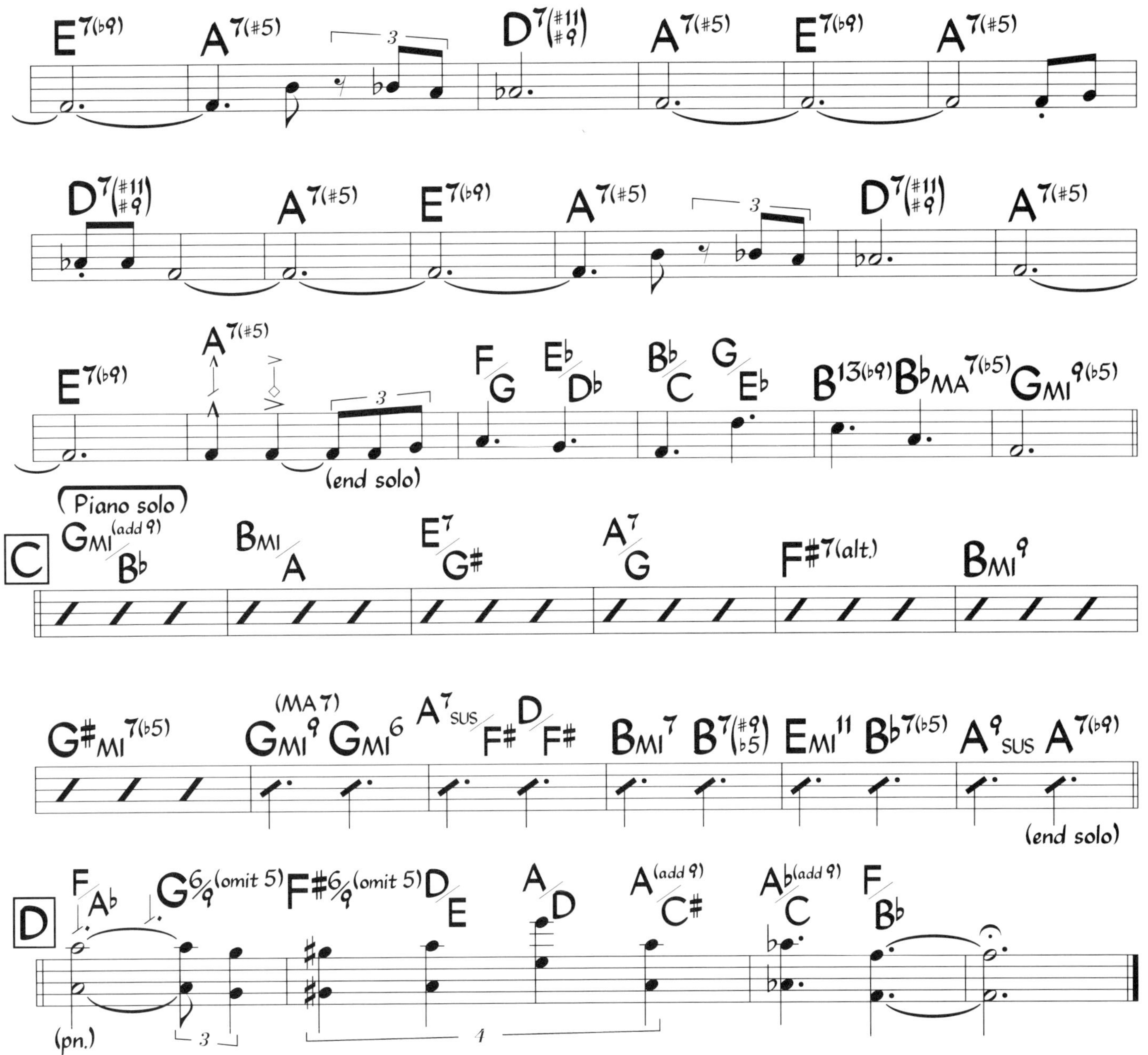

On recording, piano plays letter A (omitting the last 3 bars) out of time as an Intro.

Monk on the Run

Taras Kovayl
(As played by Othello Molineaux)

(1st x: bs. quarter note triplets, dr. hi hat 16ths
2nd x: bs. & dr. full 16th note feel)
C
GMI7 AbMA7 BbMI7 CMI7 GMI7 AbMA7 BbMI7 CMI7 DMA7 D#9(#11)
(steel dr.)
mf
gradually build
(string synth.)
1.
E9(#11) A13 DMA7 G#MI9 G9(#11) F#9
2.
E9(#11) A13 DMA7 G#MI7 G13(#11)
ff
F#9 C#7(#9 #5) C13(#11)
D
F9
C13 F13 E13
(steel dr.)
E13
(pn.)
Gb/E C/F# B/A D/C
break
F9
(Solos)
E
F9
8
EMA7
7
F#/E F#9SUS F#/E D9SUS
D9SUS
6
A/G F#/E D/C E/D
Vamp & solo till cue
(On cue)
Gb/E C/F# B/A D/C
break
F9
D.C. al Coda
(drum solo, open)
(omit 1st ending)
(Solo begins 3rd x)
FMI11 EMA9 C#MA7 BbMA9 F#MA9 EbMI9 BMA9 AbMA9
(steel dr.)
Vamp, solo & fade
(Optional ending- On cue)
EMA9(#11)
dr.
N.C.
ff
2/4
4/4
(F# bass)

Moon and Sand

Music: Alec Wilder
& Morty Palitz
Lyric: William Engvick

(F13(#11)
E9)
Ami9
D7
Bmi7
Emi9
Night is at our com - mand, Moon and
Ami9
F#mi7(b5)
B7
Emi7
sand, and the mag - ic of love.

Moonglow

Will Hudson, Eddie de Lange
& Irving Mills

Medium Ballad
Moonlight Serenade
Lyric: Mitchell Parish
Music: Glen Miller
A
(D7(b9)) G6 Bb°7 AMI7
I stand at your gate and the song that I sing is of
stars are a - glow and to - night how their light sets me
D7 D7(#5) GMA7 G6 GMA7 G6
moon - light. I stand and I wait for the
dream - ing. My love, do you know that your
GMA7 G7 E7(b9) CMI6 BMI7 E9SUS EMI7
touch of your hand in the June night. The ros - es are
eyes are like stars bright - ly beam - ing? I bring you and
AMI7(b5) AMI7 D13 D7(b9 #5) 1. GMA7 AMI7 D7(b9) 2. GMA7 G7
sigh - ing a Moon - light Ser - e - nade. The
sing you a Moon - light Ser - e - nade.
B
CMA7 F13 B7(b9 #5) B7(b9) E7(b9) E7
Let us stray till break of day in love's val - ley of dreams. Just
C#MI7(b5) F#7(b9) BMI7(b5) E7(b9) AMI7 D7(b9)
you and I, a sum - mer sky, a heav - en - ly breeze kiss - ing the trees. So
C
G6 Bb°7 AMI7
don't let me wait, come to me ten - der - ly in the
D7 D7(#5) GMA7 G6 GMA7 G6
June night. I stand at your gate and I
GMA7 G7 E7(b9) CMI6 BMI7 E9SUS EMI7
sing you a song in the moon - light; a love song, my
AMI7(b5) AMI7 D13 D7(#5) GMA7 (AMI7 D7(b9))
dar - ling, a Moon - light Ser - e - nade.

My Girl

William "Smokey" Robinson
Ronald White
(As sung by the Temptations)

2nd verse lyrics:

I've got so much honey, the bees envy me,
I've got a sweeter song than the birds in the trees.
I guess you'd say (etc.)

Never Said (Chan's Song)

Music: Herbie Hancock
Lyric: Stevie Wonder
(As sung by Diane Reeves)

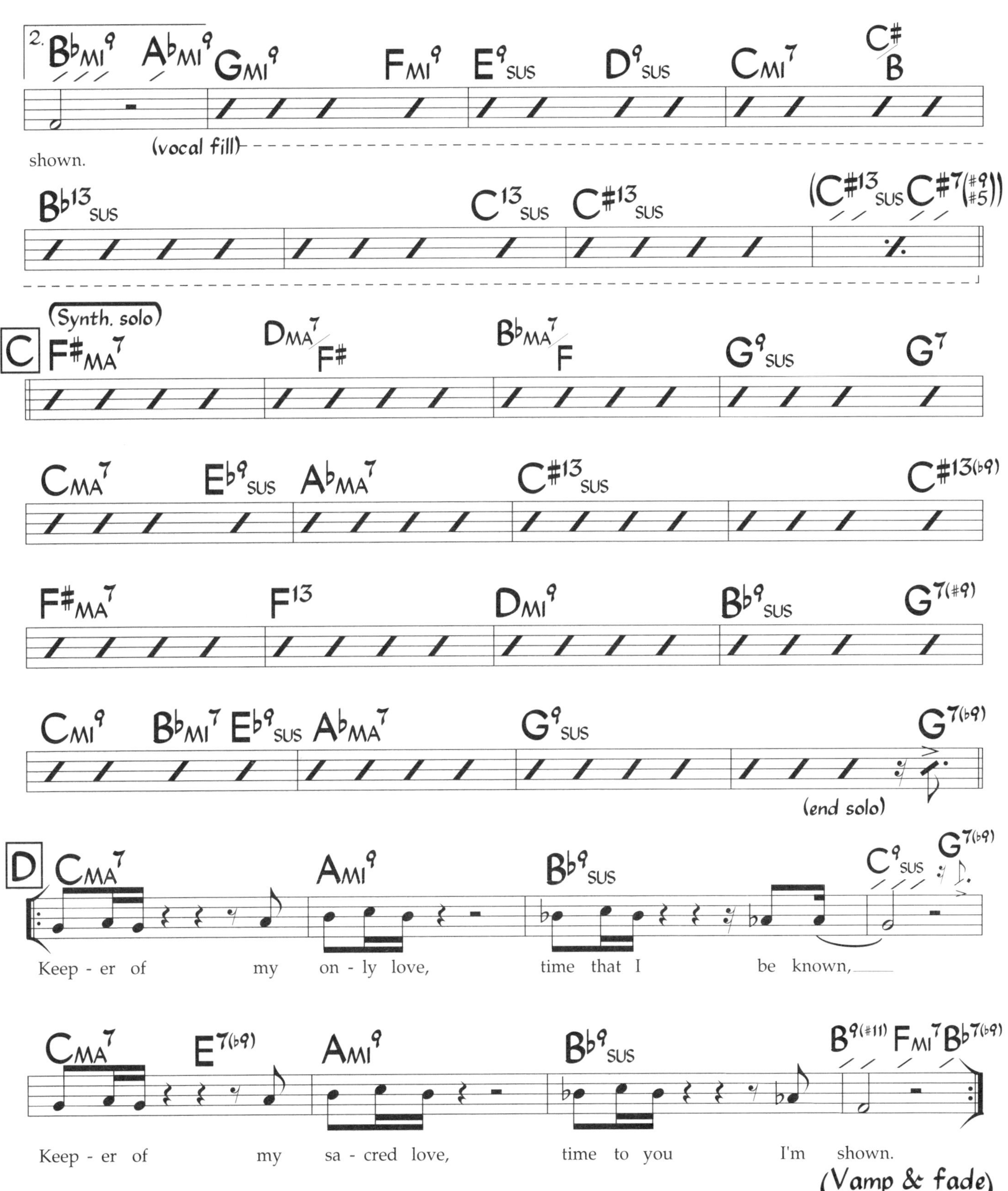

Melodic rhythm is freely interpreted.

MARIA SCHNEIDER

New Boots

Frank Gambale

Head is played twice before and after solos.
Chords in parentheses are used during solos.
No kicks or breaks during solos (except bar 1 of first solo; use '2nd x' kicks.)

Next Future

Eddie Gomez

On recording, ABCD is played out of time (no drums) as an Intro (followed by the Intro given above).
Tenor should play an octave higher than written.

No Way Out

Abel Pabón
(As played by Othello Molineaux)

E
Solos
1st x
'til cue
To letter E
for more solos
on cue (last x)
D.C. al Coda
(with repeat)
N.C.

Nowhere to Run

Eddie Holland
Lamont Dozier
Brian Holland
(As sung by Martha & The Vandellas)

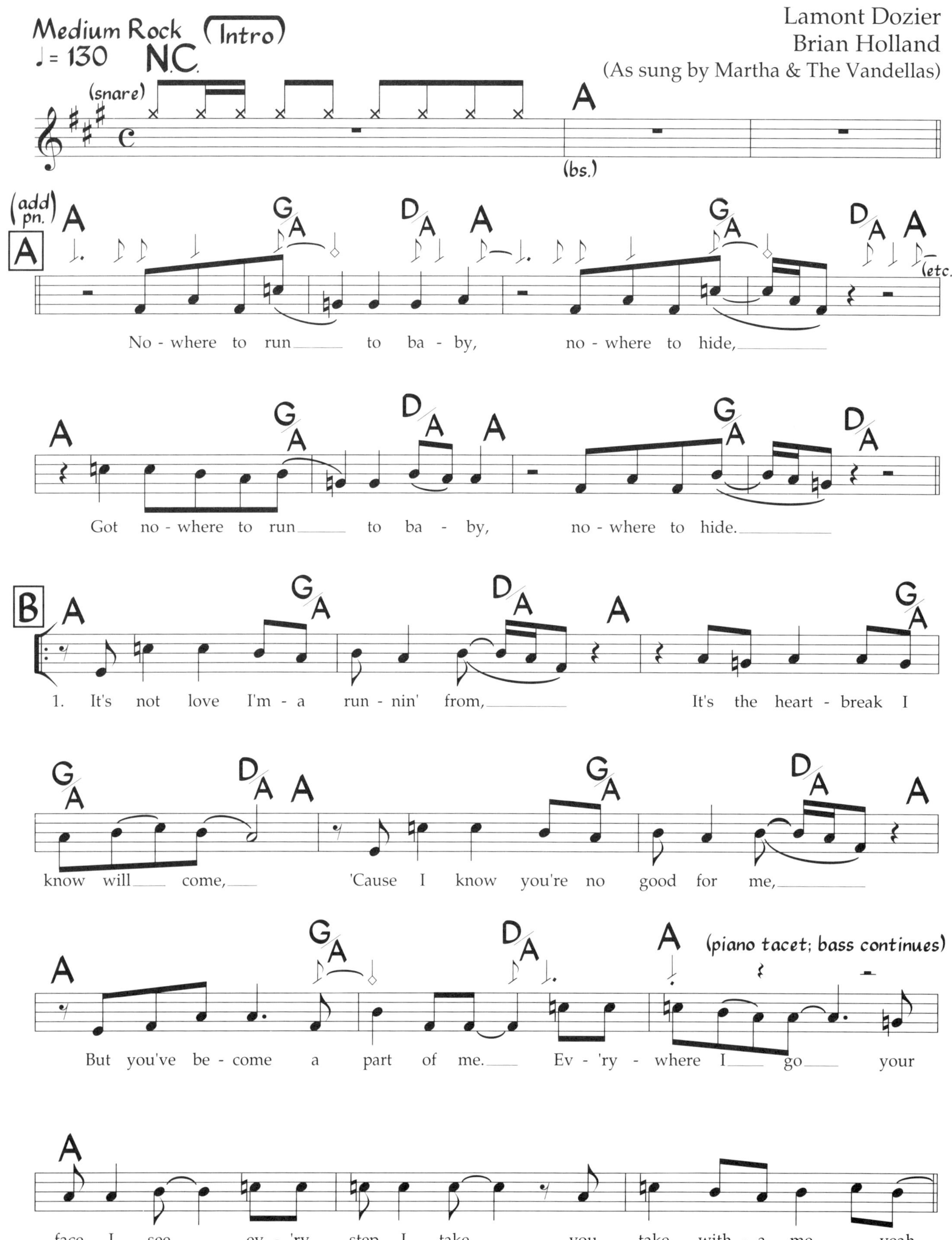

Second and Third verses

2. Each night as I sleep, Into my heart you creep.
I wake up feelin' sorry I met you,
Hopin' soon that I'll forget you.
When I look in the mirror to comb my hair
I see your face just a-smiling there.

Nowhere to run, Nowhere to hide from you, baby.
Got nowhere to run to, baby, Nowhere to hide.
I know you're no good for me,
But you've become a part of me.

3. How can I fight a love that shouldn't be,
When it's so deep, so deep,
Deep inside of me?
My love reaches so high I can't get over it.
It's so wide I can't get around it, no.

Nowhere to run, Nowhere to hide from you, baby.
Just can't get away from you, baby, No matter how I try.
I know you're no good for me,
But free of you I'll never be.

(To Coda)

Off Flow

Dave Liebman

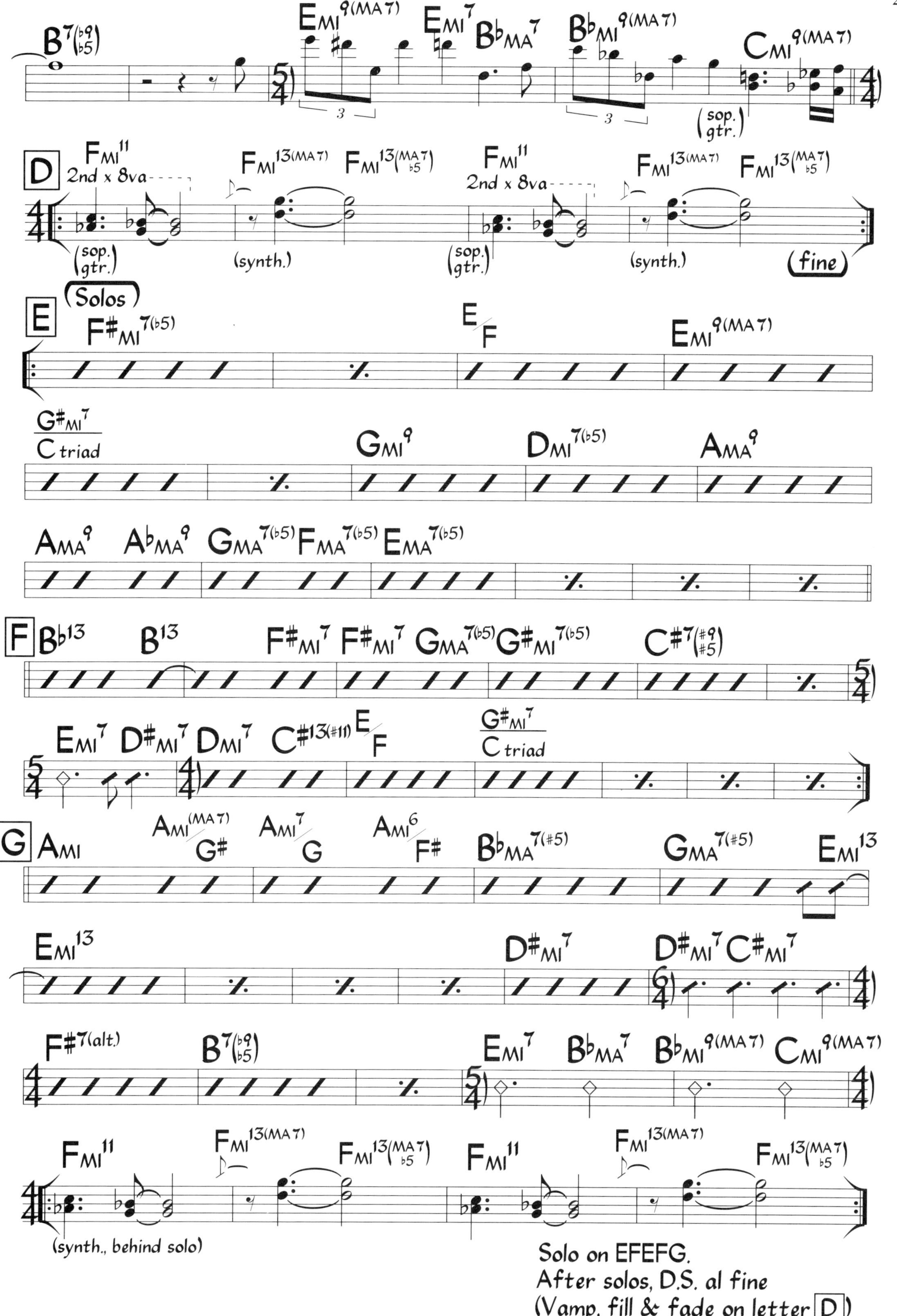
D
2nd x 8va
(sop. gtr.)
(synth.)
(fine)
(Solos)
E
F
G
(synth., behind solo)
Solo on EFEFG.
After solos, D.S. al fine
(Vamp, fill & fade on letter D)

On Green Dolphin Street

Music: Bronislau Kaper
Lyric: Ned Washington
(As played by Miles Davis)

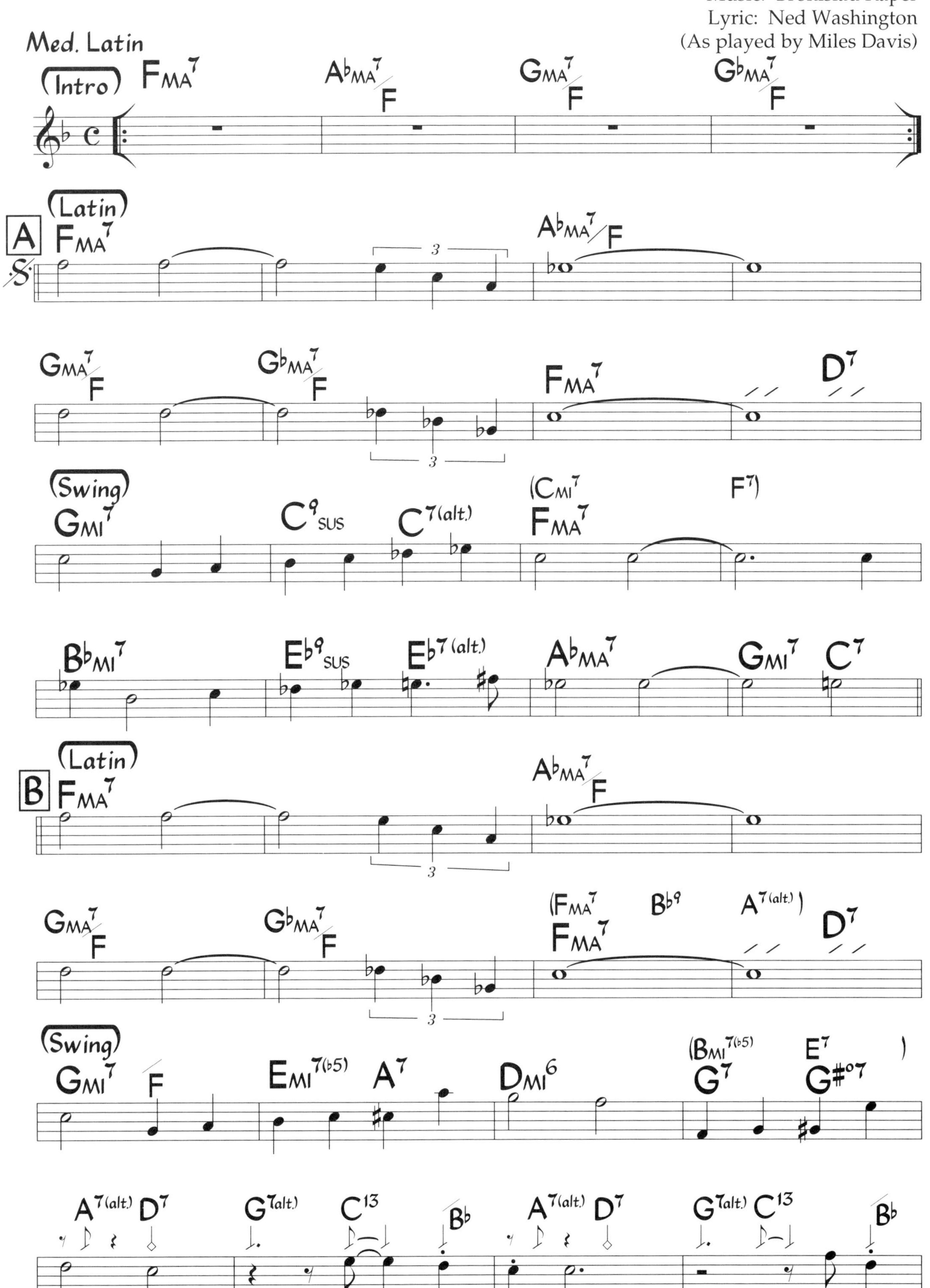

Lyric:

Lover, one lovely day
Love came planning to stay.
Green Dolphin Street supplied the setting,
The setting for nights beyond forgetting.

And through these moments apart
Memories live in my heart,
When I recall the love I found on,
I could kiss the ground on Green Dolphin Street.

One Bird, One Stone

Don Grolnick

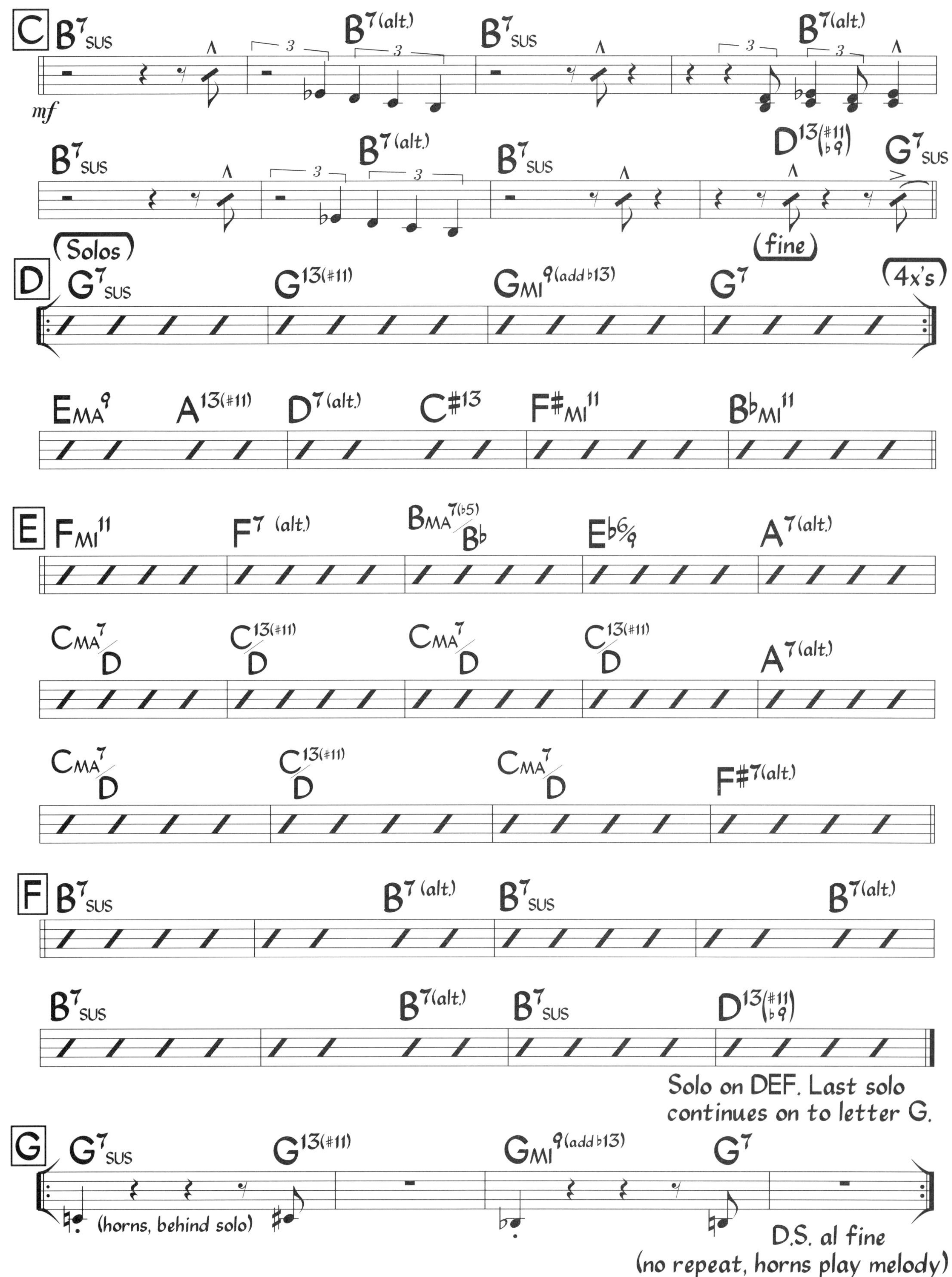

C
B7 SUS
B7(alt.)
mf
D13(#11 b9)
G7 SUS
(Solos)
D
G13(#11)
GMI9(add b13)
G7
(fine)
(4x's)
EMA9
A13(#11)
D7(alt.)
C#13
F#MI11
BbMI11
E
FMI11
F7 (alt.)
BMA7(b5)/Bb
Eb6/9
A7(alt.)
CMA7/D
C13(#11)/D
F#7(alt.)
F
Solo on DEF. Last solo continues on to letter G.
G
(horns, behind solo)
D.S. al fine
(no repeat, horns play melody)

One Bird, One Stone (horns behind solos)

D3
Third chorus
7
4
E3
8va b.
F3
8
G

Photo by Val Wilmer

HERBIE HANCOCK

One Finger Snap

Herbie Hancock

Chords in parentheses are used for solos (except A7(alt), in brackets).
Straight time for solos.

Ooo Baby Baby

William "Smokey" Robinson
& Warren Moore

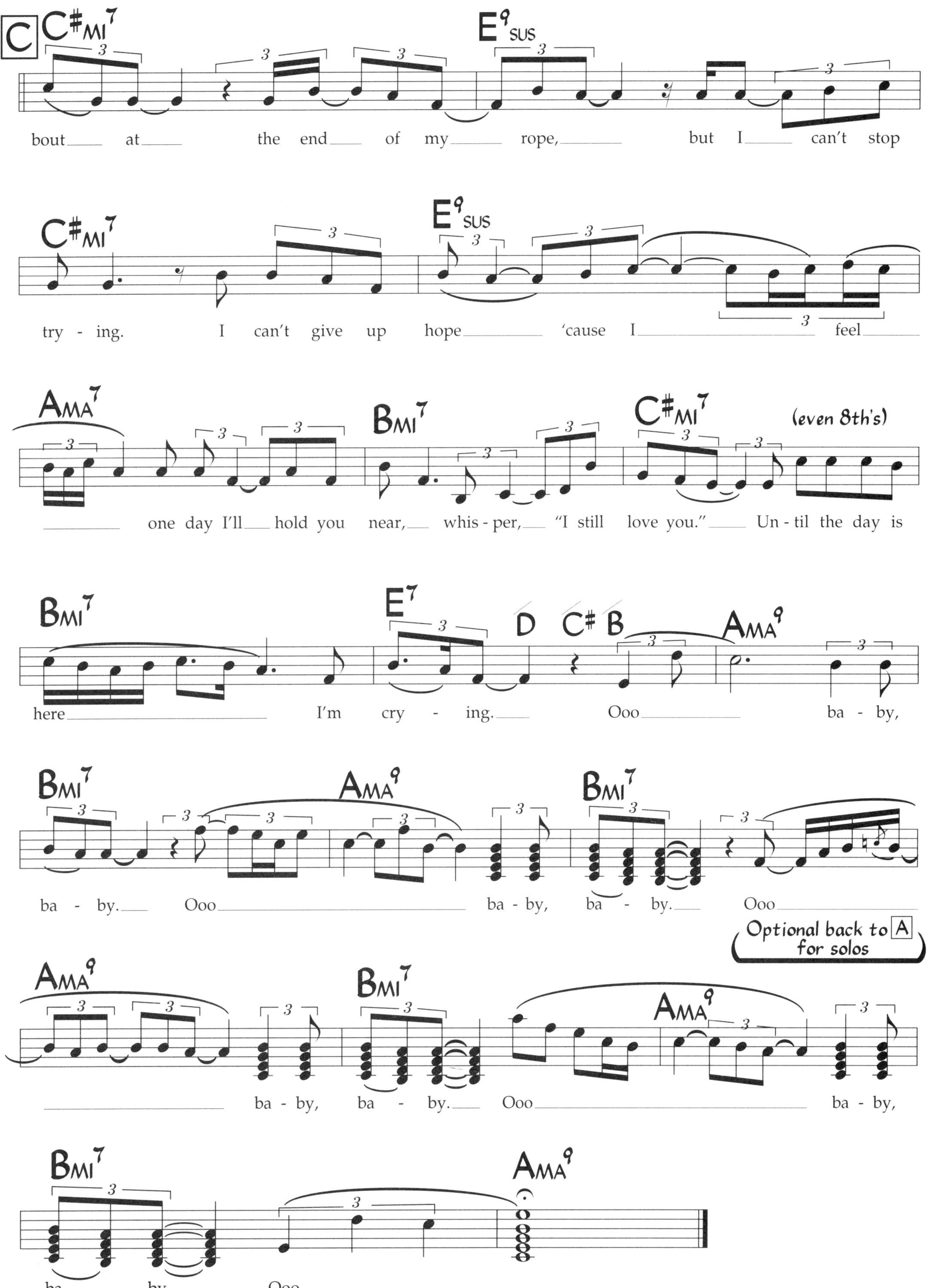

Vocal chords indicate where background vocals join lead vocal.

Opus de Funk

Horace Silver

As played by Horace Silver but transposed from concert Bb to F to be easily playable by more instruments.
Note: The head is sometimes played as two letter A's, omitting letter B.

Out A Day

Franck Amsallem

Chords in parentheses are used for solos.

Based on the changes to "Night and Day".

Photo by Francis Wolff. Courtesy of Mosaic Images

HORACE SILVER

Over the Rainbow

Lyric: E. Y. Harburg
Music: Harold Arlen

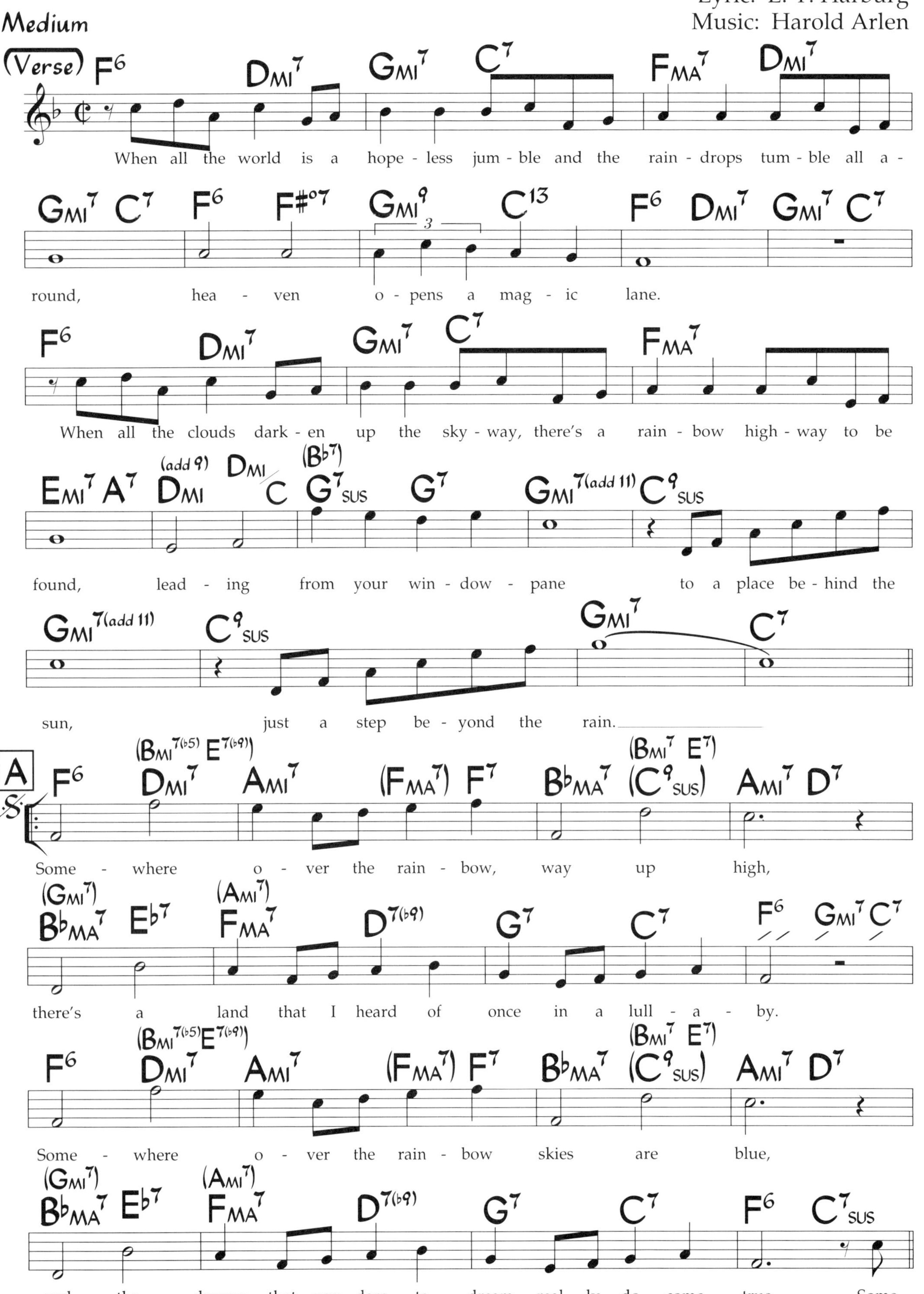

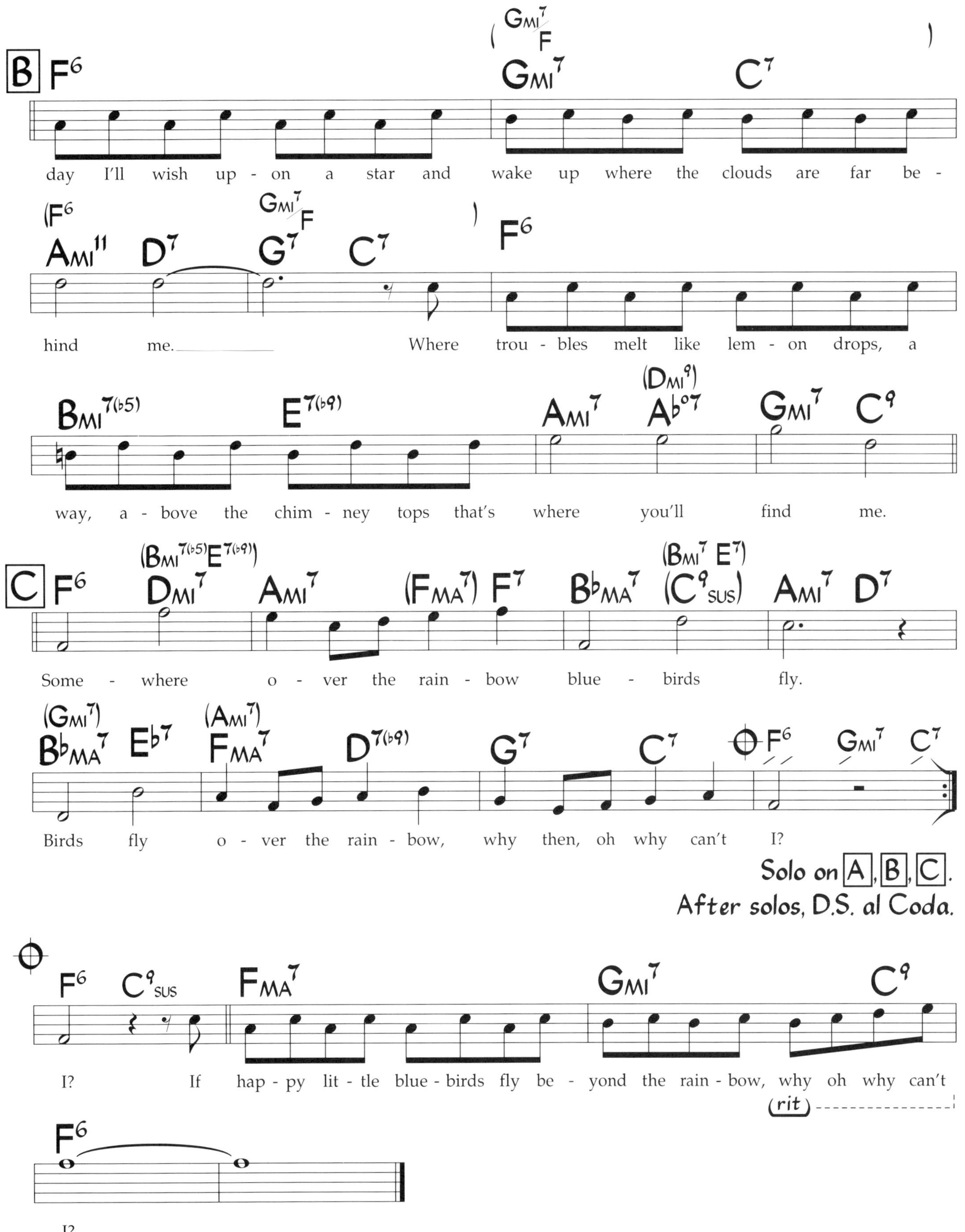
B
day I'll wish up - on a star and wake up where the clouds are far be -
hind me. Where trou - bles melt like lem - on drops, a
way, a - bove the chim - ney tops that's where you'll find me.
C
Some - where o - ver the rain - bow blue - birds fly.
Birds fly o - ver the rain - bow, why then, oh why can't I?
Solo on A, B, C.
After solos, D.S. al Coda.
I? If hap - py lit - tle blue - birds fly be - yond the rain - bow, why oh why can't
rit
I?

Part-Time Lover

Stevie Wonder

Medium Funk Shuffle (8th's swing)
♩ = 172

(Intro) 1st x: synth. 2nd x: bkgr. vocals on 'ooh')

(vocal scat, on "da", 2nd x only)

Call up, ring

A

once, hang up__ the phone__ to let me know you made__ it home,__ Don't want noth-ing to be wrong with part - time__ lov - er.__ If she's with me, I'll blink__ the lights__ to let you know to-night's__ the night__ for me and you, my part - time__ lov - er.__ We are

B

un - der - cov - er pas - sion on__ the run,__ chas - ing love up a - gainst__ the sun.__ We are strang - ers__ by day,__ lov - ers__ by night,__ know - ing it's so

2nd verse:

If I'm with friends and we should meet,
Just pass me by, don't even speak,
And know the word's "discreet" when part-time lovers.
But if there's some emergency,
Have a male friend to ask for me,
So then she won't peek, (it's really you) my part-time lover.

3rd verse:

I've got something that I must tell,
Last night someone rang our doorbell
And it was not you, my part-time lover.
And then a man called our exchange,
But didn't want to leave his name,
I guess that two can play the game of part-time lover.

Pendulum

Richie Beirach

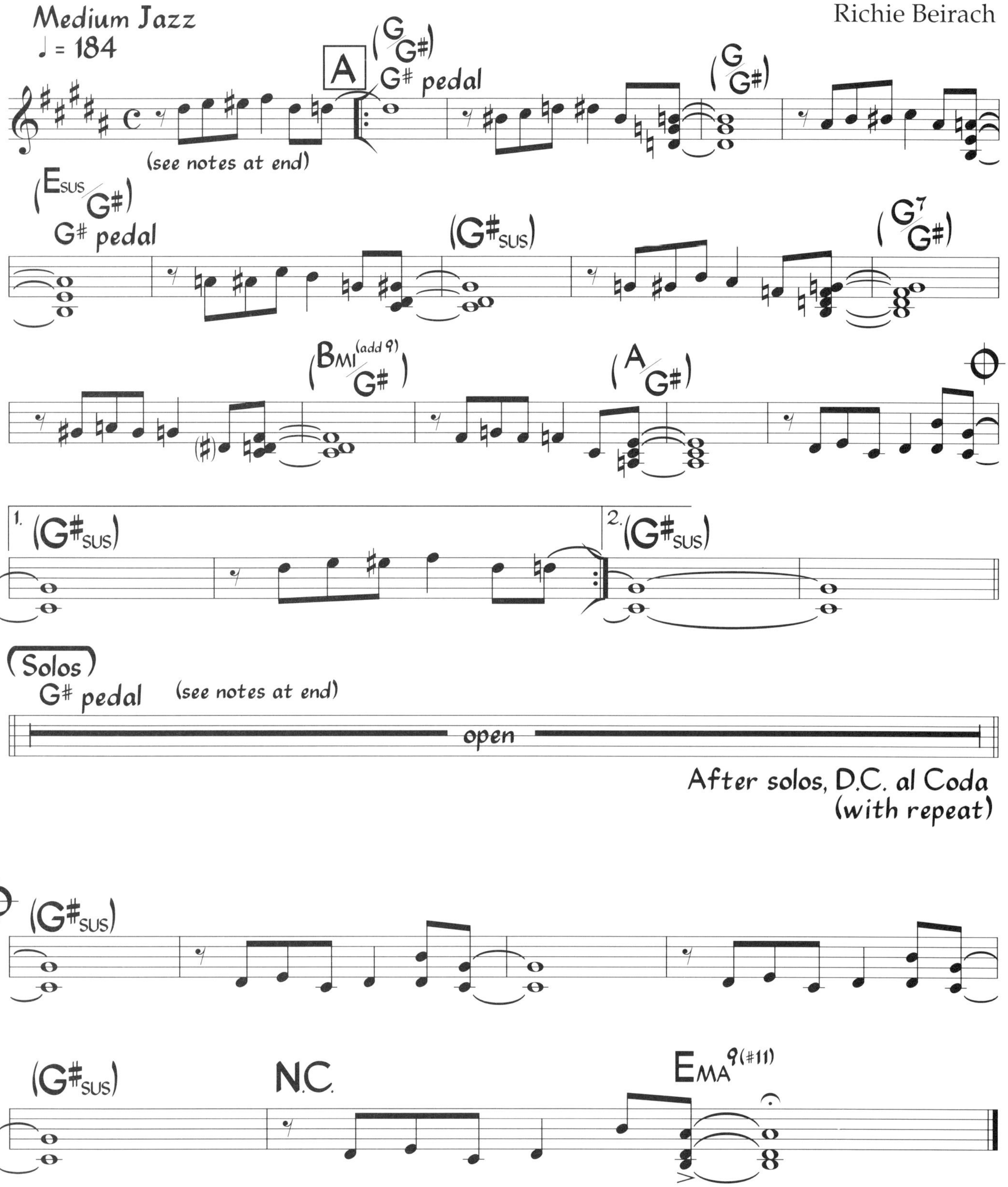

Medium Jazz
♩ = 184

A (G/G#) G# pedal — (G/G#)

(see notes at end)

(Esus/G#) G# pedal — (G#sus) — (G7/G#)

(BMI(add 9)/G#) — (A/G#) — ⊕

1. (G#sus) — 2. (G#sus)

(Solos)
G# pedal (see notes at end)

open

After solos, D.C. al Coda
(with repeat)

Note: Solos (and head) may use any harmonies over F# pedal.

Some harmonies on recording:

G#MI9, BMI9/G#, G#7, DMA7(#5)/G#, G#7sus, etc.

Prelude To A Kiss
Duke Ellington
Irving Gordon
Irving Mills
Medium Ballad
A
If you hear a song in blue, like a flow - er cry - ing for the dew,
that was my heart ser - e - nad - ing you, my pre - lude to a kiss.
If you hear a song that grows from my ten - der sen - ti - ment - tal woes,
that was my heart try - ing to com - pose a pre - lude to a kiss.
B
Though it's just a sim - ple mel - o - dy with noth - ing fan - cy, noth - ing much,
you could turn it to a sym - pho - ny, a Schu - bert tune with a Gersh - win touch. Oh,
C
how my love song gent - ly cries for the ten - der - ness with - in your eyes, my
love is a pre - lude that nev - er dies, a pre - lude to a kiss.
Alternate changes for bar 8 of letter B:

Promise

Chick Corea
(As played by Bob Berg)

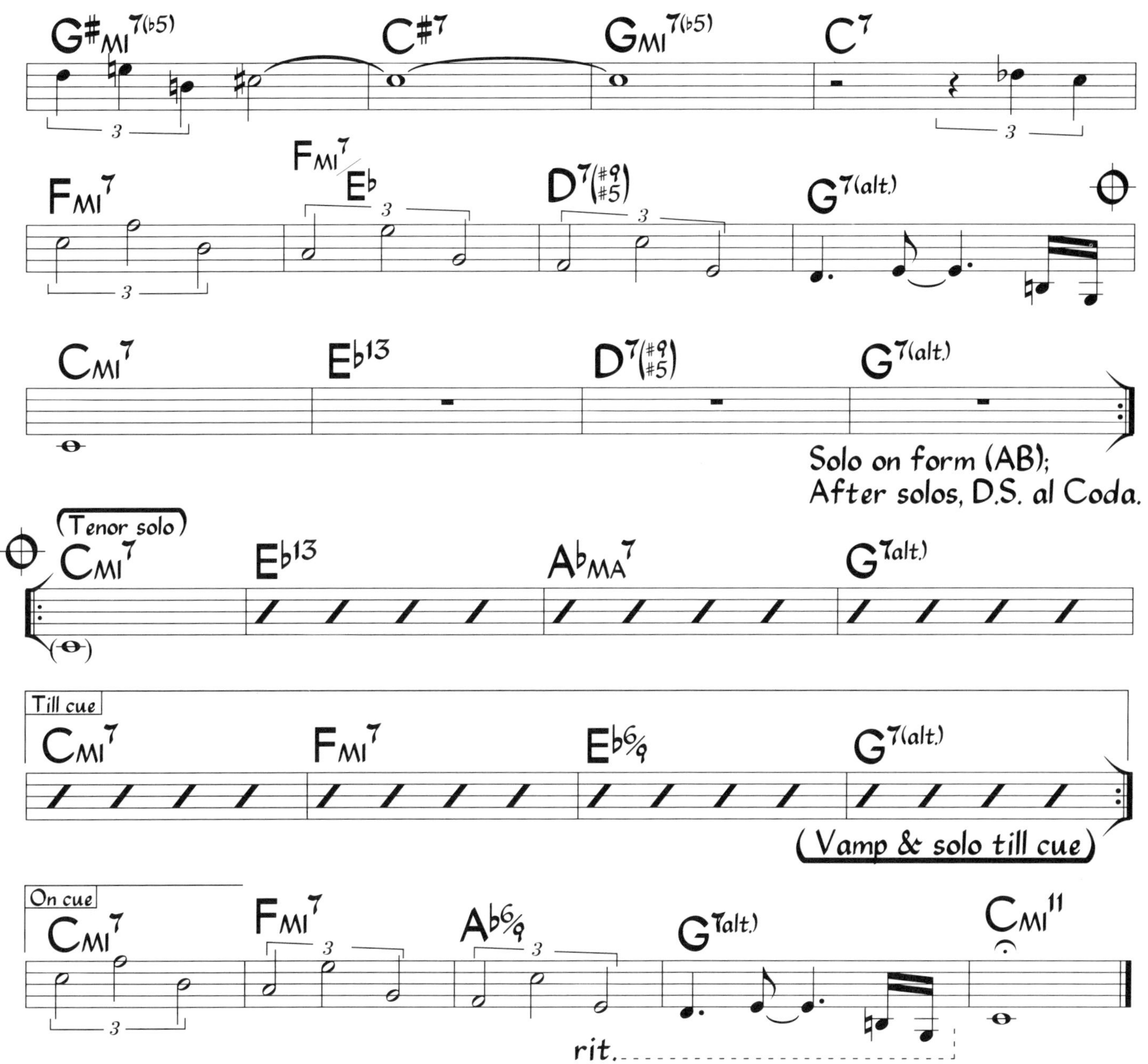

Chords in parentheses are used for solos.
Melody is somewhat freely interpreted.
Tenor plays melody one octave higher.

Punjab

Joe Henderson

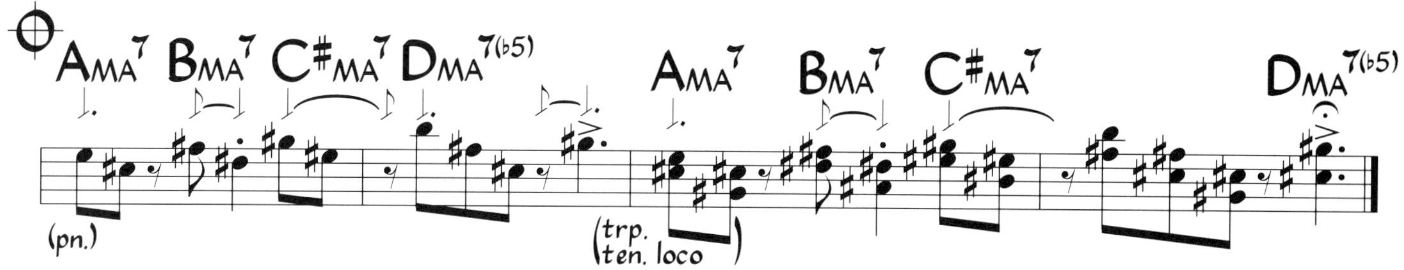

Tenor follows register notes for correct octave.

Pyramid

Horace Silver

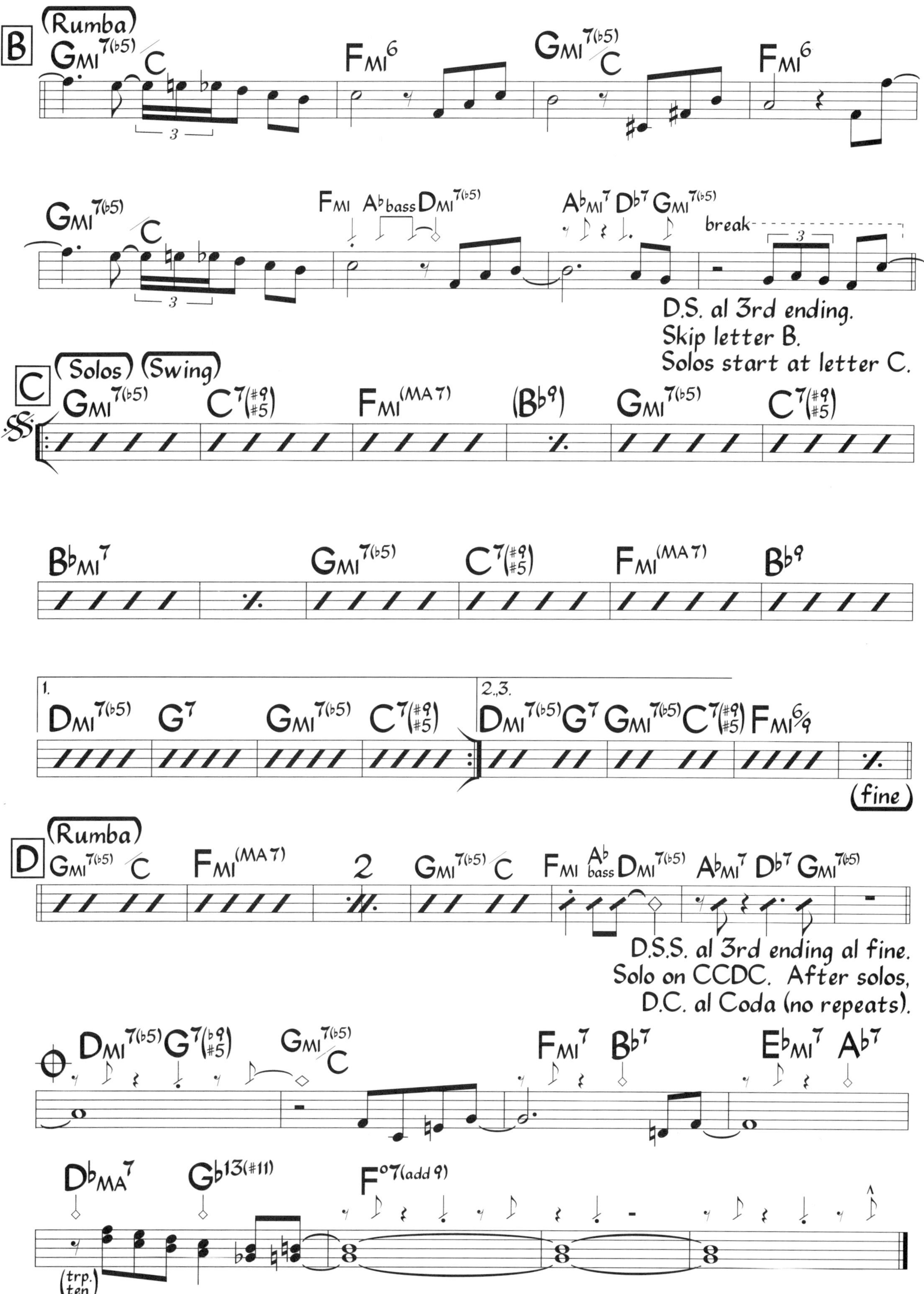

Tenor plays intro and last 4 bars of Coda an octave higher, the rest as written.

Photo by Val Wilmer

HORACE SILVER

? (Question Mark)

Nguyên Lê

Solo on A. Play B to end each solo.
To end, vamp and fade on B.
Head is played twice before and after solos.
Solos start in 2, segue to 4.

Rainland

Paul McCandless

D♭MA7(♭5)/C
DMI11
B
FMI
D♭/F
E♭/F
B♭/F
D♭MA7/F
(gtr.)
C♯/D♯
EMA7/G♯
G♯MI
D♯MI/F♯
F♯/B
EMA7
D♯MI/F♯
E/G♯
D♯MI/F♯
F♯/E
C♯/D♯
C♯MI7
EMA7/F♯
C
DMI11
(ob. w/gtr.)
A7(♯9 ♯5)
F/G
CMI11
CMI11
D♭MA7(♭5)
DMI11
Piano solo
D
CMI11
E♭MA7/F
GMI11
A7(♯9 ♯5)
FMI11
A♭MA7/B♭
CMI11
1. D7(♯9 ♯5)
2. A7(♯9 ♯5)
DMI11
DMI11/C
B♭MI6/9
E♭13
FMA7/C
D♭MA7(♭5)/C
DMI11
DMI11/C
(end solo)
(oboe)
V.S. (turn page)

E
F
(oboe w/ gtr.)

Photo by Tom Copi

MARY LOU WILLIAMS

Rainland (ostinato)

Medium Straight 8th's

♩= 138

(Intro)

(4x's)

(gtr.)

chords in parentheses are played on repeat and on D.S.

A

B

C

D.S. is letter F on melody part. Additional background line at letter E is omitted.

Reach Out, I'll Be There

Brian Holland
Lamont Dozier
Eddie Holland

(As sung by The Four Tops)

Second and Third verses

2. When you feel lost and about to give up,
'Cause your best just ain't good enough,
And you feel the world has grown cold,
And you're drifting out all on your own,
And you need a hand to hold,
Darling, Reach out (come on girl, reach out for me),
Reach out (reach out for me).

3. I can tell the way you hang your head,
You're without love and now you're afraid,
And through your tears you look around,
But there's no peace of mind to be found (I know what you're thinkin'),
You're alone now, no love of your own, but
Darling, Reach out (come on girl, reach out for me),
Reach out (reach out for me—just look over your shoulder).

I'll be there to give you all the love you need,
And I'll be there, you can always depend on me.

Real Life

Jim McNeely
(As played by Phil Woods)

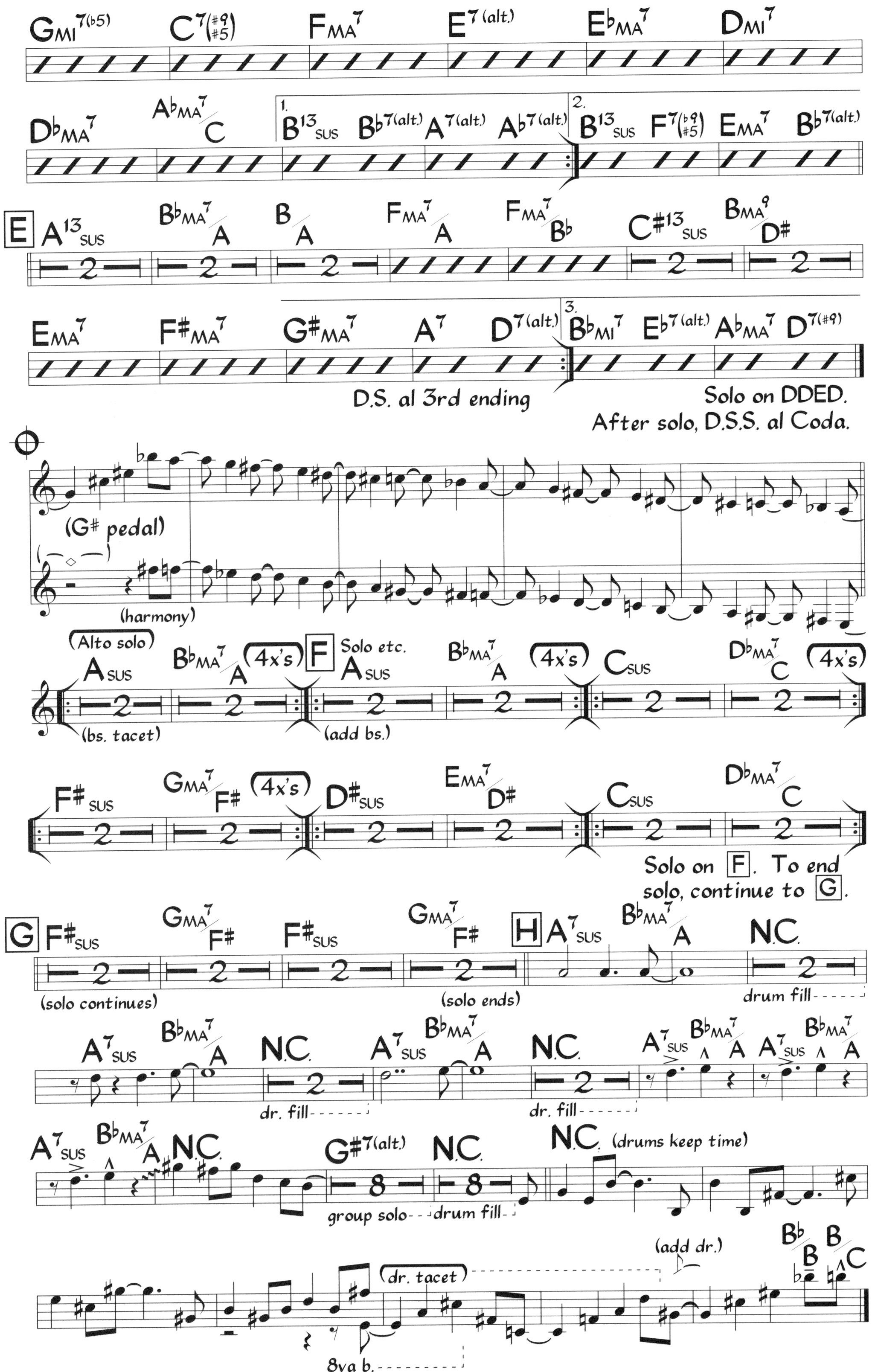

This chart has been somewhat simplified from the recording.

JERRY BERGONZI

Red's Blues

Medium Swing

Jerry Bergonzi

Head is played twice before and after solos.
Kicks are not played for solos.

During solos: On the last 4 bars of letter A, the chords begin on beat 1 of each bar.

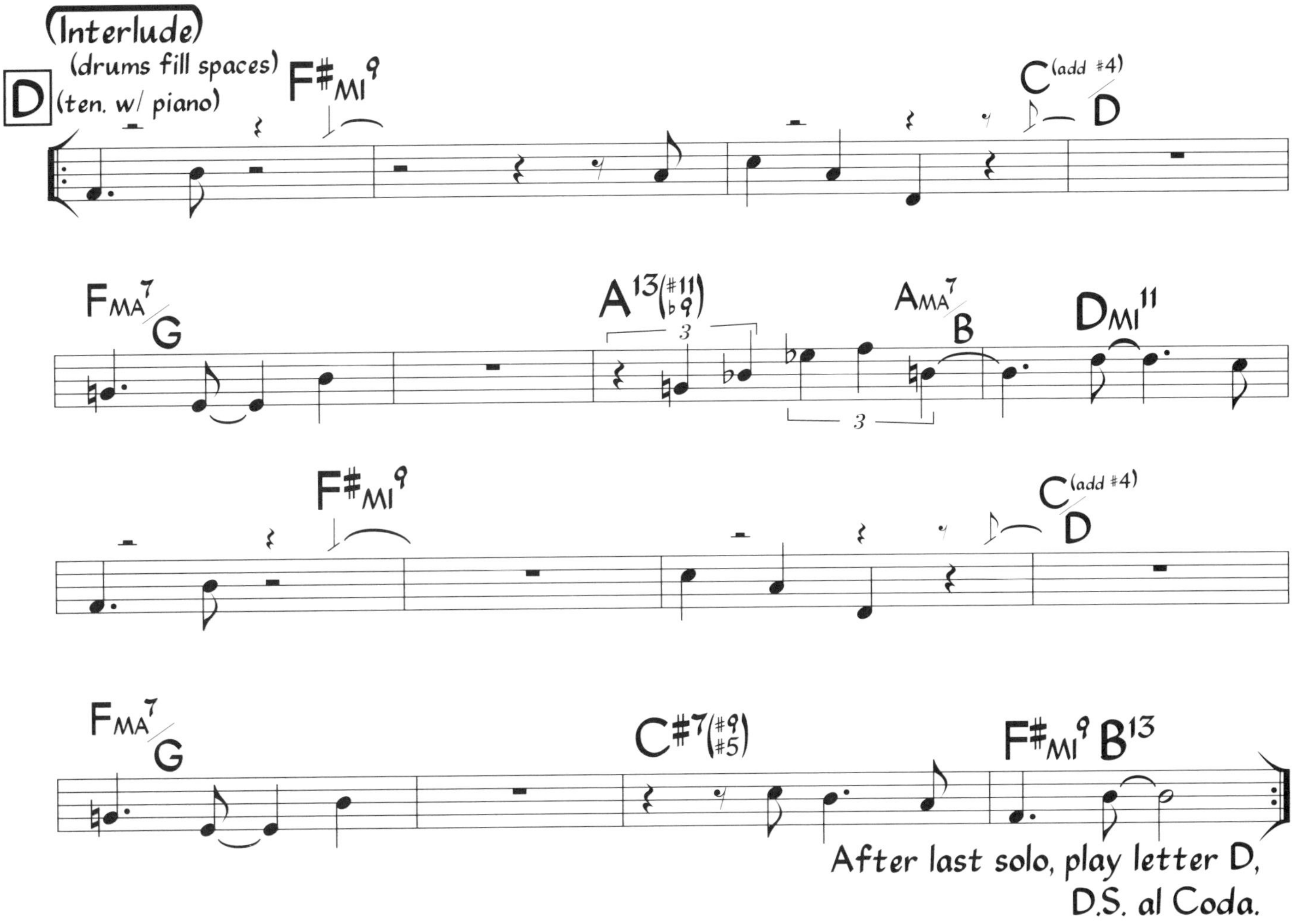

(Interlude)
(drums fill spaces)
D
(ten. w/ piano)
F#MI9
C(add #4)/D
FMA7/G
A13(#11 b9)
AMA7/B
DMI11
F#MI9
C(add #4)/D
FMA7/G
C#7(#9 #5)
F#MI9 B13
After last solo, play letter D,
D.S. al Coda.

(Tenor fills)
F#MI9
(B13)
(Vamp, fill & fade)

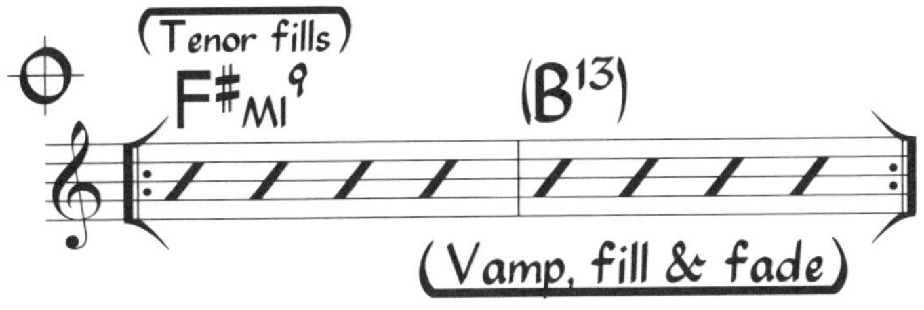

Tenor plays everything an octave higher.

Sample tenor fills at B:
EMA7/F#
F#9
F9
DMA7/E
E9
E7(#9 #5)
8va b.

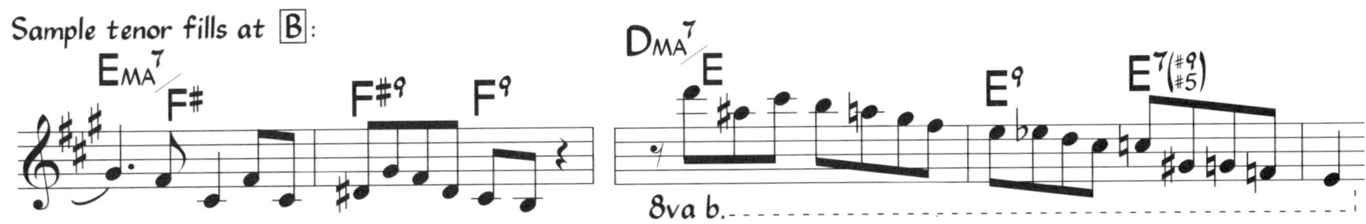

Chords at letter D are optional.

Respect
Otis Redding, Jr.
(As sung by Aretha Franklin)
Med. Motown
♩ = 112
(Intro)
D7 G7 D7 G7
(gtr.)
A
A G A
1. What you want, baby I got it, what you need,
G A G
do you know I got it? All I'm ask-in' is for a lit-tle re-
(lead vocal)
spect when you come home, Hey, ba-by, when you got home,
D7 G7
Just a lit-tle bit, just a lit-tle bit,
(3x's)
Mis-ter.
D7 G7
just a lit-tle bit, just a lit-tle bit.
B
G#MI C# G#MI A7
2 2 2 2
(sax solo)
(end solo)
C
A G A
4. Ooh, your kiss-es, sweet-er than hon-ey, and guess what
G A G
so is my mon-ey, all I want you to do for me is give it to me
3 3 3

Second and Third verses:

2. I ain't gonna do you wrong while you're gone.
I ain't gonna do you wrong, 'cause I don't wanna.
All I'm askin' is for a little respect when you come home.

3. I'm about to give you all my money,
But all I'm askin' in return, honey,
Is to give me my propers when you get home.

Revelation

Lyric: Lorraine Perry
Music: Russell Ferrante
(As played by the Yellowjackets)

re - ve - la - tion is here.
I'm so
Solos (1st solo, pn.; 2nd, sax)
D
A7 D7 C#13SUS C#13 D7 D#°7 A/E E7
(1st x only bs. tacet till repeat)
E
A D/A A G D/F# A7 A7 D7 C#13SUS C#13
D7 D#°7 A/E F°7 F#MI7 F7(#9 #5) EMI7 Eb9(#11)
(background vocal) Come take me back.
Till cue
Solo on DE
(Last solo takes "On cue" ending)
On cue
(background)
I'm so
D.S. al Coda One
(with repeat)
(here.)
D.S.S. al Coda Two
Come take me back, oh, to the one place where I come from yeah yeah
(bkgr. vocal) Come take me back where I come from a - gain
Have - n't you heard that re - ve - la - tion is here.
Say it a - gain.
(Half-time)
Have - n't you heard that re - ve - la - tion is here.
rit.

Riddles

Richie Beirach
(As played by John Abercrombie)

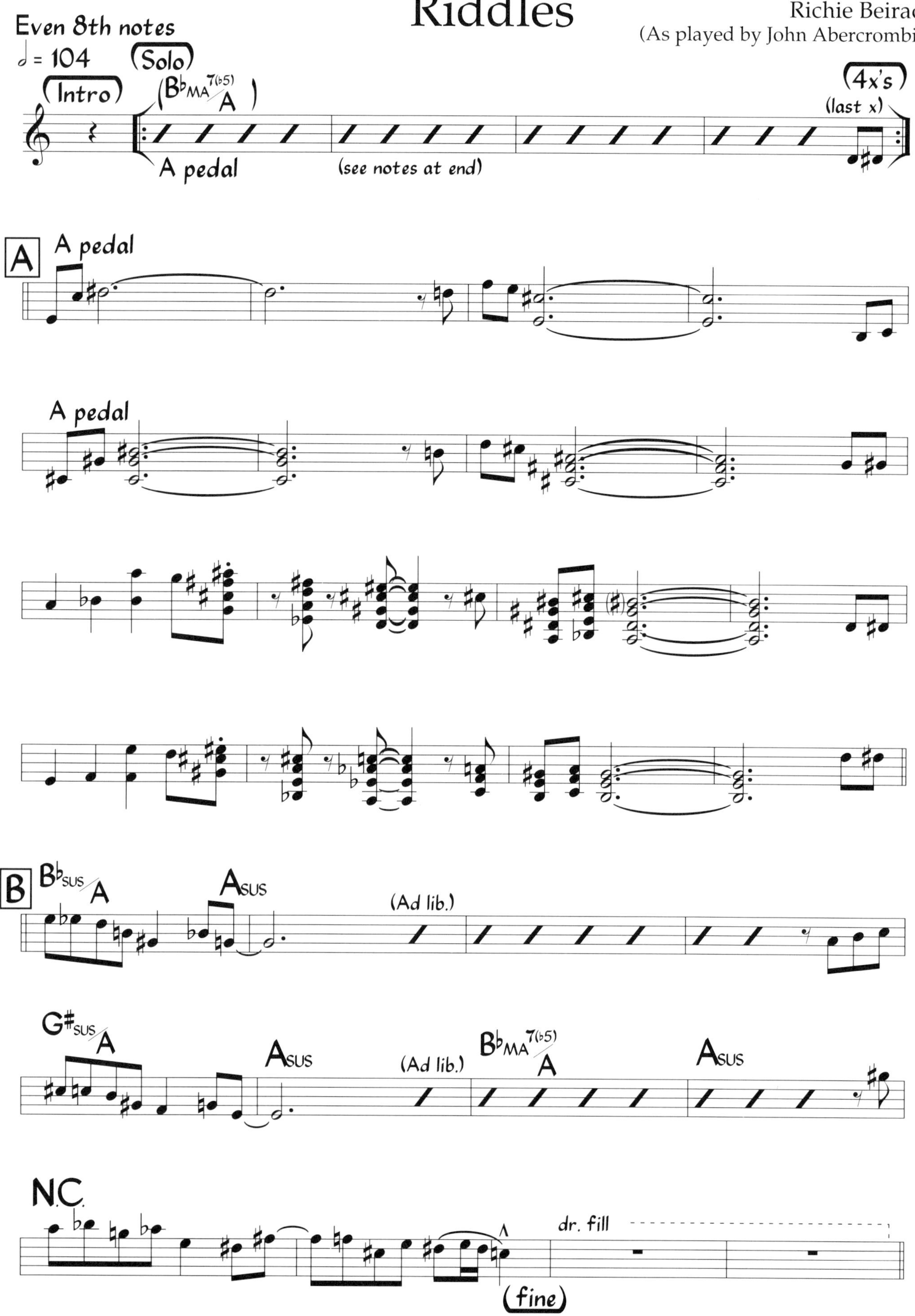

Note: Any harmonies (over A pedal) can be used on head and solos at the discretion of the musicians.

Some harmonies used on recording are:

A blues scale, B♭MA7(♭5)/A, Asus, F(add 9)/A, A♭/A, GMA7/A, etc.

(Chromatic harmonic movement is appropriate.)

Ritual

Chick Corea

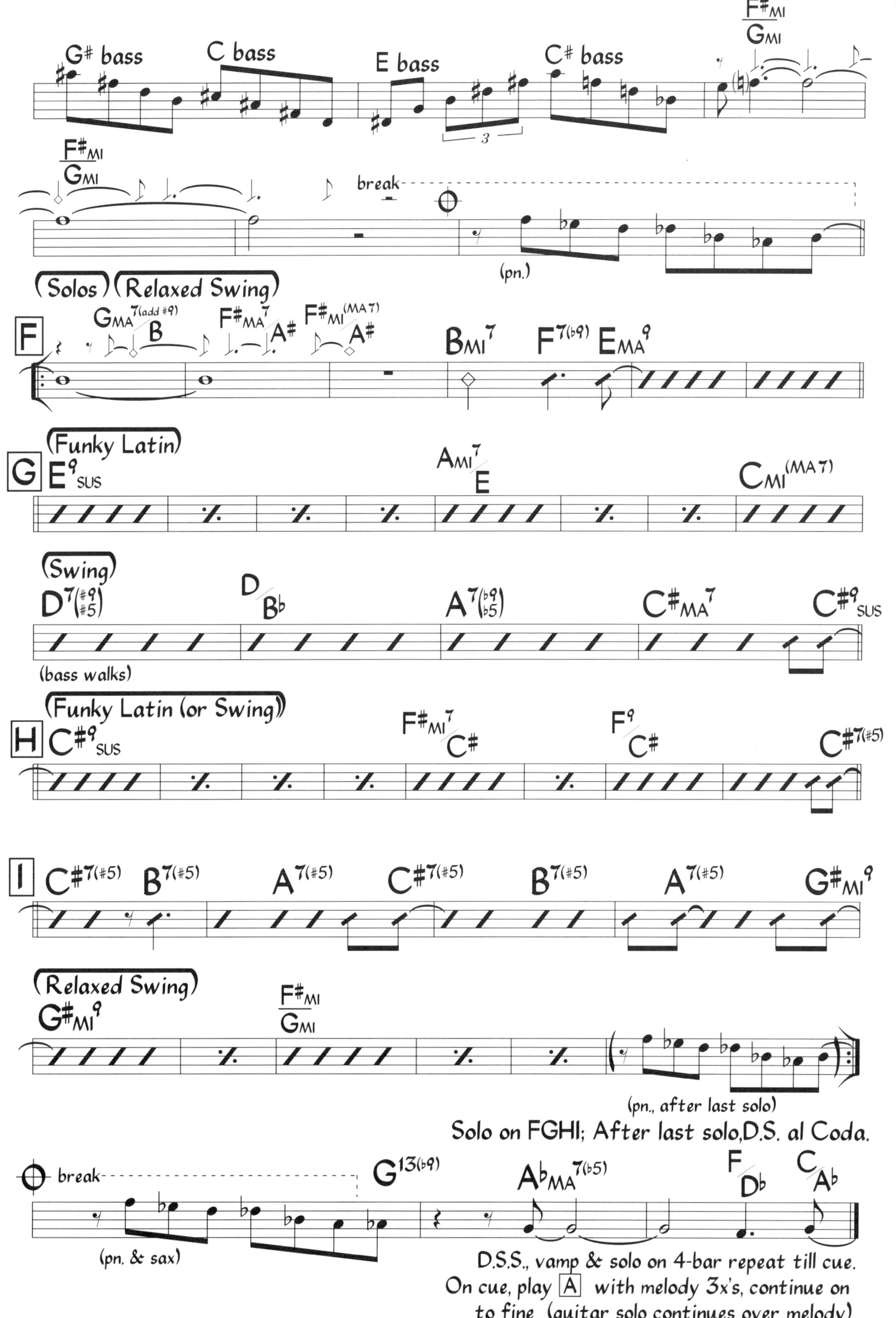
G# bass
C bass
E bass
C# bass
F#MI/GMI
F#MI/GMI
break
(pn.)
Solos
Relaxed Swing
F
GMA7(add #9)/B
F#MA7/A#
F#MI(MA7)/A#
BMI7
F7(b9)
EMA9
Funky Latin
G
E9SUS
AMI7/E
CMI(MA7)
Swing
D7(#9 #5)
D/Bb
A7(b9 b5)
C#MA7
C#9SUS
(bass walks)
Funky Latin (or Swing)
H
C#9SUS
F#MI7/C#
F9/C#
C#7(#5)
I
C#7(#5)
B7(#5)
A7(#5)
C#7(#5)
B7(#5)
A7(#5)
G#MI9
Relaxed Swing
G#MI9
F#MI/GMI
(pn., after last solo)
Solo on FGHI; After last solo, D.S. al Coda.
break
G13(b9)
AbMA7(b5)
F/Db
C/Ab
(pn. & sax)
D.S.S., vamp & solo on 4-bar repeat till cue.
On cue, play A with melody 3x's, continue on
to fine (guitar solo continues over melody).

Ruby

Lyric: Mitchell Parish
Music: Heinz Roemheld

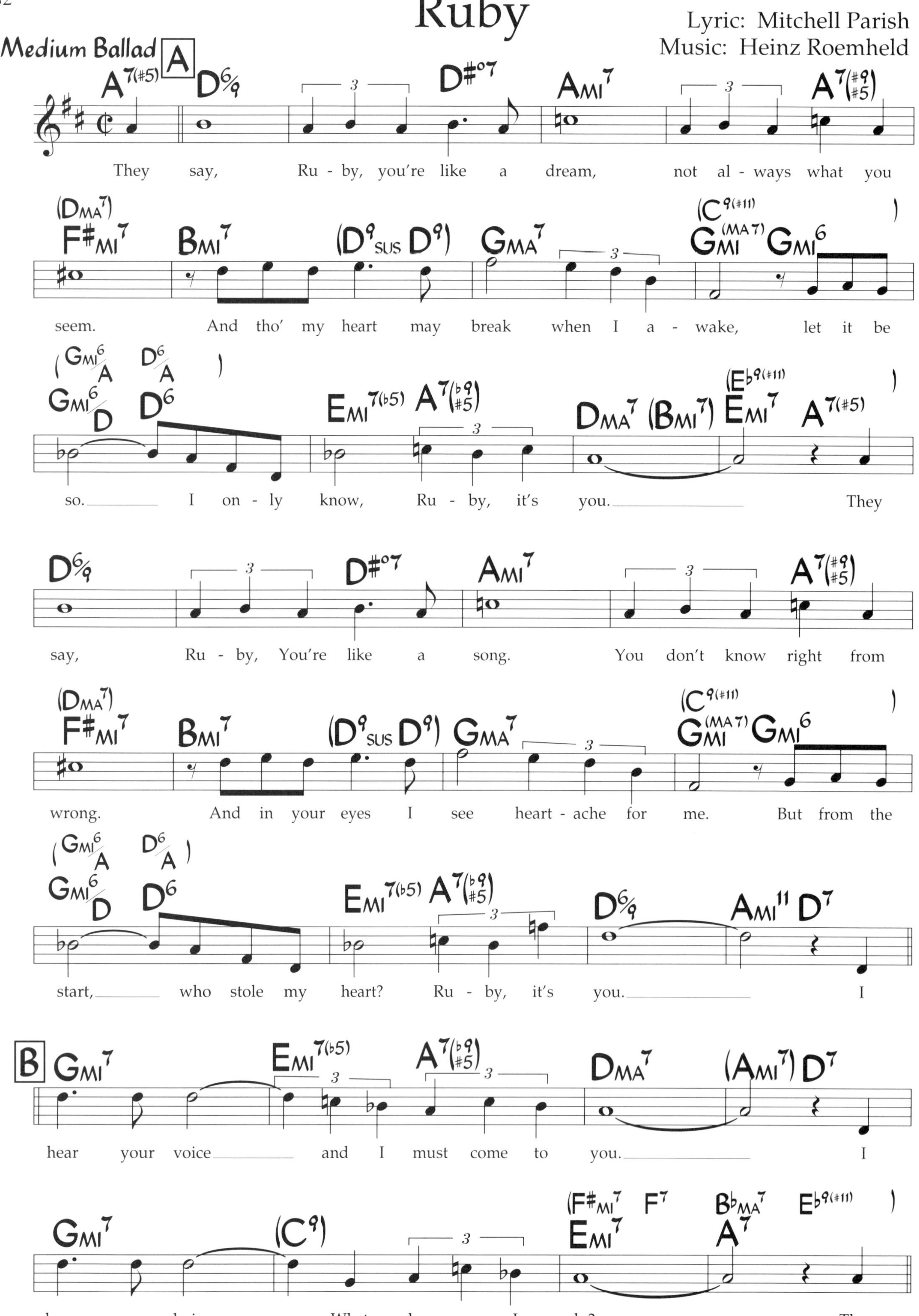

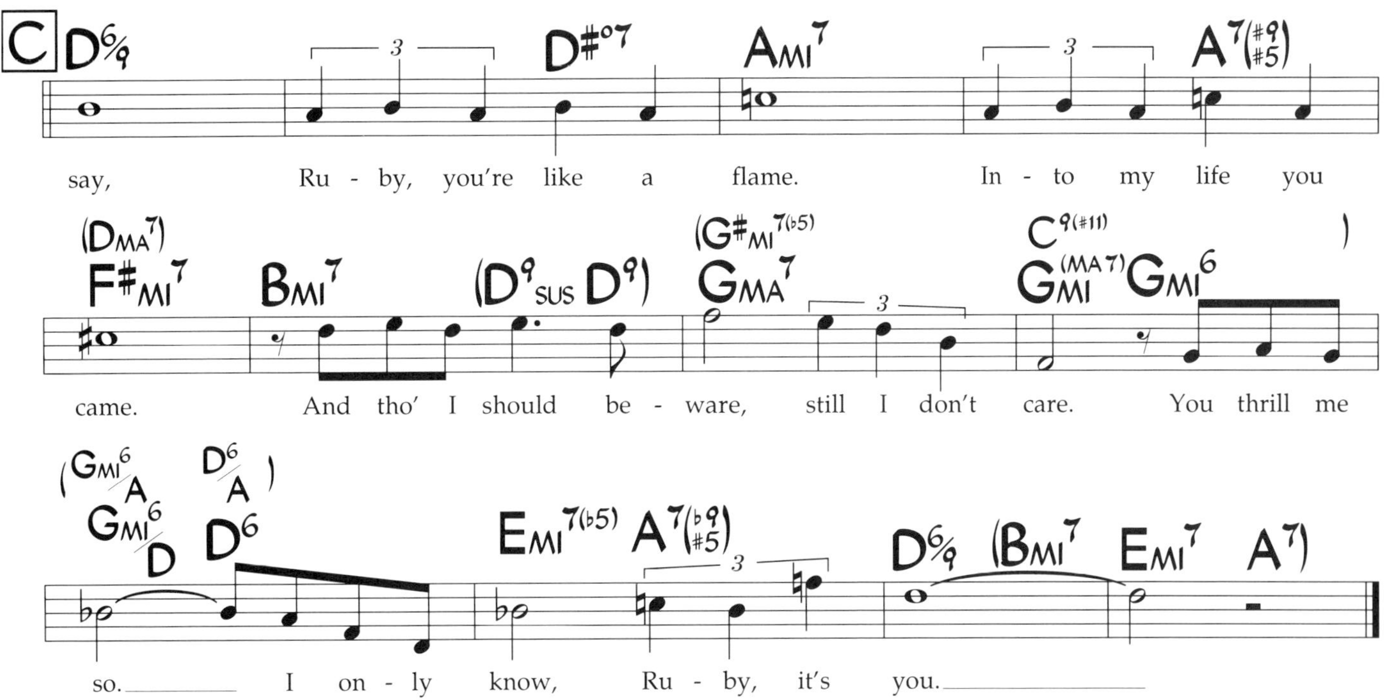
C
D 6/9
3
D#°7
AMI7
A7 (#9 #5)
say, Ru - by, you're like a flame. In - to my life you
(DMA7)
F#MI7
BMI7
(D9SUS D9)
(G#MI7(b5)
GMA7
C9(#11))
GMI(MA7) GMI6
came. And tho' I should be - ware, still I don't care. You thrill me
(GMI6/A D6/A)
GMI6/D
D6
EMI7(b5)
A7 (b9 #5)
D 6/9 (BMI7 EMI7 A7)
so. I on - ly know, Ru - by, it's you.

Sail Away
Medium Bossa
Tom Harrell
A
♩ = 139
(flug.)
B
(gtr.)
(gtr. flug.)

C
F#MI7
B7(alt.)
EMI7(11)
A7SUS(b9)
(unis.)
D6/9
BMI7
A
G#MI7
C#7(#9 #5)
D(add 9)/C
B7 (alt.)
EMI7(11)
A9SUS
A13(b9)
DMA7/A
A13SUS
DMA7/A
A13SUS
G
Solo on form (ABC).
After solos, D.C. al Coda
DMA7/A
A13SUS
DMA7/A
A13SUS
(sample flug. fill)
G
E/G#
F#MI/A
F#/A#
(etc.)
G/B
CMA7
A/C#
DMI9
(unis.)
(rit.)

THE YELLOWJACKETS

The Second Time Around

Serenata

Lyric: Mitchell Parish
Music: Leroy Anderson

(G6/B EMI7 AMI11 D9) (F9(#11))
AMI7 D9 B7 E9
loved one, Ser - e - na - ta, and say: "When you're in
A7 Eb7 D7(b9) G6/9 (AMI7 D7)
love, love finds a way."
D.S. for solos
Coda last x
G6 D7SUS(b9) GMI6 AMI7(b9/b5) D7(b9)
way." Love al - ways finds a
GMI6 AMI7(b5) D7(b9) GMA7 AMI9 D7(b9)
way. I'll win her heart some -
GMA7 (G9SUS) Ab9(#11) GMA7
day.

Photo by Tom Copi

ELLA FITZGERALD

The Shadow of Your Smile

Music: Johnny Mandel
Lyric: Paul Francis Webster

Short Story

Kenny Dorham
(As played by Joe Henderson)

Tenor plays all lines one octave higher.

Since We Met

Bill Evans

Letter D may be used as an Intro.
Chords in parentheses are used for solos.

Photo by Tom Copi

STEVIE WONDER

D.S., sing 3rd & 4th verses,
vamp & fade on letter B.

3rd & 4th verses:
A smiling face you don't have to see,
'Cause it's as joyful as a Christmas tree.
Love within, you'll begin smiling,
There are brighter days ahead.

Love's not competing, it's on your side,
You're in life's picture, so why must you cry?
So, for a friend, please begin to smile please,
There are brighter days ahead.

So Near, So Far

Crombie & Green
(As played by Miles Davis)

Chords in parentheses may be used for solos. Breaks may be played for solos.

So Near, So Far (Harmony)

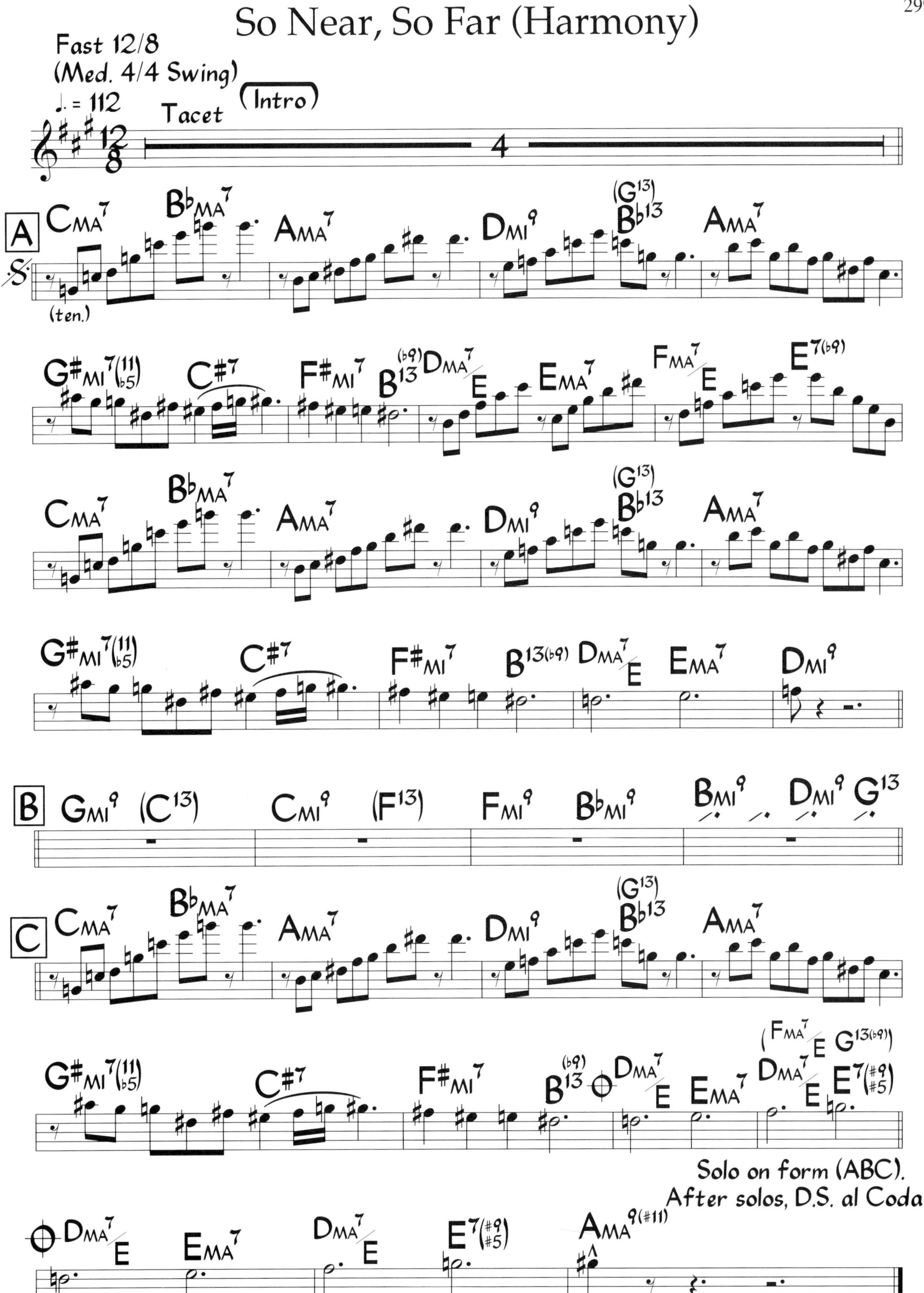

Tenor sounds one octave lower than written. Chords in parentheses may be used for solos.

Photo © Lee Tanner

FREDDIE HUBBARD

Solitude
Lyric: Eddie de Lange
& Irving Mills
Music: Duke Ellington
Medium Ballad
C7(#5) A FMA7 (DMI7 F7) (G9SUS B♭MA7) (G9 E♭9(#11) D7)
In my sol - i - tude you haunt me with
GMI7 C7 FMA7 (GMI7) C7(#5)
re - ver - ies of days gone by. In my
FMA7 (DMI7 F7) (G9SUS B♭MA7) (G9 E♭9(#11) D7)
sol - i - tude you taunt me with
GMI7 C7 FMA7 F7
mem - o - ries that nev - er die. I
B B♭6 B°7
sit in my chair, I'm filled with des - pair. There's
F6/C CMI7 F9 B♭6
no - one could be so sad. With gloom ev - 'ry - where, I
B°7 F6/C AMI7 A♭°7 GMI7 C7(#5)
sit and I stare. know that I'll soon go mad. In my
C FMA7 (DMI7 F7) (G9SUS B♭MA7) (G9 E♭9(#11) D7)
sol - i - tude I'm pray - ing, "Dear
GMI7 C7 FMA7 (F#°7 GMI7 C7)
Lord a - bove, send back my love."

Speak Like a Child
Herbie Hancock
Medium Bossa
♩ = 126
A
Eb7(alt.)
(pn.)
(Bb7(alt.)
Bb7(alt.)
F#9 SUS
Bmi7
dr. tacet
C13
C7(#5)
Cmi9
F13
Bb13 SUS
Bb13 SUS
Bb13(b9)
A7(alt.)
pn. fill
(bs. trb.)
(alto fl.)
AbMA7(#11)
Abo7(add 9)
(pn.)
(pn., melody)
F9 SUS
F13
Fmi9
E7(#9)
(alto fl.)
(alto fl.)
(D#7 (alt.)
N.C.
C7 (alt.)
GMA7 Cmi9
Bmi9
F#9 SUS
8va b.
(bs. trb.)
(flug.)
Bmi9
F#9 SUS
Bmi9
F#9 SUS
pn. fill

Chords in parentheses are used for solos.
Piano melody is freely interpreted.

Spring Is Here

Lyric: Lorenz Hart
Music: Richard Rogers
(Chords as played by Bill Evans)

* also played as a Medium Swing.

Stairway to the Stars

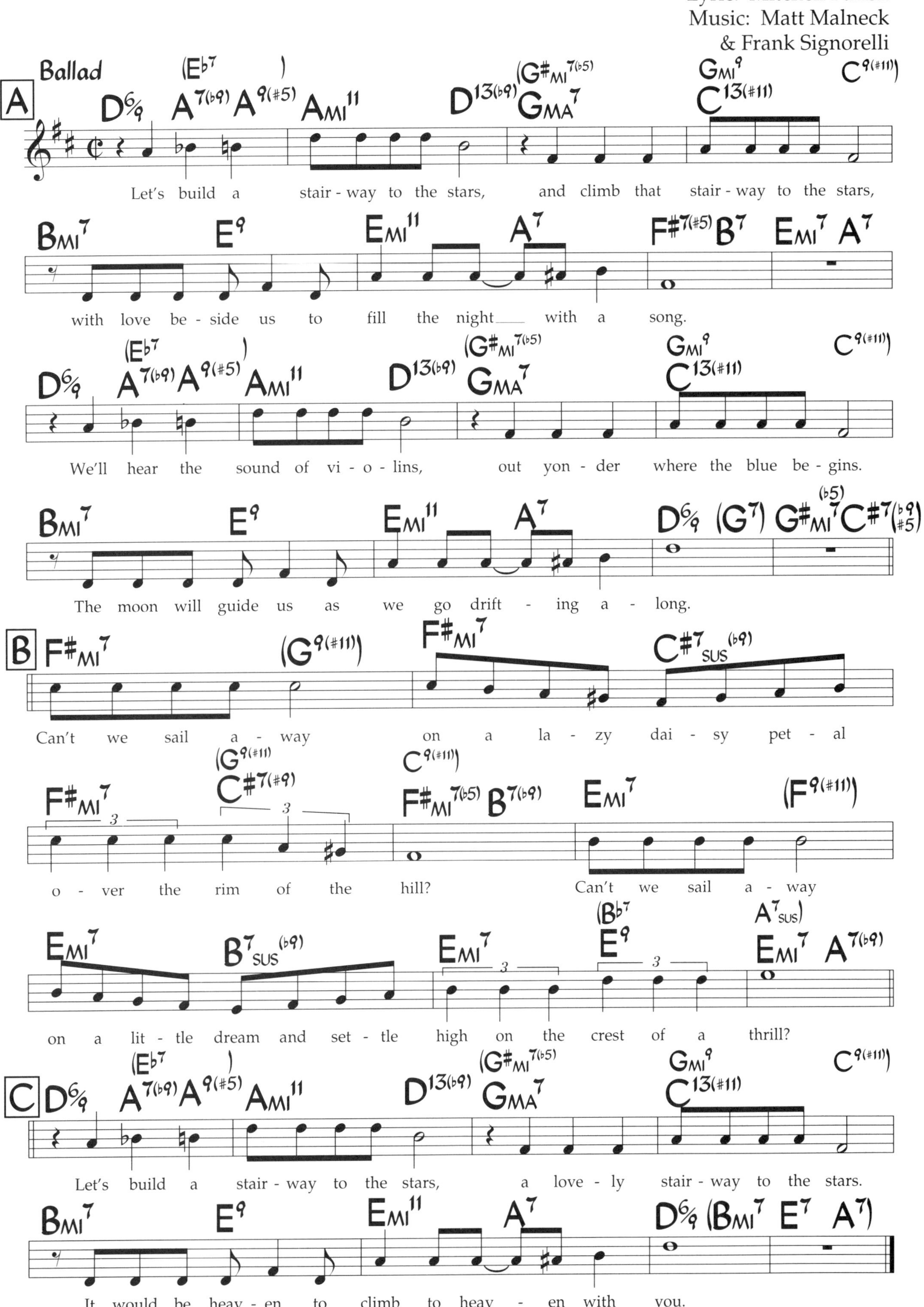

Star Eyes

Don Raye
& Gene dePaul

* also played as Bossa or Ballad.

C
(F°7(add 9) F6)
FMA7
GMI7
C13
(F°7(add 9) F6)
FMA7
FMI7
Bb7
Star eyes, when, if ev - er, will my lips know if it's me for whom those
EbMA7
AMI7(b5)
D7
GMA7
(GMI7(b5))
Db13
C13
eyes glow? Makes no diff - 'rence where you are, your eyes still hold my wish - ing
F7(#9)
E7(#9 #5)
Eb7(#9)
D7(#9)
GMI7
(G#°7
C9SUS
3
F6/9)
F6
(GMI7 C7)
star, oh, star eyes, how love - ly you are.
Solo on form (ABC)
After solos, D.S. al Coda.

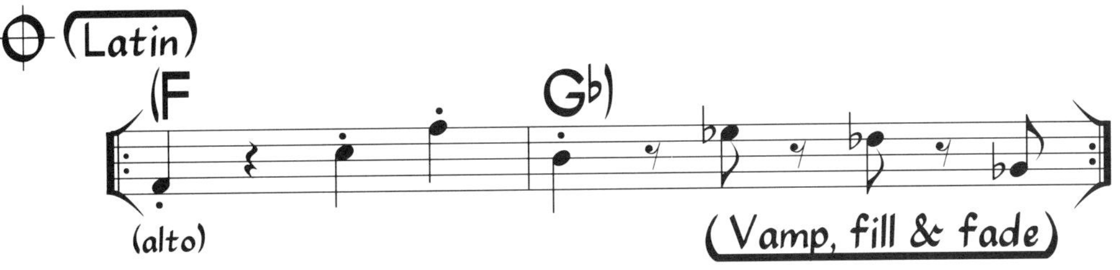
(Latin)
(F
Gb)
(alto)
(Vamp, fill & fade)

Photo © Lee Tanner

JULIAN "CANNONBALL" ADDERLEY

Stars Fell on Alabama

Lyric: Mitchell Parish
Music: Frank Perkins

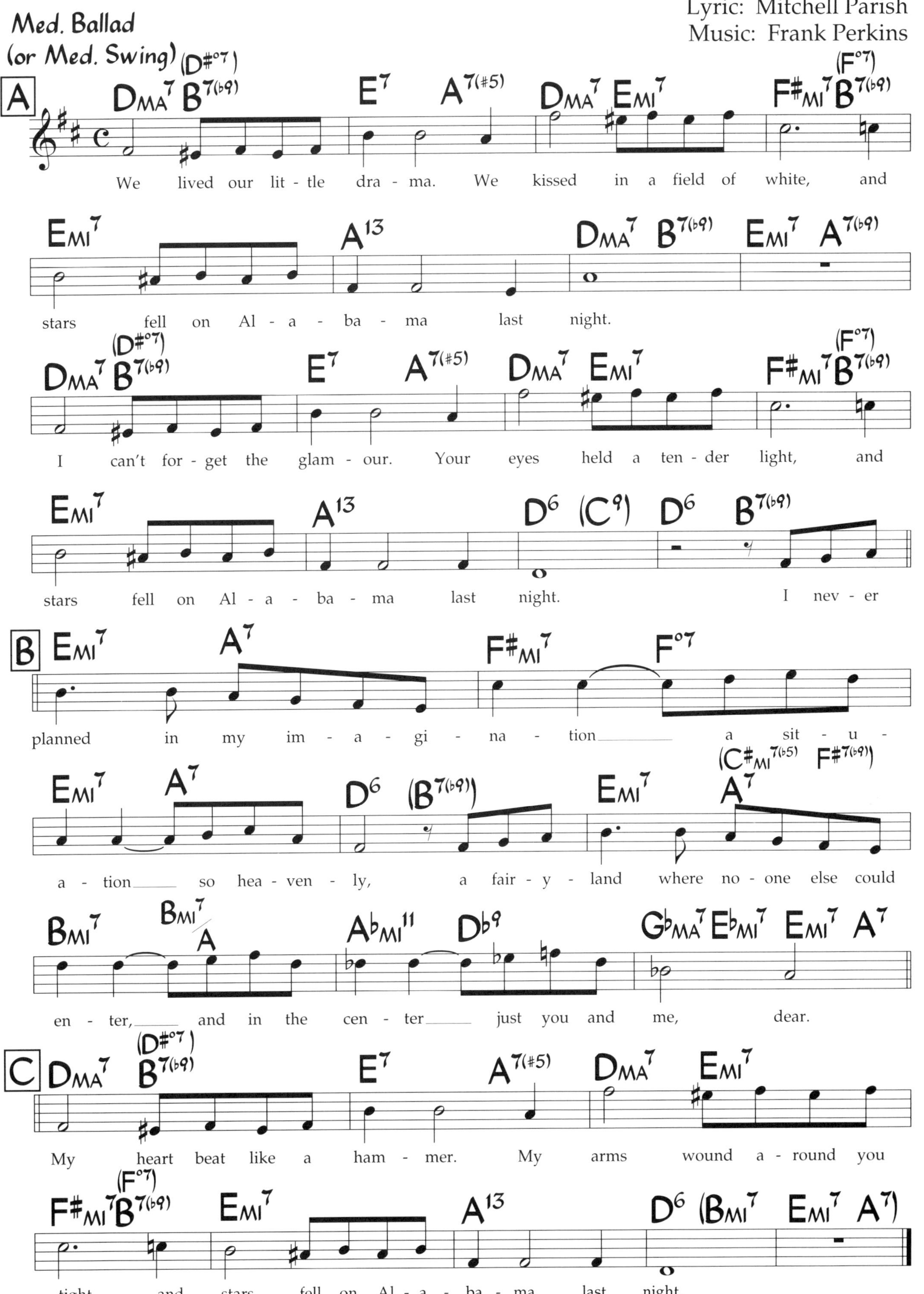

Steepian Faith

Kenny Kirkland

Bass walks in 4 for solos (and out head). Soprano doubles melody on out head.
Anticipated chords are played on beats 1 & 3 for solos.

SKY EVERGREEN

Step Lightly

Joe Henderson
(As played by Blue Mitchell)

Stompin' at the Savoy

Lyric: Andy Razaf
Music: Benny Goodman, Chick Webb & Edgar Sampson

Medium Swing

A

Bb13 | Ebma7 Bb13 | Ebma7 (Ab7(b5)) Gmi7 C7

Sa - voy, the home of sweet ro - mance, Sa - voy, it wins you at a glance, Sa - voy

Fmi7 Bb13 | Eb6 F#13 Fmi7 Bb13

gives hap - py feet a chance to dance. Your form,

Ebma7 Bb13 | Ebma7 (Ab7(b5)) Gmi7 C7

just like a cling - in' vine, your lips, so warm amd sweet as wine, your cheek,

Fmi7 Bb13 | (C#9 D13(b9) Eb6/9) Eb6 Eb7

so soft and close to mine, di - vine.

B

G#13 A13 | G#13 | C#13 (G#mi7(11/b5)) D13 | C#13

How my heart is sing - in', while the band is swing - in',

F#9 G9 | F#9 | (F#mi9 B13) B13 | (Fmi9 Bb13) Bb13

nev - er tired of romp - in' and stomp - in' with you, at the Sa - voy. What joy

Street of Dreams
Lyric: Sam F. Lewis
Music: Victor Young
Ballad or Medium Jazz*
(Verse)
Mid - night, you heav - y lad - en, it's mid - night.
Mid - night, look at the stee - ple, it's mid - night,
Come on and trade in your old dreams for new, your new dreams for old. I
un - hap - py peo - ple. It's ring - ing with joy, it's ring - ing with cheer, 'cause
know where they're bought, I know where they're sold. Mid - night,
yes - ter - day's gone, to - mor - row is near. Mid - night,
you've got to get there at mid - night, and you'll be met there by
the heart is light - er at mid - night. things will be bright - er the
oth - ers like you, broth - ers as blue, smil - ing on the street of dreams.
mo - ment you find more of your kind, smil - ing on the street of dreams.
A
Love laughs at a king, kings don't mean a thing on the street of dreams.
Dreams bro - ken in two can be made like new on the street of dreams.
B
Gold, sil - ver and gold, all you can hold is in the moon - beams.
Poor, no - one is poor, long as love is sure on the street of dreams.
(fine)
Note: This tune may be sung Verse, A, B, Verse, A, B.
* May be played as Medium Latin (2 bars per 1 written).
Solo on AB
After solos, D.S. al fine

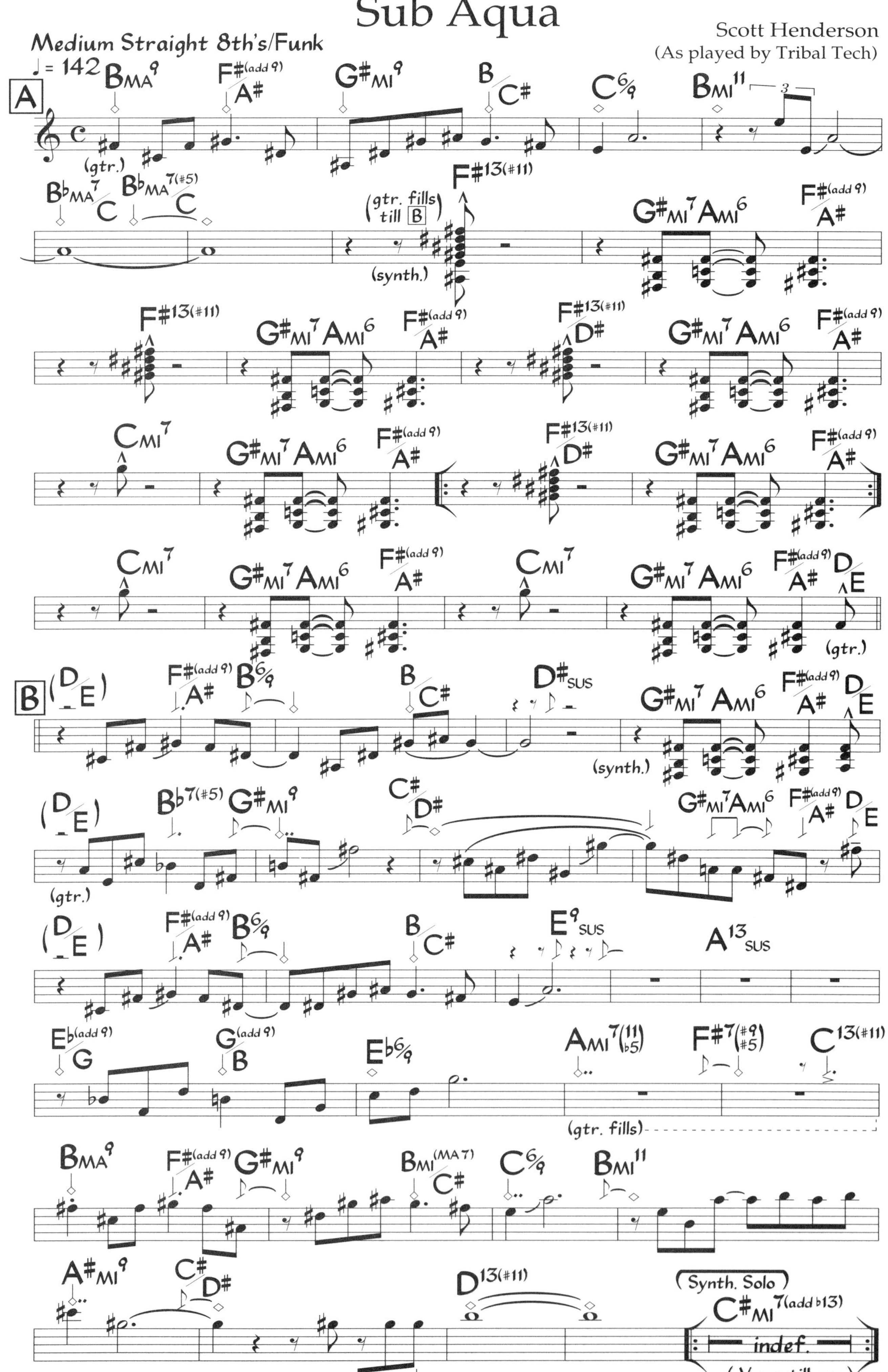
Sub Aqua
Scott Henderson
(As played by Tribal Tech)
Medium Straight 8th's/Funk
♩= 142
A
(gtr.)
(gtr. fills till B)
(synth.)
B
(synth.)
(gtr.)
(gtr.)
(gtr. fills)
Synth. Solo
indef.
(Vamp till cue)

(On cue)
(Gtr. Solo)
C
(synth.)
(top note of voicings)
D
E
(end solo)
(gtr.)
(gtr. fills)
(synth.)
F
(synth.)
gtr. fills
gtr. fills
(Vamp & fade)

Photo by Tom Copi

SONNY ROLLINS

Stanley Turrentine

Medium Jazz
♩ = 126

(Intro) Dsus A7(♭9 #5) (dr. fill) Dsus A7(♭9 #5) (dr. fill) 1. 2. Dmi7
(pn.) (trp./ten./gtr.)

A Dmi7 (Emi7(♭5)) A7(♭9 #5) Dmi7 A7(♭9 #5) Dmi7
(trp./ten./gtr.)

Dmi7 (E7(#5)) A7sus A7(♭9 #5) Dmi7

Dmi7 A♭13(#11) Gmi7 F9 Emi7(♭5)

Emi7(♭5) A7(♭9 #5) B♭9 (2nd x Solo pick-ups) Dmi7

After solos, D.S.
(fade out 2nd x through A)

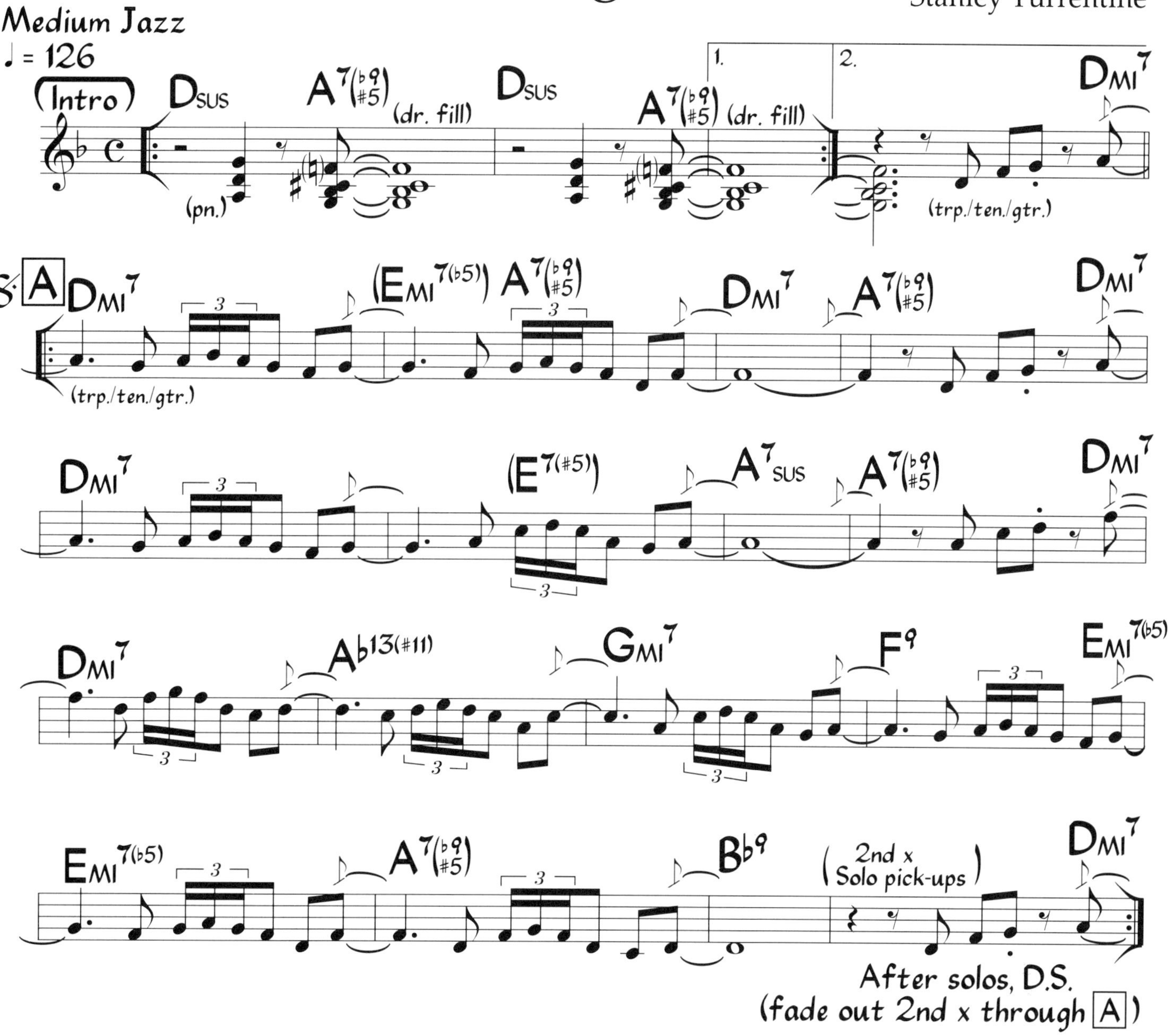

Omit anticipations during solos.
Head is played twice before & after solos.
Chords in parentheses omitted for head, optional for solos.
Tenor sounds as written. Guitar sounds 8va b.

Super Blue

Bernard Ighner
(As played by Freddie Hubbard)

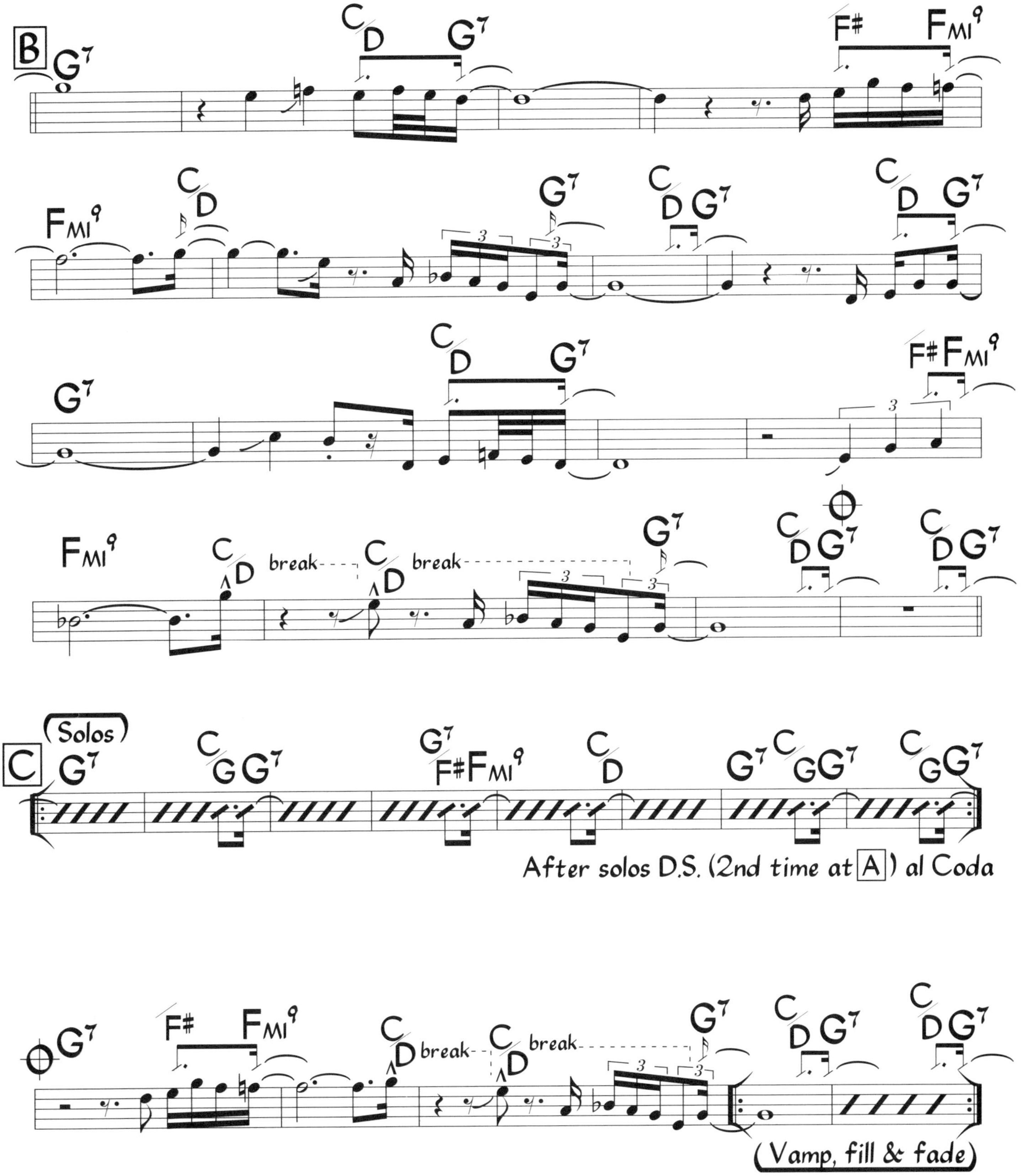

B

break

break

C

(Solos)

After solos D.S. (2nd time at A) al Coda

Sweet Lorraine

Lyric: Mitchell Parish
Music: Cliff Burwell

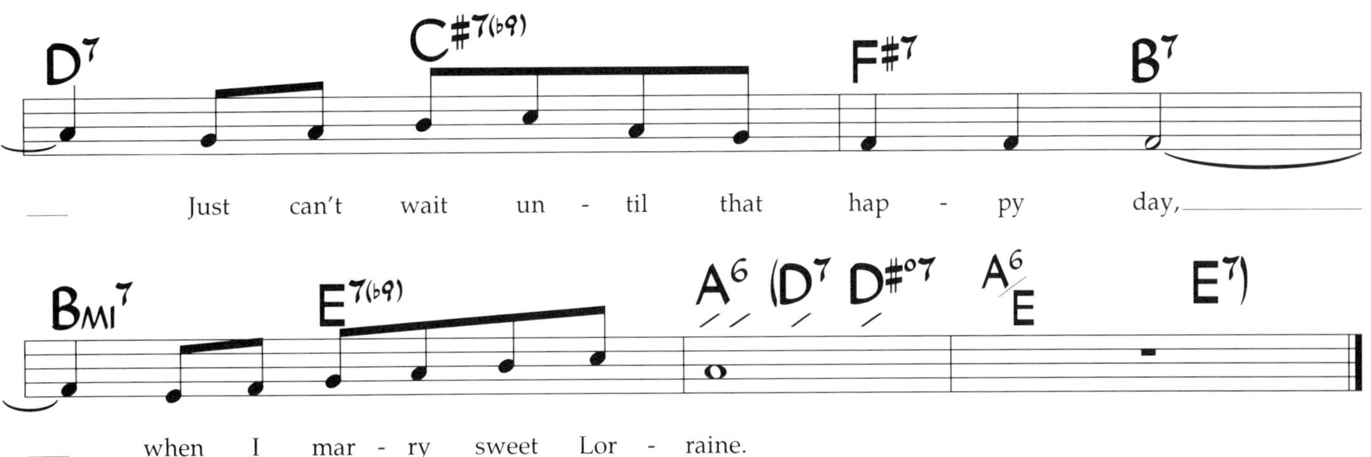
D7
C#7(b9)
F#7
B7
Just can't wait un - til that hap - py day,
BMI7
E7(b9)
A6 (D7 D#o7 A6/E E7)
when I mar - ry sweet Lor - raine.

Sweet Love

Anita Baker
Gary Bias
Louis A. Johnson
(As sung by Anita Baker)

Second and Third verses

2. Your heart has called me closer to you,
I will be all that you need,
Just trust in what we're feeling,
Never leave, 'cause baby I believe in this love.

3. How sweet this dream, how lovely, baby,
Stay right here, never fear,
I will be all that you need,
Never leave, 'cause baby I believe in this love.

Taking a Chance on Love

Lyric: John LaTouche & Ted Fetter
Music: Vernon Duke

2nd verse:
Here I come again.
I'm gonna make things hum again.
Acting dumb again,
Taking a chance on love.
Here I stand again,
about to beat the band again.
Feeling grand again,
Taking a chance on love.

I never dreamed in my slumbers
and bets were taboo.
But now I'm playing the numbers
on a little dream for two.
Wading in again,
I'm leading with my chin again.
I'm startin' out to win again,
Taking a chance on love.

3rd verse:
Here I slip again,
About to take that tip again.
Got my grip again,
Taking a chance on love.
Now I prove again
That I can make life move again.
In the groove again,
Taking a chance on love.

I walk around with a horseshoe,
In clover I lie.
And brother rabbit, of course you
better kiss your foot goodbye.
On the ball again,
I'm ridin' for a fall again.
I'm gonna give my all again,
Taking a chance on love.

That Girl

Stevie Wonder

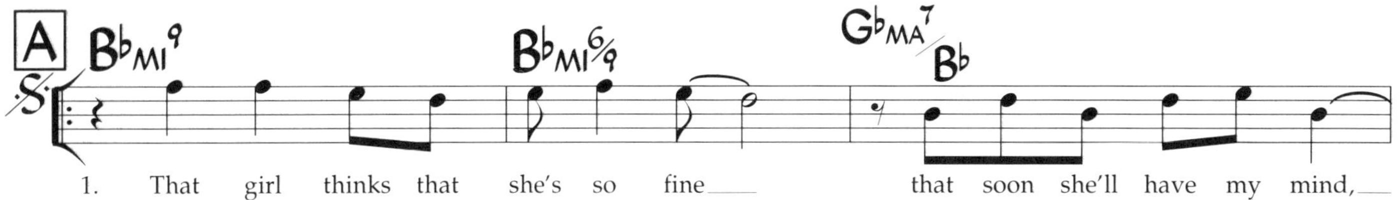

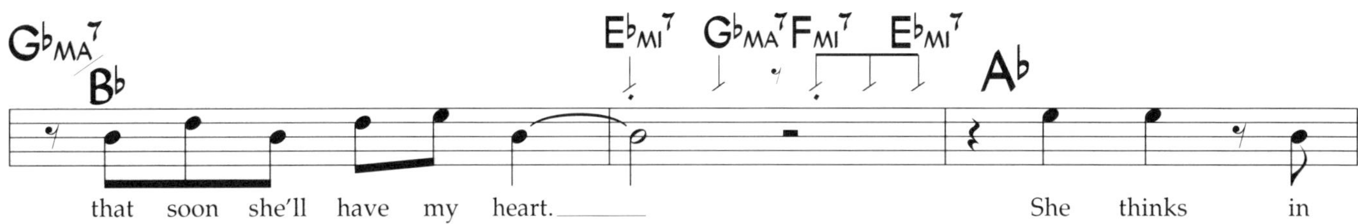

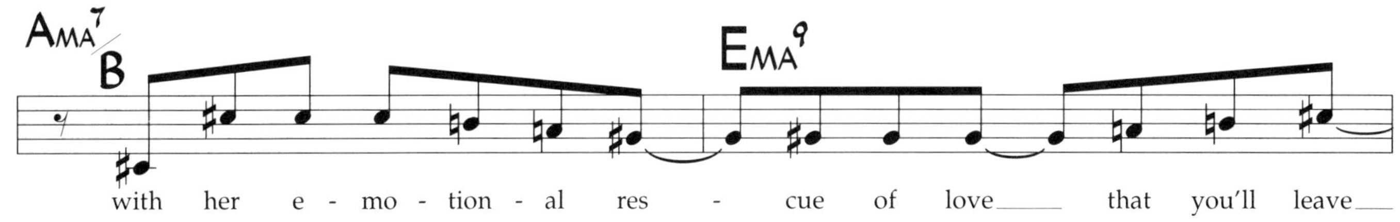

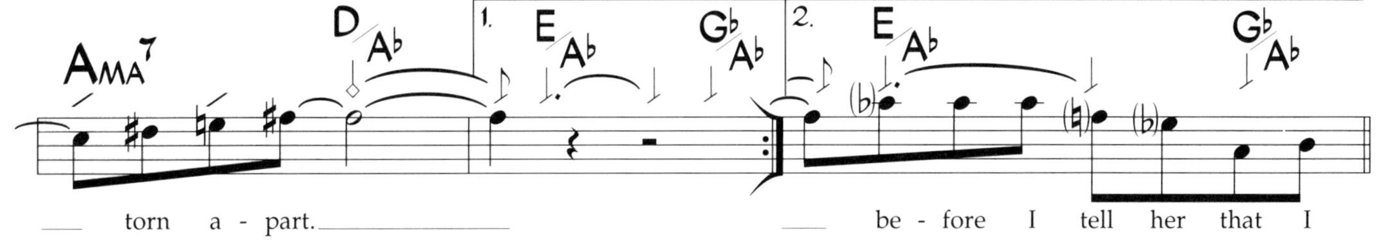

Second and Fourth verses

2. That girl thinks that she's so bad, she'll change my tears to joy from sad,
She says she keeps the upper hand, 'cause she can please her man.
She doesn't use her love to make him weak, she uses love to keep him strong,
And inside me there's no room for doubt that it won't be too long before I tell her that I…

4. That girl knows every single man would ask her for her hand,
But she says her love is much too deep for them to understand.
She says her love has been crying out, but her lover hasn't heard,
But what she doesn't realize is that I've listened to every word,
That's why I know I'll tell her that I…

Photo by Paul Hoeffler, Toronto

ART BLAKEY

That Old Feeling
(Standard Version)
Medium Ballad
(or Medium Jazz)
Lew Brown
& Sammy Fain
A
I saw you last night and got that old feel - ing.
When you came in sight I got that old feel - ing.
B
The mo - ment that you danced by I felt a thrill,
and when you caught my eye my heart stood still.
C
Once a - gain I seemed to feel that old yearn - ing,
and I knew the spark of love was still burn - ing.
D
There'll be no new ro - mance for me, It's fool - ish to start, for that
old feel - ing is still in my heart.

That Old Feeling

Lew Brown
& Sammy Fain
(As played by Art Blakey)

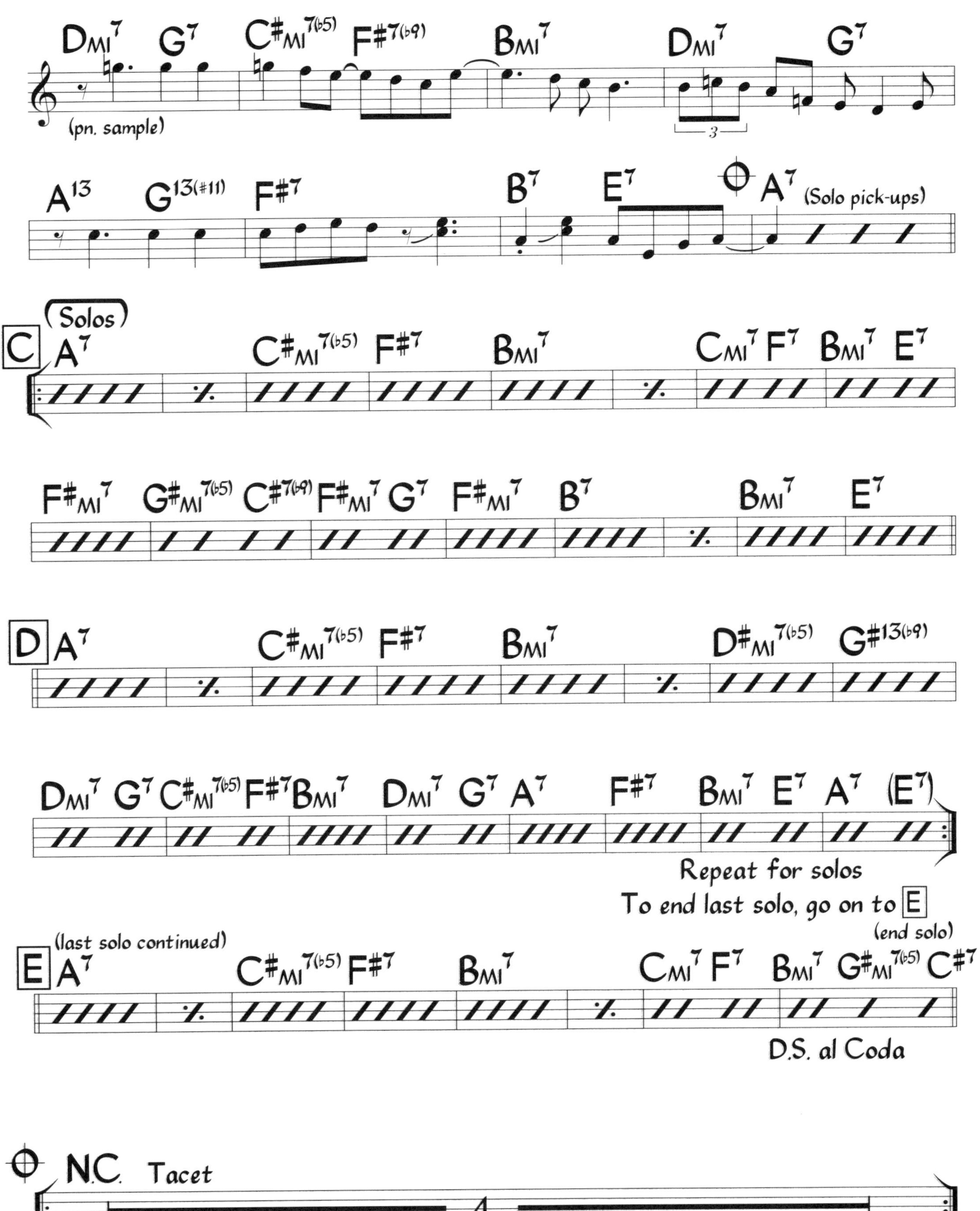

DMI7 G7 C#MI7(b5) F#7(b9) BMI7 DMI7 G7
(pn. sample)
A13 G13(#11) F#7 B7 E7 A7 (Solo pick-ups)
(Solos)
C A7 C#MI7(b5) F#7 BMI7 CMI7 F7 BMI7 E7
F#MI7 G#MI7(b5) C#7(b9) F#MI7 G7 F#MI7 B7 BMI7 E7
D A7 C#MI7(b5) F#7 BMI7 D#MI7(b5) G#13(b9)
DMI7 G7 C#MI7(b5) F#7 BMI7 DMI7 G7 A7 F#7 BMI7 E7 A7 (E7)
Repeat for solos
To end last solo, go on to E
(last solo continued)
(end solo)
E A7 C#MI7(b5) F#7 BMI7 CMI7 F7 BMI7 G#MI7(b5) C#7
D.S. al Coda
N.C. Tacet
4
D.C., vamp & fade on Intro
(with horns)

There's a Lull in My Life

Mack Gordon
& Harry Revel

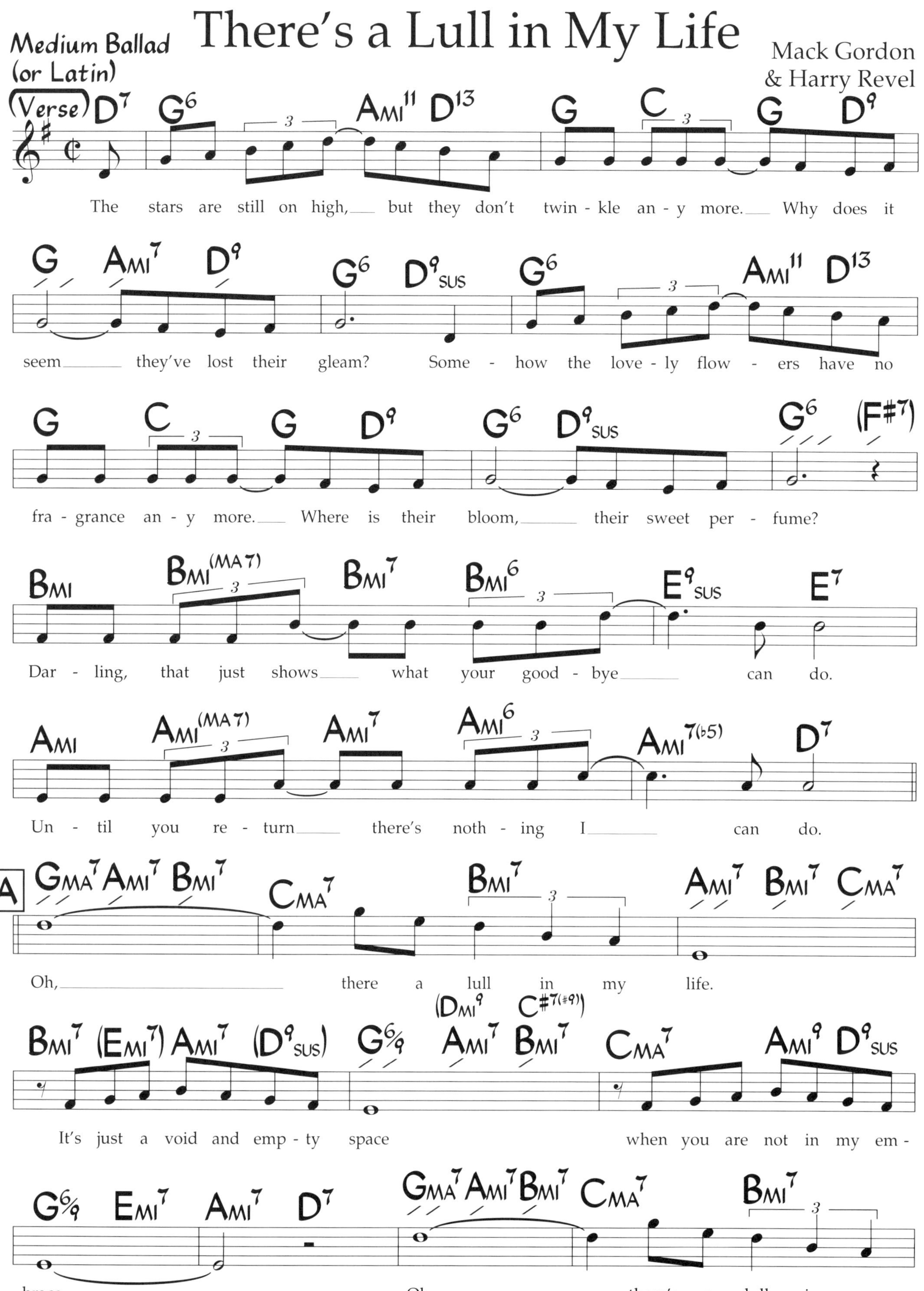

(Dmi9 C#7(#9))
Ami7 Bmi7 Cma7 Bmi7 (Emi7) Ami7 (D9sus) G6/9 Ami7 Bmi7
life. The mo - ment that you go a - way
Cma7 Ami9 D9sus G6 (F9) G6
there is no night, there is no day. The
B
Fmi11 Bb9 Fmi11 Bb9 Ebma7 Bb9sus Ebma7 (D7)
clock stops tick - ing. The world stops turn - ing.
(F#7(#5) F13 E7 Ebma9)
Gma7 G#o7 Ami11 C9 Do7 D7
Ev - 'ry - thing stops but that flame in my heart that keeps burn - ing, burn - ing. Oh, oh,
C
Gma7 Ami7 Bmi7 Cma7 Bmi7 Ami7 Bmi7 Cma7
oh, there's a lull in my life.
(Dmi9 C#7(#9))
Bmi7 (Emi7) Ami7 (D9sus) G6/9 Ami7 Bmi7 Cma7 D13sus
No mat - ter how I may pre - tend, I know that you a - lone can
Bmi11 E7 Bbmi11 Eb7
end the ache in my heart, the call of my
Ami11 D7 G6 (Ami7 D7)
arms, the lull in my life.
Solo on ABC

34 Skidoo

Bill Evans

Chords in parentheses are used for solos. Letter D may be used as an Intro (piano only).

This Is New

Lyric: Ira Gershwin
Music: Kurt Weill

Tiny Capers

Clifford Brown

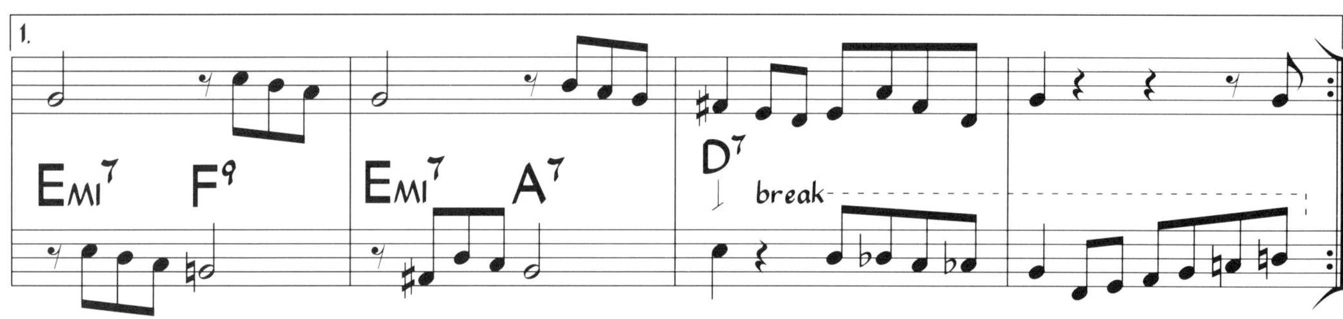

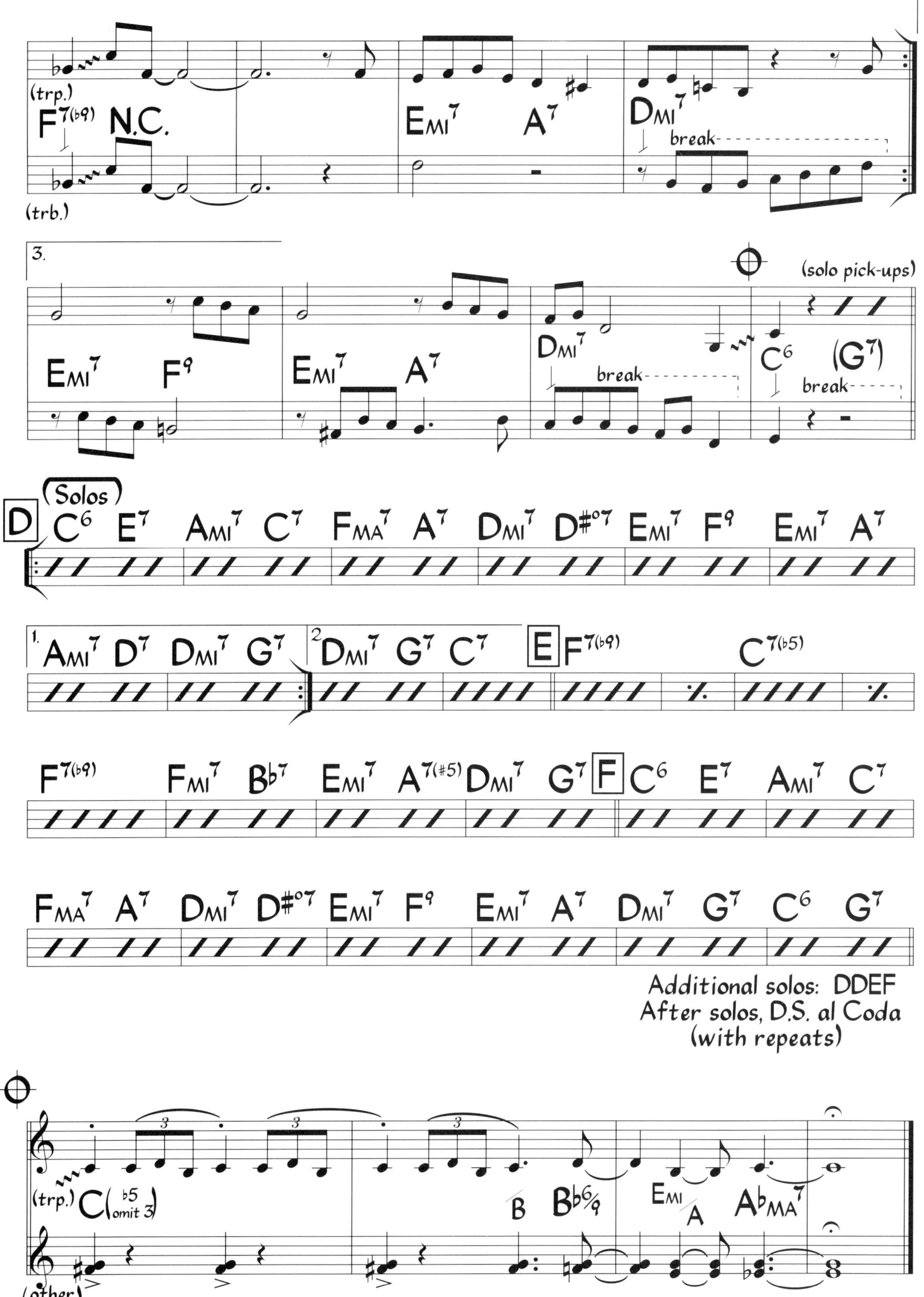

Lower lines (trombone and bari. sax) sound an octave lower than written.

Tokyo Dream

Allan Holdsworth

B(add #11)/A#
G#MI6/9
B(add 9)
C#/B
E
F#/E
F
E/F
Vamp & solo till cue.
On cue, continue to C.
C
EbMA9
AMA9
BbMA9
AMA9
(solo continues)
EbMA9
AMA9
BbMA9
AMA9
(solo ends)
D
C6/9
(gtr.)
ESUS
E(add b9)
F(add 9)/A
BbMA7(#11)/D
CMA7(#11)/E
DMI6/9/A
G7
B(add #11)/A#
G#MI6/9
3
B6/9
EbSUS
Eb(add b9)
E(add 9)/G#
C#7(#9 #5)
C#7
DMI9
G13SUS
(8x's)
DMI9
N.C.
(drums play out)

Too High

Stevie Wonder

Second and Third verses

2. I'm too high, I'm too high, but I ain't left the ground.
I'm too high, I'm too high, I hope I never come down.
She's the girl in her life,
But her world's a superficial paradise,
She had a chance to make it big more than once or twice,
But no dice, she wasn't very nice.

3. I'm too high, I'm too high, I can't ever touch the sky.
I'm too high, I'm so high, I feel like I'm about to die.
She's a girl of the past,
I guess that I got to her at last,
A-did you hear the news about the girl today?
She passed away. What did her friends say?

Photo by Tom Copi

WAYNE SHORTER

Toy Tune
Wayne Shorter
Medium Swing (in 2)
♩ = 146
A
(in 4)
B
(in 2)
C
After solos, D.C. al Coda
Chords in parentheses may be used for the head.
Piano and drums may play kicks for solos.
For solos:
Bars 1-3 & 9-11 of letter A
and bars 1-3 of letter C :
etc.

The Tracks of My Tears

William "Smokey" Robinson
Warren Moore
Marv Tarplin

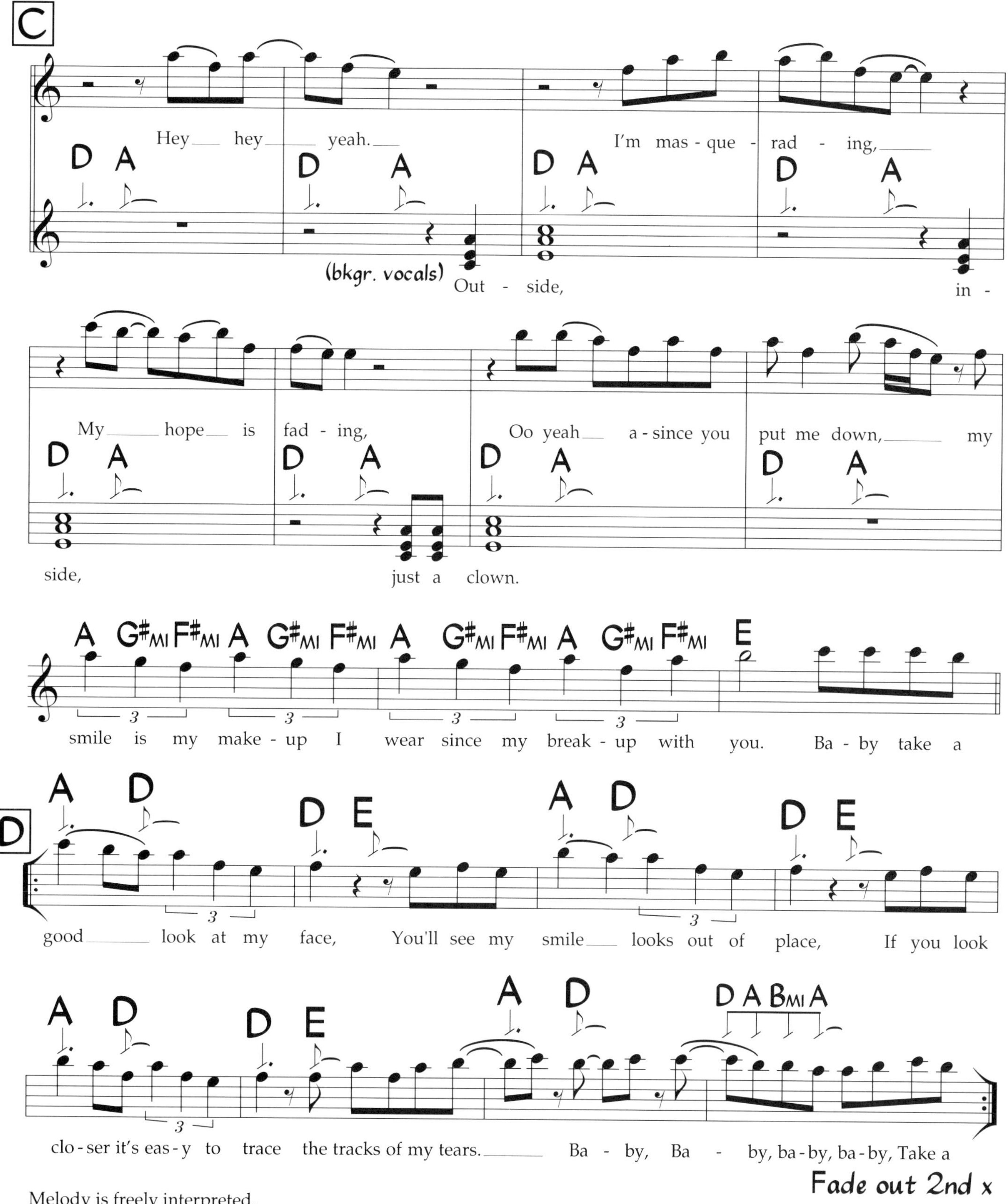

Melody is freely interpreted.

Second verse:

Since you left me, if you see me with another girl,
Seeming like I'm having fun,
Although she may be cute, she's just a substitute,
'Cause you're the permanent one. So take a…

Tuzz's Shadow

Richard Tuttobene
(As played by Warren Bernhardt)

On recording, last solo is on letters E and F, then head is played from C to D to Coda. Letter C is louder than letters A, B and D.

(Used To Be A) Cha-Cha

Jaco Pastorius

Solo on A (indef.)
B (use bass line, indef.; may use DMA7 or DMI7)
C (once)

Piccolo sounds one octave higher than written.

After solos, D.S. (w/ pickup) al fine.

Photo by Jerry Stoll

ROY ELDRIDGE, LENNY BRUCE & LORD BUCKLEY

Walk of the Negress

Robert Hurst

Warm Valley

Duke Ellington

Melody may be freely interpreted.

Wee
(a.k.a. Allen's Alley)
Denzil Best
(As played by Stan Getz
and Dizzy Gillespie)
Fast Be-Bop
(Intro/Ending)
N.C.
12
(drums play time)
N.C.
G bass F bass
(fine (on repeat))
A
B
C
Solo on form (ABC, rhythm changes).
After solos, D.S., play head (ABC), then
D.C. al fine (repeat before fine)

What Are You Doing the Rest of Your Life?

Music: Michel Legrand
Lyric: Alan & Marylin Bergman

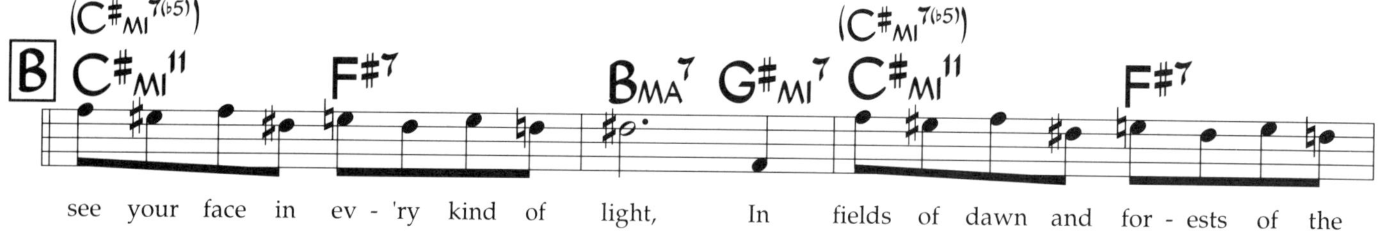

Alternate changes, bars 3-6 of letters A & C, and bars 11-14 of letter A.

What's Going On

Marvin Gaye,
Al Cleveland & Renaldo Benson

3rd verse:

Mother, mother, ev'rybody thinks we're wrong.
Ah, but who are they to judge us simply 'cause our hair is long.
You know we've got to find a way (to) bring some understanding here today. (to letter B)

What's Love Got To Do With It

Graham Lyle
& Terry Britten
(As sung by Tina Turner)

Second verse:

It may seem to you that I'm acting confused when you're close to me,
If I tend to look dazed, I've read it someplace, I've got cause to be,
There's a name for it, there's a phrase that fits,
But whatever the reason, you do it for me.

When I Look In Your Eyes

Leslie Bricusse

C
BMI
B♭+
BMI7/A
E/G♯
Au - tumn comes, sum - mer dies, I see the pass - ing of the years in your eyes,
GMA7
F♯7
BMI
BMI7/A
(GMI7 C7)
C/G
F♯7(♭9 ♭5)
And when we part there'll be no tears, no good - byes, I'll just look in - to your
BMI
E/B
EMI/B
BMI
BMI7/A
eyes. Those eyes so wise, so
E/G♯
EMI/G
BMI/F♯
F♯7(♭9 ♭5)
BMI
warm, so real, How I love the world your eyes re - veal.

When Lights Are Low

Lyric: Spencer Williams
Music: Benny Carter

Optional: Use chords in parentheses for solos.

When Lights Are Low

Music: Benny Carter
(As played by Miles Davis)

Where Are You?

Lyric: Harold Adamson
Music: Jimmy McHugh

You Are So Beautiful

Pop Ballad

Billy Preston
& Bruce Fisher

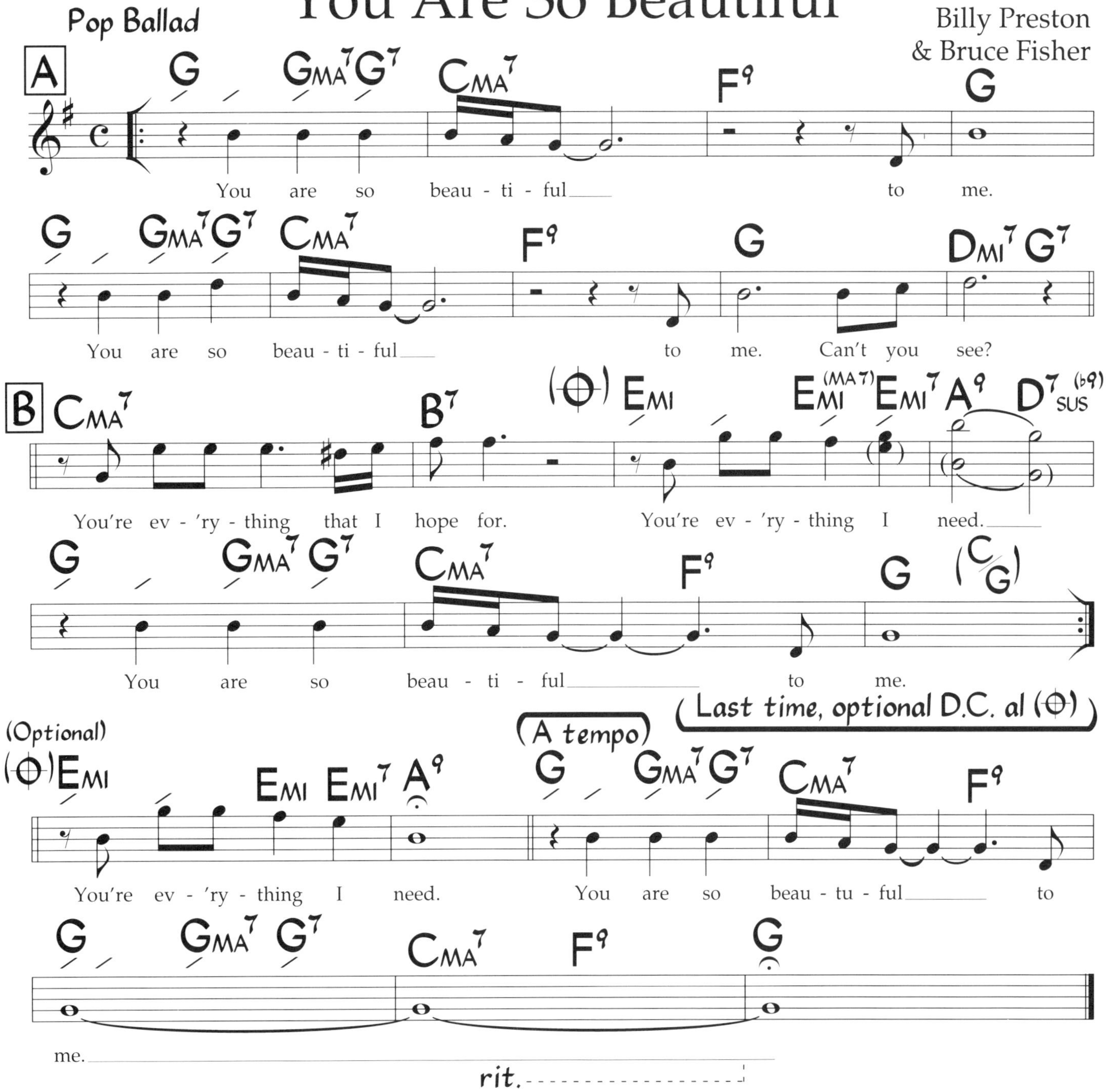

A

G GMA7 G7 CMA7 F9 G

You are so beau - ti - ful ___ to me.

G GMA7 G7 CMA7 F9 G DMI7 G7

You are so beau - ti - ful ___ to me. Can't you see?

B

CMA7 B7 (⊕) EMI EMI(MA7) EMI7 A9 D7SUS(♭9)

You're ev - 'ry - thing that I hope for. You're ev - 'ry - thing I need. ___

G GMA7 G7 CMA7 F9 G (C/G)

You are so beau - ti - ful ___ to me.

(Last time, optional D.C. al ⊕)

(Optional)

(⊕) EMI EMI EMI7 A9 (A tempo) G GMA7 G7 CMA7 F9

You're ev - 'ry - thing I need. You are so beau - tu - ful ___ to

G GMA7 G7 CMA7 F9 G

me. ___

rit.

2nd verse: Such joy and happiness you bring.
Such joy and happiness you bring. Just like a dream,
You're like a guiding light, shining in the night.
You're heaven's gift to me.
You are so beautiful to me.

Note: Letter A is sometimes sung (or played) as follows:

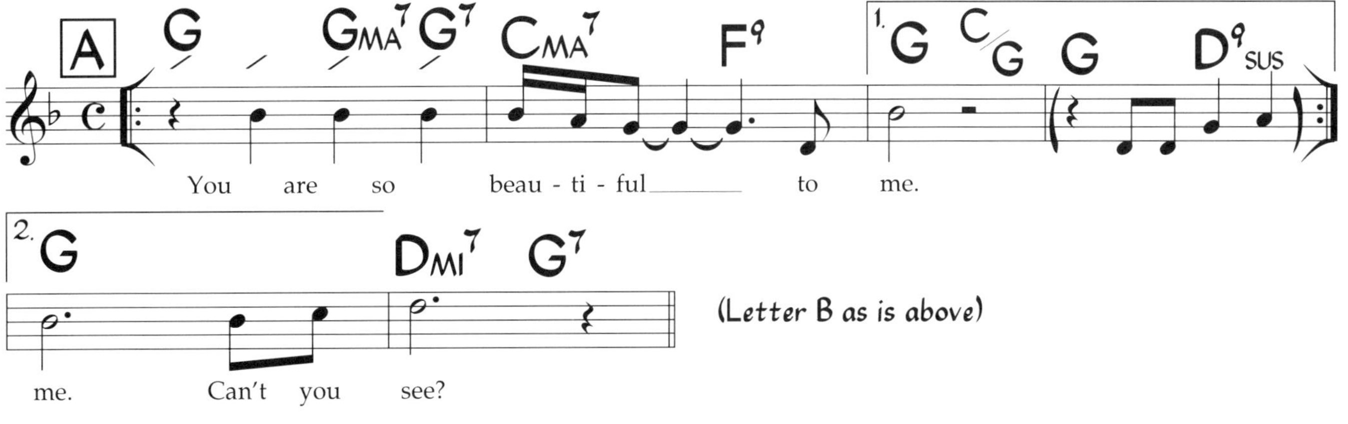

You Must Believe in Spring

Lyric: Alan & Marilyn Bergman
Music: Michel Legrand

Chords in parentheses incorporate Bill Evans' changes.

You Stepped Out of a Dream

You've Changed
Lyric: Bill Carey
Music: Carl Fischer
Ballad
A
You've changed, that spar - kle in your eyes is gone. Your
smile is just a care - less yawn. You're break - ing my heart, you've changed.
You've changed, your kiss - es now are so bla -
sé. You're bored with me in ev - 'ry way. I
can't un - der - stand, you've changed. You've for -
B
got - ten the words, "I love you," each mem - o - ry that we've shared.
You ig - nore ev - 'ry star a - bove you. I can't
re - a - lize you ev - er cared.
C
You've changed, you're
not the an - gel I once knew. No need to tell me that we're
through. It's all o - ver now, you've changed.

APPENDIX - SOURCES

A wide selection of published music, manuscripts, records and other sources was used in creating the charts in this book. Below is an alphabetical listing of tunes with the major sources used for each.

Sources on paper fall into four categories:

1) Published sheet music - usually a full piano/vocal arrangement, though only melody and chord symbols in some instances.

2) Published transcription - a literal transcription from a specific recorded version.

3) Publisher's lead sheet - an in-house document created by staff transcribers or an outside transcription service with or without the composer's input; it usually reflects a single recorded version.

4) Composer's lead sheet - an original lead sheet in the composer's own hand.

The recorded sources for each tune are listed in order of contribution - records listed first contributed more to the final chart than those records which follow. Often other recordings were listened to but are not listed if they added no new information to the charts. The various recordings of a tune are always our primary source for these charts.

A number of other sources used are not listed here. These include fake books, legal and illegal (never used as primary sources for chord progressions), composer's approval of and/or input for lead sheets we sent them, and suggestions from local musicians who proofread the book.

1. ACTUAL PROOF - Herbie Hancock's "Thrust"
2. THE AERIE - Composer's lead sheet. Peggy Stern & Lee Konitz's "Lunasea"
3. AJA'S THEME - Composer's lead sheet. Eddie Daniel's "Breakthrough"
4. AIN'T THAT PECULIAR - Published sheet music. Marvin Gaye on "The Motown Sound - Vol.6"
6. ALMOST LIKE BEING IN LOVE - Published sheet music. "Chet Baker Plays The Best Of Lerner And Lowe", Etta Jones' "Something Nice", Sonny Rollins' "The Complete Riverside Recordings".
7. AMERICAN GOTHIC - Composer's lead sheet. Bob Berg's "Back Roads"
8. AND IT ALL GOES ROUND AND ROUND - "Jaye P. Morgan", Sheila Jordan and Mark Murphy's "One For Junior".
9. ANOTHER STAR - Published sheet music. Stevie Wonder's "Songs In The Key Of Life".
10. ANOTHER TIME - Composer's lead sheet. Alan Broadbent's "Another Time".
11. APPOINTMENT IN GHANA - Jackie McLean's "Jackie's Bag".
12. ARIETAS - Freddie Hubbard's "Ready For Freddie".
13. AUTUMN SERENADE - Published sheet music. "John Coltrane and Johnny Hartman".
14. B-STING - Composer's lead sheet. Brandon Fields' "Everybody's Business".
15. BABY COME TO ME - Published sheet music. Patti Austin's "Every Home Should Have One".
16. BACKSTAGE SALLY - Art Blakey's "Buhaina's Delight".
17. A BALLAD FOR DOLL - Jackie McLean's "Jackie's Bag".
18. BALLAD FOR TWO MUSICIANS - Composer's lead sheet. Trilok Gurtu's "Crazy Saints".
19. BIRD OF BEAUTY - Published sheet music. Stevie Wonder's "Fulfillingness' First Finale".
20. BLACK NILE - Composer's lead sheet. Wayne Shorter's "Night Dreamer".
21. BLUE MOON - Published sheet music. Nat King Cole's "The Billy May Sessions", Ella Fitzgerald's "Jazz Round Mid night", Art Blakey's "Three Blind Mice", Art Tatum's "Complete Pablo Solo Masterpieces", Earl Bostic's "14 Original Greatest Hits".
22. BLUE TUESDAY - "Jessica Williams At Maybeck"
23. BLUE SPIRITS - Freddie Hubbard's "Blue Spirits"
24. BODY AND SOUL - John Coltrane's "Coltrane's Sound", Coleman Hawkins' "Body And Soul", Billie Holiday's "The Silver Collection".
25. BROTHERS OF THE BOTTOM ROW - Julian Joseph's "The Language Of Truth".
26. BU'S DELIGHT - Art Blakey's "Buhaina's Delight".
27. BUD POWELL - Composer's lead sheet. "Chick Corea and Gary Burton In Concert. Zurich, Oct. 28, 1979"
28. BUTTERFLY - Norman Conners' "This Is Your Life", Herbie Hancock's "Earth Run".
29. CAN'T STOP THE WIND - Paul McCandless' "Premonition".
30. CARAVAN - Published sheet music. Duke Ellington's "Private Collection" and "Duke Ellington and Friends"; Art Blakey's "Caravan", "Ella Fitzgerald Sings The Duke Ellington Songbook", Nat 'King' Cole's "The After Midnight Sessions", Tommy Flanagan's "Jazz Poet".
31. CEORA - Lee Morgan's "Cornbread".
32. CHAIRS AND CHILDREN -Composer's lead sheet. Gary Burton's "Reunion".
33. CHICK'S TUNE - Published sheet music. Blue Mitchell's "The Thing To Do".
34. CIRCULAR MOTION - Composer's lead sheet. Phil Markowitz' "Sno' Peas".
35. CIRRUS - Bobby Hutcherson's "Cirrus".
36. CLOSE YOUR EYES - Published sheet music. Cleo Laine's "Woman To Woman", Gene Ammons' "Boss Tenors", "Oscar Peterson and Dizzy Gillespie", Pat Martino's "Exit".
37. COOL GREEN - Jackie McLean's "Bluesnik".
38. CREEPIN' - Published sheet music. Stevie Wonder's "Fulfillingness' First Finale".
39. D MINOR MINT - Freddie Hubbard's "The Best Of Freddie Hubbard".

40. DADDY'S GIRL CYNTHIA - Composer's lead sheet. Donald Brown's "Cause And Effect".
41. DANCING IN THE STREET - Published sheet music. Martha Reeves And The Vandellas on "The Motown Sound - Vol.3".
42. DARIUS DANCE - Composer's lead sheet. Marc Copland's "Two Way Street".
43. DAY DREAM - Published sheet music. Duke Ellington's "And His Mother Called Him Bill", Phil Woods' "Flowers For Hodges", "Ella Fitzgerald Sings The Duke Ellington Songbook", Mark Levine's "Smiley And Me", Tommy Flanagan's "The Tokyo Recital", 44. DEXTER - Composer's lead sheet. Joey Calderazzo's "To Know One".
45. DIENDA - Branford Marsalis' "Royal Garden Blues".
46. DIVERTAMENTO - Composer's lead sheet. Eddie Daniels' "Breakthrough".
47. DOLPHIN DANCE - Herbie Hancock's "Maiden Voyage".
48. DON'T ASK WHY - Composer's lead sheet. Alan Broadbent's "Everything I Love".
49. DON'T BE THAT WAY - Published sheet music. Benny Goodman's "Let's Dance", Ella Fitzgerald's "First Lady Of Song", Ella Fitzgerald and Louis Armstrong's "Ella And Louis Again", Dee Bell's "One By One".
50. DON'T BLAME ME - Published sheet music. Nat 'King' Cole's "The Very Thought Of You", "The Complete Coleman Hawkins", Thelonious Monk's "Standards", Tete Monteliu's "A Spanish Treasure".
51. THE DOUBLE UP - Lee Morgan's "Carumba".
52. DREAMIN' - Published sheet music. Vanessa Williams' "The Right Stuff".
54. EL GAUCHO - Wayne Shorter's "Adam's Apple".
55. EMILY - Published sheet music. Bill Evans' "Autumn Leaves", "Buenos Aires Concert - 1973", and "You're Gonna Hear From Me",
56. EVERYTHING I HAVE IS YOURS - Published sheet music. Billie Holiday's "Billie's Best", Art Tatum's "The Complete Pablo Solo Masterpieces", Barney Kessel's "Spontaneous Combustion", Charlie Shoemake's "Strollin' ", Sarah Vaughn's "Live In Japan".
57. FALL WITH ME - Composer's lead sheet. Jude Swift's "Common Ground".
59. FOR ALL WE KNOW - Published sheet music. "Stan Getz With Cal Tjader", Johnny Hartman's "Once In Every Life", Billie Holiday's "Lady In Satin",
60. FREEDOMLAND - Composer's lead sheet. The Yellowjackets' "Greenhouse".
61. FROM DAY TO DAY - Composer's lead sheet. Mulgrew Miller's "From Day To Day".
62. THE GENTLE RAIN - Luiz Bonfa's "Non-Stop To Brazil", Irene Kral's "Gentle Rain", Sarah Vaughn's "Copacabana", Joe Pass' "Tuto Bem".
63. GET READY - Published sheet music. "The Temptations' Greatest Hits - Vol.1".
64. A GHOST OF A CHANCE - Published sheet music. Clifford Brown's "The Complete Emarcy Recordings", Ella Fitzgerald's "Fine And Mellow", Wes Montgomery's "Movin' Along".
66. GRAND CENTRAL - "Cannonball And Coltrane".
67. HARD EIGHTS - Lyle Mays' "Fictionary".
68. GUSH - Composer's original score. Maria Schneider's "Evanescence".
69. HEAT WAVE - Published sheet music. Martha Reeves and the Vandellas on "The Motown Sound - Vol.2".
70. HERZOG - Bobby Hutcherson's "Total Eclipse".
71. HOLD ON, I'M COMING - Published sheet music. Same & Dave's "Hold On, I'm Coming" (45rpm).
72. HOW SWEET IT IS - Published sheet music. Marvin Gaye on "The Motown Sound, Vol. 5".
73. I CAN'T HELP IT - Michael Jackson's "Off The Wall".
74. I FALL IN LOVE TOO EASILY - Published transcription. Miles Davis' "Seven Steps To Heaven", Chet Baker's "Let's Get Lost", Bill Evans' "The Complete Riverside Recordings", Enrico Pieranunzi's "New Lands", Fred Hersh's "Dancing In The Dark".
76. I GOT IT BAD - Published sheet music. Duke Ellington & Louis Armstrong's "The Great Reunion", "Ella Fitzgerald Sings The Duke Ellington Songbook", Bill Evans' "New Jazz Conceptions", Carmen McRae's "Song Time", Jessica Williams' "The Next Step".
77. I HEAR A RHAPSODY - Bill Evans' "Montreux II", Bill Evans & Jim Hall's "Undercurrent", Keith Jarrett's "Tribute", "Jim Hall Live".
78. I HEARD IT THROUGH THE GRAPEVINE - Published sheet music. "Every Great Motown Hit of Marvin Gaye".
80. I WANTED TO SAY - Composer's lead sheet. Kenny Barron's "Quickstep".
83. IF YOU COULD SEE ME NOW - Bill Evans' "Blue In Green", "The Complete Riverside Recordings" and "Jazz Round Midnight", Sarah Vaughn's "Send In The Clowns", Etta Jones' "If You Could See Me Now".
84. I'M GETTING SENTIMENTAL OVER YOU - Published sheet music. Ella Fitzgerald and Count Basie's "A Classy Pair", Bill Evans' "A Simple Matter Of Conviction", "Jessica Williams Live At Maybeck", John Hicks and Elise Wood's "Luminous".
86. I'M LOSING YOU - Published sheet music. The Temptations on "The Motown Sound - Vol.8".
87. I'M THROUGH WITH LOVE - Published sheet music. "Sarah Vaughn", "More of the Great Lorez Alexandria", Etta Jones' "So Warm".
88. IN A MELLOW TONE - Published sheet music. Duke Ellington's "The Blanton-Webster Band", "Ella Fitzgerald Sings The Duke Ellington Songbook", "The Complete Galaxy Recordings of Art Pepper", Ernestine Anderson's "Be Mine Tonight".

89. IN A SENTIMENTAL MOOD - Published sheet music. "The Best Of Duke Ellington", "Ella Fitzgerald Sings The Duke Ellington Songbook", Bill Evans' "Eloquence", "Duke Ellington and John Coltrane".
90. IN CASE YOU MISSED IT - Bobby Watson's "Post-Motown Bop", Art Blakey's "Album Of The Year".
91. IN LOVE WITH NIGHT - Composer's lead sheet. Andy LaVerne's "Double Standard".
92. INNER URGE - Joe Henderson's "Inner Urge" and "The Standard Joe Henderson".
93. INVITATION - Published sheet music. Joe Henderson's "Tetragon" and "In Search Of Blackness", Bill Evans' "Invita tion", Jack Wilkins' "You Can't Live Without It", Tom Lellis' "Double Entendre".
95. ISOAR - Composer's lead sheet. Nguyen Le's "Zanzibar".
96. ISOTOPE - Joe Henderson's "Inner Urge".
97. IT ALWAYS IS - Tom Harrell's "Sail Away".
100. JEAN DE FLEUR - Grant Green's "Idle Moments".
101. JITTERBUG WALTZ - Roland Kirk's "Bright Moments", "Eric Dolphy", Dinah Washington's "The Fats Waller Songbook", Fats Waller, "The Last Years, 1940-1943", "Bill Mays At Maybeck",
102. JOHN'S WALTZ - John Abercrombie & Andy LaVerne's "Now It Can Be Played".
103. JUST FRIENDS - Published sheet music. Chet Baker's "Let's Get Lost", "The Original Recordings of Charlie Parker", Cannonball Adderley on anthology "Jazz Of The '60s", Irene Kral's "Better Than Anything", "Paul Chambers - 1935-1969".
104. JUST SQUEEZE ME - Published sheet music. "The New Miles Davis Quintet", Duke Ellington & Louis Armstrong's "The Great Reunion", "Ella Fitzgerald Sings The Duke Ellington Songbook", Duke Ellington's "Duke's Big 4".
105. JUST YOU, JUST ME - Published sheet music. Nat 'King' Cole's "The After Midnight Sessions", Ella Fitzgerald's "Ella SwingsLightly", Carmen McCrae's "You're Lookin' At Me".
106. KAHLIL THE PROPHET - Jackie McLean's "Destination Out".
107. KNOCK ON WOOD - Published sheet music. Eddie Floyd's "Knock On Wood".
108. THE LAMP IS LOW - Published sheet music. Carmen McRae's "Sarah - Dedicated To You", "Bill Henderson With The Oscar Peterson Trio", "George Shearing And The Montgomery Brothers", Bobbe Norris and Larry Dunlap's "Hoisted Sails".
109. LAST NITE - Larry Carleton's "Last Night" and "Sleepwalk".
110. LAST SEASON - Composer's original score. Maria Schneider's "Evanescence".
111. LAURA - Published sheet music. Charlie Parker's "Jazz Round Midnight", Ella Fitzgerald's "For The Love Of Ella", Bill Evans' "A Simple Matter Of Conviction", "The Complete Emarcy Recordings Of Clifford Brown".
112. LET'S STAY TOGETHER - Published sheet music. Al Green's "Let's Stay Together" (45 rpm).
113. LITHA - Chick Corea's "Inner Space", Stan Getz' "Sweet Rain".
114. LONELY WOMAN - Composer's lead sheet. Horace Silver's "Song For My Father", Pat Metheny's "Rejoicing".
115. LOOK AT THE BIRDIE - Art Blakey's "Roots And Herbs".
116. LOVE LETTER - Composer's lead sheet. Eddie Gomez' "Next Future".
118. LOVE'S HAUNTS - Composer's lead sheet. Aydin Esen's "Anadolu".
120. LULLABY IN RHYTHM - Published sheet music. "Charlie Ventura In Concert", "The Four Freshmen and Five Saxes", Art Tatum's "Complete Pablo Solo Masterpieces".
121. MAIDEN VOYAGE - Herbie Hancock's "Maiden Voyage".
122. MAMACITA - Joe Henderson's "The Kicker".
123. MAN FACING NORTH - Composer's lead sheet. The Yellowjackets' "Like A River".
124. METAMORPHOSIS - Composer's lead sheet. Horace Silver's "The Stylings Of Silver" and "Explorations By The Horace Silver Quintet".
125. MIDNIGHT SILENCE - "Kenny Kirkland".
126. MONK ON THE RUN - Composer's lead sheet. Othello Molineaux' "It's About Time".
127. MOON AND SAND - Published sheet music. Keith Jarrett's "Standards - Vol.2", Kenny Burrell's "Moon And Sand", Jackie & Roy's " An Alec Wilder Collection" ," Chet Baker' Sings And Plays From The Film 'Let's Get Lost' ".
128. MOONGLOW - Published sheet music. Sarah Vaughn's "You're Mine, You", Count Basie's "The Standards", Art Tatum's "The Complete Pablo Solo Masterpieces", Django Reinhardt's "Django '35-39. The Quintet of the Hot Club of France".
130. MOONLIGHT SERENADE - Published sheet music. Glenn Miller's "In The Digital Mood", Frank Sinatra's "The Reprise Collection".
131. MY GIRL - Published sheet music. The Temptations on "The Motown Sound - Vol.5".
134. NEVER SAID (Chan's Song) - "Diane Reeves", Herbie Hancock & Bobby McFerrin on "Round Midnight - Vol.2".
135. NEW BOOTS - Composer's lead sheet. Mark Varney's "Truth In Shreading".
136. NEXT FUTURE - Composer's lead sheet. Eddie Gomez' "Next Future".

138. NO WAY OUT - Composer's lead sheet. Othello Molineaux' "It's About Time".
139. NOWHERE TO RUN - Published sheet music. Martha Reeves and the Vandellas on "The Motown Sound - Vol.5".
140. OFF FLOW - Composer's lead sheet. Dave Liebman's "Turn It Around".
141. ON GREEN DOLPHIN STREET - Published sheet music. Miles Davis' "The '58 Sessions", Bill Evans' "On Green Dolphin Street", Jimmy Heath's "Fast Company" , Mel Torme and George Shearing's "An Evening At Charlie's", Mark Murphy's "Rah".
142. ONE BIRD, ONE STONE - Don Grolnick's "Nighttown".
143. ONE FINGER SNAP - Herbie Hancock's "Empyrean Isles".
144. OOO BABY BABY - Published sheet music. Smokey Robinson & The Miracles' "Ooo Baby Baby" (45 rpm).
145. OPUS DE FUNK - Composer's lead sheet. "The Horace Silver Trio", Milt Jackson's "From Opus De Jazz To Jazz Sky line", "Art Pepper Plus 11".
146. OUT A DAY - Composer's lead sheet. Franck Amsallem's "Out A Day".
148. OVER THE RAINBOW - Published sheet music. Ella Fitzgerald's "The Harold Arlen Songbook - Vol.II", Sarah Vaughn's "In The Land Of Hi-Fi" and "Live In Japan", "More Of The Great Lorez Alexandria", Buddy Collette's "Nice Day".
149. PART-TIME LOVER - Published sheet music. Stevie Wonder's "In Square Circle".
150. PENDULUM - Composer's lead sheet. Richie Beirach's "Elm".
151. PRELUDE TO A KISS - Published sheet music. Jim Hall's "All Across The City", Duke Ellington's "Duke's Big Four" , "Ella Fitzgerald Sings The Duke Ellington Songbook", Rahsaan Roland Kirk's "Bright Moments", Kenny Barron's "One Plus OnePlus One", " Duke Ellington And Friends".
152. PROMISE - Bob Berg's "Enter The Spirit".
153. PUNJAB - Joe Henderson's "In And Out".
154. PYRAMID - Composer's lead sheet. "Further Explorations By The Horace Silver Quintet".
155. QUESTION MARK - Composer's lead sheet. Nguyen Le's "Miracles".
156. RAINLAND - Paul McCandless' "Premonition".
157. REACH OUT, I'LL BE THERE - Published sheet music. The Four Tops on "The Motown Sound - Vol.9".
158. REAL LIFE - Phil Woods' Little Big Band's "Real Life".
159. RED'S BLUES - Composer's lead sheet. Jerry Bergonzi's "Lineage".
160. RELENTLESS - Composer's lead sheet. Bob Mintzer's "I Remember Jaco".
161. RESPECT - Published sheet music. Aretha Franklin's "Respect" (45 rpm), Otis Redding's "Respect" (45 rpm).
162. REVELATION - Composer's lead sheet. The Yellowjackets' "Shades".
163. RIDDLES - Composer's lead sheet. Richie Beirach & George Coleman's "Convergence", "The John Abercrombie Quartet".
164. RITUAL - Chick Corea's "Paint The World".
165. RUBY - Published sheet music. Ray Charles' "The Legend Lives", Jimmy Ponders' "To Reach A Dream".
166. SAIL AWAY - Tom Harrell's "Sail Away".
167. THE SECOND TIME AROUND - Published sheet music. Frank Sinatra's "The Reprise Collection", Bill Evans' "Quin tessence", Shirley Horn's "Loads Of Love", Etta Jones' "Ms. Jones To You".
168. SERENATA - Published sheet music. "Nat Cole Sings, George Shearing Plays", "Cannonball Takes Charge - VRG", Cal Tjader's "A Fuego Vivo", Frank Foster's "No Count".
169. THE SHADOW OF YOUR SMILE - Published sheet music. "The Complete Galaxy Recordings Of Art Pepper", Wes Montgomery's"Compact Jazz", Frank Sinatra's "The Reprise Collection", "The Best Of Eddie Harris".
170. SHORT STORY - Joe Henderson's "In And Out".
171. SINCE WE MET - Publisher's lead sheet. Bill Evans' "Since We Met" and "Eloquence".
172. SMILE PLEASE - Published sheet music. Stevie Wonder's "Fulfillingness' First Finale".
173. SO NEAR, SO FAR - Miles Davis' "Seven Steps To Heaven".
174. SOLITUDE - Published sheet music. Duke Ellington's "Money Jungle", "Ella Fitzgerald Sings The Duke Ellington Songbook", Billie Holiday's "The Complete Decca Recordings".
175. SPEAK LIKE A CHILD - Herbie Hancock's "Speak Like A Child".
176. SPRING IS HERE - Published sheet music. Bill Evans' "Bill Evans At Town Hall" and "The Complete Riverside Re cordings", John Coltrane's "The Stardust Sessions".
177. STAIRWAY TO THE STARS - Published sheet music. Johnny Hartman's "I Just Stopped By To Say Hello", Bill Evans' "Undercurrent", John Coltrane's "The Coltrane Legacy".
178. STAR EYES - Published sheet music. "The Cannonball Adderley' Quintet Plus", Bill Evans' "A Simple Matter Of Conviction", Cal Tjader's "La Onda Va Bien", Irene Kral's "Kral Space", "Art Pepper Meets The Rhythm Section".
179. STARS FELL ON ALABAMA - Published sheet music. Cannonball Adderley & John Coltrane's "The Dreamweavers", Anita O'Day's "Pick Yourself Up", Art Tatum's "The Complete Pablo Solo Masterpieces".
180. STEEPIAN FAITH - "Kenny Kirkland".
182. STEP LIGHTLY - Blue Mitchell's "The Thing To Do".
183. STOMPIN' AT THE SAVOY - Published sheet music. "The Complete Emarcy Recordings Of Clifford Brown", Ella Fitzgerald & Louis Armstrong's "Ella And Louis Again", Cal Tjader's "Black Orchid", Benny Goodman's "After You've Gone", "Bill Mays At Maybeck", Mark Levine's "Smiley & Me".

184. STREET OF DREAMS - Published sheet music. Frank Sinatra's "The Reprise Collection", Ernestine Anderson's "Big City", Art Tatum's "The Complete Pablo Solo Masterpieces", Nancy Harrow's "Street Of Dreams".
185. SUB AQUA - Scott Henderson & Gary Willis & Tribal Tech's "Primal Tracks".
186. SUGAR - Stanley Turrentine's "Sugar".
187. SUPER BLUE - Freddie Hubbard's "Super Blue".
188. SWEET LORRAINE - Published sheet music. Nat 'King' Cole's "The After Midnight Sessions", Carmen McRae's "You're Looking At Me", Count Basie & Oscar Peterson's "Night Rider".
189. SWEET LOVE - Published sheet music. Anita Baker's "Rapture".
190. 34 SKIDOO - Published sheet music. Bill Evans' "Blue In Green", "How My Heart Sings", and "Montreux II", Billy Childs' "Portrait Of A Player", Eddie Daniels' "This Is New".
191. TAKING A CHANCE ON LOVE - Published sheet music. Ella Fitzgerald's "Sweet And Hot", George Shearing's "Grand Piano Live", Jessica Williams' "The Next Step", Ray Brown's "Bass Face".
193. THAT GIRL - Published sheet music. Stevie Wonder's "Musiquarium I, Vol.2".
195. THAT OLD FEELING - Published sheet music. Art Blakey's "Three Blind Mice". Standard version is from "The Com plete Pacific Jazz Recordings Of Chet Baker", Art Tatum's "Complete Pablo Solo Masterpiueces", Stan Getz' "Getz And Friends".
196. THERE'S A LULL IN MY LIFE - Published sheet music. Bobbe Norris' "You And The Night And The Music", "Nat 'King' Cole Sings, George Shearing Plays", Stan Getz' "Getz And Friends", Anita O'Day's "Pick Yourself Up".
197. THIS IS NEW - Published sheet music. Dave Catney's "Jade Visions", Ed Bickert's "This Is New", Chick Corea's "Chick Corea, Herbie Hancock, Keith Jarrett, McCoy Tyner", Kenny Drew's "Trio/Quartet/Quintet".
198. TINY CAPERS - "Clifford Brown & Max Roach".
199. TOKYO DREAM - Published sheet music. Alan Holdsworth's "Road Games".
200. TOO HIGH - Published sheet music. Stevie Wonder's "Inner Visions".
201. TOY TUNE - Wayne Shorter's "Etcetera", Dave Kikoski's "Persistent Dreams".
202. THE TRACKS OF MY TEARS - Smokey Robinson & The Miracles on "The Motown Sound - Vol.5".
203. TUZZ'S SHADOW - Composer's lead sheet. Warren Bernhardt's "Reflections".
205. (USED TO BE A) CHA CHA - "Jaco Pastorius", Michel Camilo's "Suntan".
206. WALK OF THE NEGRESS - Composer's lead sheet. "Robert Hurst Presents Robert Hurst".
207. WARM VALLEY - Published sheet music. Duke Ellington's "The Best Of Duke Ellington" and "Money Jungle", Kenny Barron's "The Only One", Jerome Richardson's "Roamin' With Richardson".
208. WEE (aka Allen's Alley) - Dizzy Gillespie, Sonny Stitt and Stan Getz' "For Musicians Only", Dizzy Gillespie and Charlie Parker's "Jazz At Massey Hall", "The Complete Galaxy Recordings Of Art Pepper".
209. WHAT ARE YOU DOING THE REST OF YOUR LIFE? - Published sheet music. Bill Evans' "Blue In Green" and "Live In Paris 1972, Vol.1", "Sarah Vaughn With Michel Legrand", Frank Sinatra's "The Reprise Collection", "The Best Of Joe Pass", Carmen McRae's "The Great American Songbook".
210. WHAT'S GOING ON? - Published sheet music. Marvin Gaye's "What's Going On?"
211. WHAT'S LOVE GOT TO DO WITH IT - Published sheet music. Tina Turner's "Private Dancer".
212. WHEN I LOOK IN YOUR EYES - Published sheet music. Irene Kral's "Where Is Love?", "Helen Merrill & Gordon Beck", Wes Montgomery's "Down Here On The Ground".
213. WHEN LIGHTS ARE LOW - Published sheet music. Miles Davis' "The Complete Prestige Recordings", Art Blakey's "Three Blind Mice", Kitty Margolis' "Evolution", Oscar Peterson's "Exclusively For My Friends", Benny Carter's "BBB & Co.".
214. WHERE ARE YOU - Published sheet music. "The Best Of Dinah Washington", Dexter Gordon's "I Want More", "The Red Garland Quartet".
215. YOU ARE SO BEAUTIFUL - "The Best Of Billy Preston", Joe Cocker's "You Are So Beautiful" (45 rpm), Arthur Prysock's "Today's Love Songs, Tomorrow's Blues", Woddy Herman's "Live At The Concord Jazz Festival", Teramasa Hino's "Unforgettable".
216. YOU MUST BELIEVE IN SPRING - Published sheet music. Bill Evans' "You Must Believe In Spring", Karin Krog's "You Must Believe In Spring", Frank Morgan's "You Must Believe In Spring".
217. YOU STEPPED OUT OF A DREAM - Published sheet music. Nat 'King' Cole's "Lush Life", Shirley Horn's "You Won't Forget Me", "The Oscar Peterson Trio Plays", Stan Getz' "Quartets".
218. YOU'VE CHANGED - Published sheet music. Billie Holiday's "Lady In Satin", Dexter Gordon's "Nights At The Keystone", "Alan Broadbent Live At Maybeck", Elvin Jones' "Going Home".

Latin Music Books & CDs from Sher Music Co.

The Latin Real Book (C, Bb or Eb)

The only professional-level Latin fake book ever published! Over 570 pages. Includes detailed transcriptions sof tunes, exactly as recorded by:

Ray Barretto
Eddie Palmieri
Fania All-Stars
Tito Puente
Ruben Blades
Los Van Van
NG La Banda
Irakere
Celia Cruz
Arsenio Rodriguez
Tito Rodriguez
Orquesta Aragon
Beny Moré
Cal Tjader
Andy Narell
Mario Bauza
Dizzy Gilllespie
Mongo Santamaria
Manny Oquendo & Libre
Puerto Rico All-Stars
Issac Delgaldo
Ft. Apache Band
Dave Valentin
Paquito D'Rivera
Clare Fischer
Chick Corea
Sergio Mendes
Ivan Lins
Djavan
Tom Jobim
Toninho Horta
Joao Bosco
Milton Nascimento
Leila Pinheiro
Gal Costa
And Many More!

Muy Caliente!

Afro-Cuban Play-Along CD and Book
Rebeca Mauleón - Keyboard
Oscar Stagnaro - Bass
Orestes Vilató - Timbales
Carlos Caro - Bongos
Edgardo Cambon - Congas
(Over 70 min. of smokin' Latin grooves)

The Latin Real Book Sampler CD

12 of the greatest Latin Real Book tunes as played by the original artists: Tito Puente, Ray Barretto, Andy Narell, Puerto Rico Allstars, Bacacoto, etc. $16 list price. Available in U.S.A. only.

101 Montunos

by Rebeca Mauleón
The only comprehensive study of Latin piano playing ever published.

- Bi-lingual text (English/Spanish)
- 2 CDs of the author demonstrating each montuno
- Covers over 100 years of Afro-Cuban styles, including the danzón, guaracha, mambo, merengue and songo—from Peruchin to Eddie Palmieri.

The True Cuban Bass

By Carlos Del Puerto, (bassist with Irakere) and **Silvio Vergara**, $22.

For acoustic or electric bass; English and Spanish text; Includes CDs of either historic Cuban recordings or Carlos playing each exercise; Many transcriptions of complete bass parts for tunes in different Cuban styles – the roots of Salsa.

The Brazilian Guitar Book

by Nelson Faria, one of Brazil's best new guitarists.

- Over 140 pages of comping patterns, transcriptions and chord melodies for samba, bossa, baiaõ, etc.
- Complete chord voicings written out for each example.
- Comes with a CD of Nelson playing each example.
- The most complete Brazilian guitar method ever published! $26 including surface postage.

Joe Diorio – "Nelson Faria's book is a welcome addition to the guitar literature. I'm sure those who work with this volume wiill benefit greatly"

The Salsa Guide Book

By Rebeca Mauleón
The only complete method book on salsa ever published! 260 pages. $25

Carlos Santana – "A true treasure of knowledge and information about Afro-Cuban music."
Mark Levine, author of The *Jazz Piano Book*. – "This is the book on salsa."
Sonny Bravo, pianist with Tito Puente – "This will be the salsa 'bible' for years to come."
Oscar Hernández, pianist with Rubén Blades – "An excellent and much needed resource."